MOB DEEP

Benjamin Holmes

NEWMAN SPRINGS PUBLISHING
320 Broad Street
Red Bank, NJ 07701

First originally published by Newman Springs Publishing 2019

ISBN 978-1-64531-031-0 (Paperback)
ISBN 978-1-64531-032-7 (Digital)

Printed in the United States of America

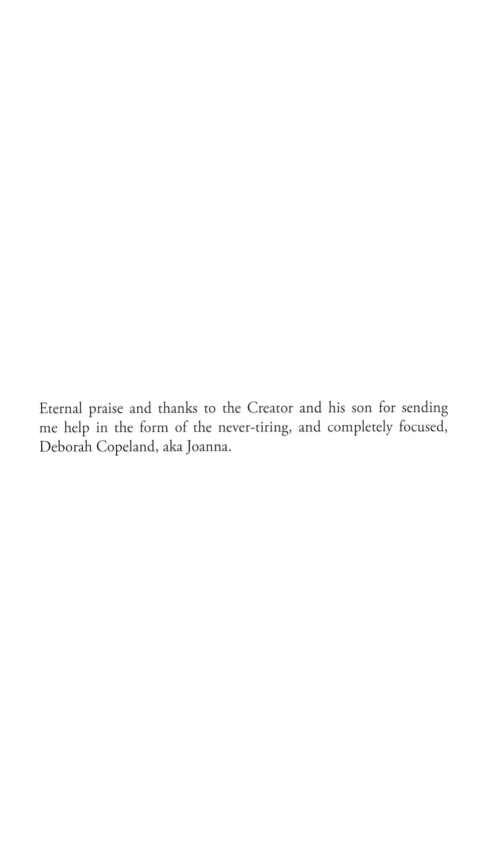

Eternal praise and thanks to the Creator and his son for sending me help in the form of the never-tiring, and completely focused, Deborah Copeland, aka Joanna.

Racing Car Mufflers

The candy-apple-red Camaro roared like a thousand hungry lions, as Lying Johnny floored its gas pedal and made the fire-breathing monster leap out of the door of my shop. Over the head of the door of my shop was a sign that said, "We sell speed!" Lying Johnny pulled the Camaro onto the street in front of my shop and floored the gas pedal once again. The beast took off up the street with so much noise that it caused the neighbors to think that their windows would shatter. Lying Johnny laughed and shifted to second gear, as the candy-apple-red Camaro disappeared around the corner. A few minutes later Lying Johnny pulled the loud Camaro back onto the lot and ran into the shop. A police cruiser pulled onto the lot a few seconds later and an officer demanded to know who had just driven the car around the block. Lying Johnny walked up to the officer and admitted that he had just test-driven the car. The officer stated that the automobile was in violation of the noise ordinance, and he ordered Lying Johnny to start the car. Lying Johnny started the Camaro for the officer, and the car was as quiet as a church mouse. I was about to pop a rib out of place, as I tried to keep from laughing at the surprised look on the policeman's face. The completely confused officer got into his cruiser and sped away, totally disgusted. Lying Johnny had struck again.

Lying Johnny was given that name because he made a habit of telling the other racing car fanatics that his 455 cubic inch racing engine was actually a 350 cubic inch engine. Lying Johnny was credited with many other similar deeds that earned him that title, including the ability to beat the lie detector machine. That was one of the benefits of his intelligence training in Vietnam. At a much later date, I would thank him a thousand times for teaching me the technique.

In the late spring of 1977, I was in the business of installing my version of the Hemi-racing-car muffler on automobiles that should have been used for the racing track only. The Hemi-racing-car muffler was designed to quiet the vehicle enough to pass the legal noise ordinance limits, but still retain the raw power needed in a high-performance racing machine. My version of the Hemi-racing-car muffler went a step beyond the traditional system invented by the Chrysler-Plymouth-Dodge Corporation. My system employed remote-cable-controlled cutouts that allowed a racer to pull a cable under the dashboard of his car, which allowed him or her to select a quiet exhaust system or the all-out-race car exhaust system. Even though it was 1977 and the prices of gasoline were sky-high, auto racing was still very popular in some areas. Formerly, side bets were made at the racing tracks whenever two racers decided to have a grudge match race. My selective exhaust system made it possible to drive racing cars on city streets, to a pre-determined location, select the full-race car exhaust mode, race the car, then return to the street legal exhaust mode by pulling a cable, and then drive the vehicle home. This eliminated the need to tow racing cars from place to place.

Just three days before, Timmy Brooks's Nova gave Art Grant's GTO a three-car head start, and Timmy still beat Art by five car lengths. The bet was for five hundred dollars. Street racing was not only very exciting, it was also very profitable to the winners and the parts suppliers. Not only was I supplying the parts, I was also making the parts and installing them. Every weekend, and sometimes on weekdays, some secluded street would be blocked off for a few seconds so that a quick race could take place. One racer called "The Greek" was reputed to only race for one thousand dollars and up. Often cars were driven from the area of my shop in Youngstown, Ohio, to Akron or Cleveland, Ohio, and back. Street racing was a thriving business in Akron and Cleveland, and still is today. After working all day in dirt and grease at my shop, I did what everyone else did, who was in a similar line of work in my area. The engineers, mechanics, tow truck drivers, landscapers, carpenters, painters, and anyone else who worked by the sweat of their brow all had the unique habit of washing off the day's dirt and grime, and then dressing in the finest suits and ties available to the civilized world.

Truck drivers were often seen after work in Armani suits, while driving Lincoln Continentals, Cadillacs, Jaguars, or Mercedes Benz. After work, I drove my Jaguar Sedan, and Lying Johnny drove his Lincoln Continental. The mixture of racing cars, luxury cars, foreign cars, trucks, motorcycles, and classic collectors' cars made my shop, and Youngstown in general, a mecca for automobile enthusiasts. After work, everyone was looking for somewhere to hang out. This need to hang out gave rise to several very nice nightclubs and restaurants.

One of the nicest nightclubs was just one block away from my shop. It was called Dee's Lounge. From time to time, Dee's Lounge featured some very attractive dancing girls. Lying Johnny and I were regulars at Dee's and we often brought friends and customers there from my shop, but in 1977 I was only thinking of one girl; she was my new bride, Addie. We were approaching our first year anniversary and I was convinced that the Creator had sent this woman to me, until death do us part. She was perfect in mind and body. I wasn't content unless I was with her. I felt that we were truly soul mates. I would have gladly given my life for her. The strange mix of a variety of car enthusiasts included the foreign luxury car crowd, of which I was included. Most of the Jaguars and Mercedes Benz were owned by a group of gentlemen who claimed to be Black Muslims. After checking with some friends who were very serious about the Islamic religion, I came to the realization that some of these gentlemen had misrepresented themselves and were actually Muslims in name only. They hung around my shop like everyone else did, and seemed to get along with everybody. The day after Lying Johnny had stymied the policeman over the exhaust system on the candy-apple-red Camaro, two of the usual gentlemen who represented themselves as Black Muslims approached me about the merits of a Mercedes over a Jaguar.

Our conversation soon turned to the use of my version of the Hemi-racing muffler to quiet full-race engines enough to pass street-legal noise ordinances. Mikah Muhammad and Raul Muhammad showed me several blueprints of firearm silencers, and asked if I could read the blueprints. I admitted that I could read the blueprints and that they were remarkably similar to my muffler blueprints. The next question from them was, "Can you make one for us?" I replied that I could make the silencer but that I didn't want to get involved in anything illegal. I did agree to correct and perfect their blueprints, and then to instruct them on making the silencer themselves. The final blueprint utilized a lawn mower muffler that was extensively modified and customized to fit a particular weapon. I pre-fitted all of the parts and stopped just short of actually assembling the device. That, I left to them, away from my shop. I kept a copy of the final blueprint for myself and gave them two copies and the pre-fitted parts. Two weeks of the usual routine of working all day and then going home to the company of my lovely wife had passed, when Lying Johnny suggested that we stop at Dee's Lounge for a drink, some ribs, and to see the three new dancing girls.

As Lying Johnny and I walked into Dee's Lounge, I thought about the rumors that the alleged owner of the bar, Joey Naples, the reputed "Mob Boss" of the area, had machine-gun toting guards hiding behind the two-way mirrors of the bar, waiting for raids, robberies, or hits. The loud and friendly voice of Eddie Truelove reverberated about the bar as he called my name. "Brother Holmes, Benny, Benny the Blood," Truelove yelled. Truelove was the manager and bartender of Dee's Lounge. I met him through Jay Brownlee, who worked with me at Ohio Edison, the local electric company. Jay Brownlee owned a strip club downtown called Satan's Inferno, and it really got hot there. Dee's Lounge and Satan's Inferno were both hangout spots of the local car fanatics, who were also fans of the dancing girls. The dancers always seemed to be turned on by the powerful, expensive, and shiny racing cars.

Eddie Truelove and Jay Brownlee were known to bet thousands of dollars on automobile or motorcycle races, and they always had several over-friendly, scantily-clad, and beautiful girls accompanying them. I went to Dee's Lounge several times a day for a sandwich and a beer during my breaks from work at my shop. Eddie was always there and we eventually came to the point that we called each other "buddies." As I sat at the bar next to Lying Johnny, Truelove motioned me on down to the far end of the bar, where no one could hear our conversation. "Why are you helping the other side? I thought that we were friends. These Black Muslims are running off at the mouth and telling people that they're going to own this town because you're doing things for them exclusively that you won't do for us."

I tried to explain to Truelove that I simply reworked some blueprints for the Muhammad brothers, and that I had not made any silencers for them, nor did I intend to take a part in a power struggle or a turf war. I quickly added that I would gladly provide the same blueprints and pre-fitted parts to him that I had provided to the Muhammad brothers. Eddie seemed to be satisfied with that promise for the time being. After getting me to say that I would provide the blueprints and parts in a few days, he plied Lying Johnny and me with food and drinks all night long. After I provided the blueprints and the parts for the silencer, nothing else was mentioned about it for a while. I came and went like I always had at Dee's lounge. I had no clue that forces were at work that I couldn't even begin to fathom.

On November 22, of that year, 1977, just a few months after I had given Truelove the blueprints, my home in Hubbard was burglarized. I had a camera rigged to the doors and I knew who it was who had stolen from me. The burglars were two neighborhood thugs who had returned home from Vietnam with heroin addictions. They stole to supply their habits. I later found that the quiet suburban township that I had chosen for me and my lovely wife was filled with drug addicts and drug dealers, who were also Vietnam veterans. These thugs were armed to the teeth with everything from magnum pistols to rocket launchers. It was time to get serious about arming myself. I had accumulated a small arsenal of seventeen firearms. Most of them were hunting rifles and shotguns. The pride of my collection was a pre-Civil War 12-gauge shotgun, which was given to my great-grandfather by his slave master upon releasing him. My second finest collectible was an 1876 30-30 Winchester "Buffalo Soldier" rifle. My third finest gun was a World War II German Luger pistol. Each of these items was worth more than five thousand dollars.

The burglars, Jesse Green and Melvin Brooks, went to my home while I was across town, at a hospital, receiving physical therapy for a bad back and leg. My beautiful wife was at home and answered the door. The pair of burglars lied to her by telling her that they were supposed to go hunting with me that morning. My wife, Addie, knew that I would never go hunting with a pair of strangers and told them to come back later. Addie then called me at the hospital and informed me of what was going on. I told her to take the snub-nosed .38 caliber handgun, and to come to get me from the hospital immediately. We were a little too late. By the time we got a half a block away from our home, we saw Jesse and Melvin pulling away from our home. The front door was lying flat on the floor of our house. My wife started to pursue the pair of thieves, but Jesse pointed one of my high-powered rifles out the window of their car at Addie and me. I told her to stop the chase. I had her to drive back to our house to call the Hubbard Police, while I rode around to some of the local fence joints to see if the pair of thieves had already fenced my property or traded my property for drugs.

I followed the pair of thieves to one of the local drug dealers' houses. They were in the driveway of the house, with their needles in their arms, when I surprised them. They had already stashed or fenced my seventeen firearms, a portable television, and some jewelry. I showed them the pictures from the camera I had rigged to the door they kicked in. The deal was to return all of my property in the same condition they found it, repair the door, and never let me see them near my home again. In exchange, I would not press charges against them. Out of gratitude, or just out of a propensity to lie, the pair of thieves claimed that they were recruited by members of the Hubbard Police Department, to break into my home to check for a silencer shop and a drug laboratory. They found neither. I dismissed their claim as that of caught rats, willing to say anything to save their tails. It was a matter of record that these very same burglars had pistol-whipped a Hubbard Police officer and then broke his leg. It was ridiculous to believe that this pair of miscreants was recruited by those same policemen to spy on me, but truth is stranger than fiction.

I returned home to my wife and waited to see who would show up first, the thieves returning my property or the Hubbard Police Department. An assortment of characters I had never seen before simply walked up to the front porch and placed a television, a gun, or a piece of jewelry on the front steps. After every bit of my property was returned, the Hubbard Police finally arrived at the scene of the crime. Several hours had passed. I had met these same officers several times before, when they would drop by my home to see me loading my racing car on the trailer to take it to the racing track. Policemen hung out at my home like everybody else did; everybody expressed an interest in high-performance automobiles. I had already told the police officers that since I had gotten my property back and the perpetrators were willing to compensate me for the door, I had no interest in prosecuting them. The policemen insisted on inspecting my returned property. They pretended to look over the jewelry and to inspect the portable television, but they were really only interested in the collection of firearms that were returned to me. They were particularly interested in the World War II German luger. One of the officers held the luger in his hands and massaged the threads on the end of the barrel of the gun. "I've got to get me one of these," he exclaimed. I played dumb and asked if he was interested in German handguns. He replied, "No, I meant that I'd like to get my hands on a silencer." I asked if silencers were legal and he replied, "Yes and no." I left the subject alone and told them that I had to take some medication. For the time being, I was free of this amateurish chess match, but many more chess matches lay in wait for me. Forces were in effect that I had not even dreamed of.

The Hubbard policemen made a point of stopping at my house whenever I was taking out the trash, shoveling snow, or working on one of our cars in our double-car garage. The double-car garage was attached to our home and led into the main foyer of the house. One could easily stand in the garage and get a good look into the kitchen or the basement of the home. Whenever an officer dropped by to just "kill time," I always got suspicious enough to scan the area he was in with an electronic listening device detector; also called a "bug detector." Yes, I was concerned about being bugged by the police and anyone else.

Sometimes the policemen's feigned friendliness extended to their offering me time on their shooting range. Talk of doing favors for favors was abundant. I often thought that the time would come when I would have wished that I had recorded some of these conversations, and so I began to do just that. A small, pocket-sized, voice-activated, micro recorder became my constant companion. Not only did I never leave home without it, but I got to the point that I didn't feel dressed without it. Often, when I replayed the tapes, I noticed certain insinuations in the officers' voices that I had not paid attention to when the conversations actually happened.

These officers were insinuating that I was getting away with something, and they wanted a piece of whatever it was. Conversations generally started off about cars but quickly led to guns, silencers, drugs, prostitution, and gambling. There were always the profound statements: "You've got to pay to play," and "It all depends on who you know." My guess was that you had to pay the police, and they were the right ones to know. I didn't see a need to get involved and I told them so many times, but they insisted that I was aligned with the Black Muslims, who were continuously running their mouths about taking over the rackets from "the Mob." Through the Christmas and New Year Holidays, Eddie Truelove told me that he needed me to actually make a silencer for him, and to let an understudy watch me do it. He told me that the weakness of his operation was the unavailability of good silencers.

Truelove told me that we could both get rich if I played ball. I refused him for what seemed like the thousandth time. My garage was doing well and my wife had a good job at General Motors. I didn't want to get involved in anything that would cause me to worry about her safety, or cause me to look over my shoulder for the rest of my life.

What I didn't want is exactly what I ended up getting. Profits from the garage allowed Addie and me to have a very good Christmas. I started buying land around our home in Hubbard Township. I made plans to buy the shop I had been renting, and I had blueprints made to build an addition onto our home. My best laid plans went astray on February 13, 1978, when the Ohio Bureau of Criminal Investigation; the Alcohol, Tobacco, and Firearms Department; the Drug Enforcement Administration; the Trumbull County Sheriff's Department; and the Hubbard Township Police raided my home. Addie and I were arrested for having a drug and silencer laboratory, even though no drugs or silencers were found in our home. The warrants claimed that information from a confidential informant was the basis for the warrants and the ensuing raid. Helicopters circled our home, dogs sniffed through our garbage and around our house. Addie and I had shotguns put to our heads, as we were forced to lie spread-eagle, face-down, to the floor. Everything in our home was torn apart and searched. Our brand-new television was turned over on its screen and the circuits were torn out of it. After no drugs or silencers were found, the raid turned into a "free-for-all." Everything Addie and I owned was stolen by the raiders. All seventeen of my guns were taken for no cause.

Addie's wedding dress was taken. Several of our leather coats were taken. My glass bell collection was stolen. Addie's figurines and statuettes were all stolen. African carvings and paintings were stolen. Even men's and women's shoes, hats, and scarves were taken.

Addie and I spent the night in jail, while the raiders continued to loot our home. We were finally released from jail only to find that our home had been fitted with concealed listening devices in the ceilings. Once I found the "bugs," I destroyed them, but we assumed that there were other "bugs" in our home that were too sophisticated to be detected by my primitive "bug" detector. We had to post bond to be released from jail, but the charges were dropped in three days. Outraged by the event, Addie and I sued everyone involved in the raid. We sued for violating our civil rights, illegal search and seizure, since the search warrant wasn't even available when the raid occurred, and theft. None of our property was ever returned and no receipt was ever given for any of the items taken. Three more burglaries occurred from that time through late 1979. Each time my camera was rigged to the door and the resulting photograph was the cause of my property being returned. In each case, the perpetrators claimed to have been recruited for the task by Hubbard policemen. I really didn't know whether I could believe the thieves or just dismiss their claims as parts of a con.

On New Year's Day of 1979, Addie and I flew to New York to meet her brother's four-year-old daughter, Yoshica. Addie's brother lived in Alaska and worked on the Alaskan pipeline. His wife was dying from leukemia. Both of them agreed that the child would be better off with Addie and me. We loved Yoshica as if she were our own daughter, and she had the best of everything. We never accepted a single penny from her mother or father for her care. She went to a private school and wore the very best of clothing. When Addie went to work at General Motors, Yoshica went with me wherever I went, including my shop. Tired of the break-ins at my shop and my home, I decided to give up my shop across town and to work out of the huge extra garage that was attached to my home in Hubbard. Because my home was situated in the middle of a large wooded area, the idea of the "auto ranch" was conceived. I intended to convert the extra land that I bought around my property into car lots, on which I would place a variety of automobiles for sale. Yoshica sometimes spent the night at some of her cousins' homes, but she called our house her home. Burglars plagued us through the spring and summer of 1979. Whenever I'd leave my home for car parts and supplies, the thieves would help themselves to small petty items; they seemed more interested in having a look around than in actually stealing anything. My state-of-the-art burglar alarm did me no good, because the burglars had always gone through the house and left by the time the police got there. To circumvent the cameras on the doors, the thieves used the basement windows. I was about to invest in a total home surveillance camera system when the nightmare of all nightmares befell me. Forces that had simply been intrusions on my life would now prove to be very serious threats on my life.

The constant break-ins led me to send other people to the car parts stores, while I stayed close to our home; there was always someone hanging out there anyway. I was never any further away than a few blocks. The CYP Club (Cars of Youngstown's Prominents) was only walking distance from my home. I often took a break from work to go there for a sandwich and a beer. This car club was very popular and it was always filled with interesting people from all avenues of life. The CYP Club replaced Dee's Lounge as the place where I took my breaks from work. All through the day, someone was at the club arguing about who made the superior American automobile: General Motors, Ford, or Chrysler. Then the debate switched to the pros and cons of foreign automobiles. I almost saw two best friends come to physical blows over an argument about a Harley Davidson motorcycle compared to a Kawasaki. Yarns abounded about the shear brute strength and traction derived from four-wheel-drive vehicles. Cars were not the only topics. Inevitably, some Vietnam veteran would mention the superiority of the Communists' AK-47 machinegun when compared with the American M-16 machinegun. War stories abounded and often overtook conversations about cars. Everyone's favorite topic wasn't cars or guns; the topic of choice was females. Even women at the club liked to talk about other females. A male would mention some woman that he thought was attractive, only to get a pack of shewolves attacking him for his choice. On one occasion, I actually witnessed a woman expose her breasts to give a gentleman some idea of what a real woman looked like. The CYP Club never failed to get my attention. Every minute of every day offered something new and exciting. Tonight was Halloween, and the club was having a masquerade party at 10:00 p.m.

CHAPTER 2

Trick or Treat

I was really looking forward to going to the Halloween party. Yoshica was staying at her cousins' house after their little Halloween party for toddlers. Addie was working the afternoon shift at General Motors and wouldn't be home until 12:30 a.m. I could go to the party for two hours and still be at home to meet my better half when she got there; she was afraid to come home to an empty house, since the thieves walked in anytime they felt like it.

I didn't have a costume, so I decided to wear a dark, burnt-orange, business suit with a mask, and tell everybody that I was disguised as a pumpkin. When I went home to get dressed for the party, I took a friend from the club who wanted to use my bathroom to clean up and get dressed for the same masquerade party at the CYP Club. Children dressed in their goblins, ghosts, and witches outfits filled the streets in my neighborhood. As I stood looking at my dark house, I wondered why the inside lights weren't on as I had left them earlier in the day. One of the neighborhood kids came up to me in her Miss America costume and said, "Trick or treat." I didn't have a piece of candy on me, in my car, or in the house, so I reached into my pockets for some change to give her. For some unknown reason she blurted out that she had seen some men in a pink Cadillac park in my driveway and then enter my house.

When they left the house they turned the lights off. Her father joined her in giving a description of the men and their pink Cadillac. Now, instead of giving the child some change from my pockets, I gave her three dollars. I wondered what had the thieves stolen this time.

I stepped through the door and into the pitch-black foyer of *my* side door entrance into my home. My buddy from the club was standing outside the doorway, waiting for me to find the light switch. When I flipped the light switch, all hell broke loose. I heard a small popping sound, followed by the loudest sound I have ever heard in my life. In a split second, I saw moonlight, as the roof of the foyer and of the garage separated from the foundation of the house. A ball of fire was dropping from the light fixture in the ceiling and it was engulfing *me*. I put my hands up to my face and tried to duck the approaching shower of fire, but it was too late. I held my breath as my mind screamed "Jesus Christ." I was a ball of fire. I could smell my own flesh burning and the smell made me sick to my stomach. I knew I was dying and the thought flashed through my mind that I would never see my beautiful wife again. My wife was pregnant with our first child and I begged the Creator to let me live to see my unborn baby. The fire felt like a thousand hot knives ripping my flesh from head to toe. Everything around me was on fire. I remember thinking that this must be what hell is like. I tried to scream but no words would come out. Fire was in my mouth and up my nose. I was breathing fire. Another explosion knocked me off my feet and into unconsciousness. When I opened my eyes, I realized that the second explosion had temporarily blown out the fire around me. I looked around for my buddy from the club and found him on his stomach, in a semi-conscious state. I helped him to his feet and we stumbled out of the rubble that used to be my home. A crowd had gathered around my home and they were trying to will us to walk out of the inferno on our own, because no one would dare to approach that much heat to help us. I thought what my burned throat couldn't say, "Father in heaven, help us."

As soon as we stepped out of the remains of my home, it swelled into a ball of fire again. At the same time, it started raining and snowing outside. Both of us fell to the ground and rolled in the puddles of rain and snow. Our clothing hissed as the rain and snow extinguished our burning clothing. I didn't care that my home was gone; I didn't care that I was burned from head to toe; I was alive. Praise God for answering my prayer! The crowd of neighbors and I heard several loud pops that sounded like gunfire. I wondered if I had any ammunition in the house that was being detonated by the fire. Then I remembered that all of my guns and ammunition were taken when my home was raided by the authorities.

Someone was shooting at us. The neighbors and I ducked for cover, as a series of gunshots rang out in the night. When the onslaught of gunfire subsided, all of us ran down the street to another neighbor's home to call the ambulance, the fire department, and the police. It was there at the neighbor's home that I first got a look at myself in his mirror. I didn't recognize the pink and bloody mass standing before the mirror. The pink face had no skin, eyebrows, eyelashes, or mustache. The shoulder-length hair was nowhere to be seen. I didn't know who or what I was looking at, but whatever it was, its clothing had been burned off. The pink, bloody, hairless mass was naked. A sheet and blanket were placed around me to prevent me from going into shock. I was assured that an ambulance was on the way. I went outside on the front porch to breathe some cold air into my singed lungs, as the freezing night rain cooled my burned flesh. For me, pain was confirmation that I was still alive.

A familiar car passed me as I sat on my neighbor's front porch. It was my father and my cousin. They were going to my house to ask me to ride to Mississippi with them to attend my uncle's funeral. Can you imagine the looks on their faces when they discovered my home leveled to the ground? Not one cement block, red brick, or piece of lumber remained above ground level. Everything that had made my home had fallen into the basement and burned.

My basement was now a gigantic hole for waste and debris. In the days to come, some neighbors actually dumped their trash into my basement. Anything salvable was looted by the neighbors. I later found out that a light bulb bomb, also called a fire shower, was installed in the ceiling light fixture in the foyer. A light bulb was cut at its base with a glass cutter, filled with gasoline, then glued back together with super glue, and screwed into my light socket. When I hit the light switch, the electricity ignited the gasoline and gave me a fire shower.

The burn pattern on my body is an eternally mapped testimony that verifies what I have stated about the fire. A variety of other types of explosives were also found to have been used on my home. When my father and my cousin came back down the street to where I was, I stepped out into the street and stopped them by waving my white sheet. Can you imagine the look on my father's face when he saw a pink glob approaching his car waving a sheet? He didn't even recognize me. My throat was still very sore and the sound that came out sounded like a dog barking. My father looked at me with tears in his eyes, as he said, "Ben, is that you?" By that time the ambulance was on the scene and the paramedics put me and the other burn victim into the ambulance. The fire wagon went on down to the house, but there was nothing that they could do. The house was gone; the smoldering remains of my home were contained within the cement-block foundation of my basement.

The fire was no longer a threat to anyone; it had done its damage and then it died.

Trick or treat! This was one Halloween I would never forget. For years to come, I would always be extra cautious on Halloween, one of the most sacred holidays of witches, goblins, ghouls, and ghosts. This Halloween I almost became a ghost myself. I was taken to the Akron Burn Clinic, and not expected to live. I was burned over sixty percent of my body. The other burn victim was burned over forty percent of his body. Despite what the doctors told our friends and families about our small chances of survival, we never had any doubts about living. The hardest part was done when we walked out of that ball of fire. After that, everything else was a breeze. I was amazed that a burn victim who was admitted to the hospital at the same time that we were had died from a burn on his foot and leg. I had been burned from my head to my feet, wrapped like a mummy, and I was complaining about not going home in three days' time. This seemingly fit gentleman didn't have a fourth of the burns that I did, yet he panicked, went into shock, and died. So much for the will to live.

The second day of my stay at the Akron Burn Center, the Hubbard Police came to visit me in the hospital. They asked me the general questions concerning the fire and the explosion. One of my car parts chasers, a person who ran to the car parts store for me, was present in my room when the officers visited me. My parts chaser had driven my car to the hospital to see me, and I let him use my car while I was hospitalized. Every day he came to the hospital and hung out with me and the other burn victim. One day the police came to the hospital and informed me that they had a witness who was supposed to be a friend of mine, and that the witness was prepared to testify in court that I had burned my own home to the ground in order to collect the insurance money from it. I wasn't placed under arrest, but a policewoman was placed in my room. She was dressed as a nurse and she told me that she was placed there to make sure that I did not flee from the hospital. After several days, she disappeared from the hospital and the Hubbard Police told me the witness had no credibility, so the accusation was dropped for the time being. I continued to try to heal my burned body. At one time, I was actually prescribed a six-pack of beer a day, to increase my caloric intake, so that my skin would grow back faster.

It seemed like I was in the hospital for a lifetime. Finally, I was released. The other bum victim had been released a week before. True to form, my parts chaser visited me regularly in the hospital, and after my release he visited me at my mother's home. Since my wife had a car, and I was in no shape to drive, I let the parts chaser continue to drive my car. His driving record was so bad that his parents wouldn't let him drive their car, except on very rare occasions. He had been an alcoholic and a heroin user, and had wrecked his own automobile and his parents' several times before. I was the only one who trusted his driving. I remember his teasing of my wife, when she couldn't find a spot on which to kiss me, because I was wrapped from head to toe like a mummy. Everyone thought that he had beaten his heroin and alcohol addictions. Creeping back to some normalcy, I began to feel pretty good, physically and mentally. I had just received a notice from the United States District Court, stating that I was to give an oral deposition in court, on January 23, 1980, in support of my lawsuit because of the raid that took place at my home on February 13, 1978. Three weeks later, the Hubbard Police charged me with burning my home to the ground to collect the insurance money. The date of the charges was the second anniversary of the raid.

Imagine my surprise when my parts chaser called me at my mother's home, after I had posted bond and was released from jail. He told me that he was the confidential informant mentioned in the warrant for my arrest. My buddy from the club, who was also burned in the fire, was also charged with arson. The parts chaser revealed that he was at the Akron Burn Center to visit us, when a Hubbard policeman, nicknamed "The Pitbull," asked him about the track marks on his arms. Track marks are the telltale marks of the needle that are left on an intravenous drug user's arms. The Pitbull spotted the marks and posed some hypothetical scenarios in which the parts chaser would be jailed until he got "sick" from not getting his drugs. This is called "cold turkey," and it is a junkie's worst nightmare. Most junkies die during cold turkey. The parts chaser revealed that while the police were satisfied with the carefully scripted and perjured testimony they forced from him, he had the presence of mind to include some easily refuted statements in that perjured testimony. The parts chaser drove my car to the Akron Burn Clinic every day to visit us, but he intentionally testified that he was kidnapped by my father and mother for four days, to keep him from telling the truth about the arson. My father went to Mississippi to bury his dead brother the next day after the explosion and the fire. Hundreds of witnesses and a program listing the pallbearers and family members in attendance are a matter of public record. My mother was wheelchair-bound at the time, because of a debilitating stroke that left her crippled for life. The parts chaser knew all of this and claims that he intentionally crafted his entire testimony in such a way that it could easily be refuted. Not bad thinking for a burned out junkie, but the simple truth should have sufficed. He told the truth at first, but that was not what the police wanted.

The Pitbull made it a habit of stopping by or calling my mother's home, where Addie, Yoshica, and I were living after the fire. Again there was the talk of doing favors for favors.

Once he pretended to be doing me a favor by telling me that some of the Hubbard policemen believed that my lawsuit was the equivalent of spitting in their faces. The parts chaser revealed many other easily refuted statements from his perjured testimony, to me and to the other burn victim. The rumor on the street was that the parts chaser's brother had been kidnapped because the parts chaser had shorted someone of a considerable amount of money during a drug deal. The other burn victim and I were questioned about the disappearance of the parts chaser's brother, and then we were dismissed by the authorities. The two gentlemen who misrepresented themselves to me as Black Muslims, the Muhammad brothers, made a telephone call to the parts chaser, in which they asked him to do the right thing and to tell the truth. Their conversation was recorded by the police, who had bugged the parts chaser's phone. One of the Muhammad brothers was charged with Obstruction of Justice, because a claim was made by a Youngstown prosecutor that Muhammad attempted to persuade the parts chaser to change his testimony.

To give you some idea of how intricate this web of deception was that was being woven around me, consider this: the Muhammad brother who claimed to be a Black Muslim attempting to take the rackets away from "The Mob" was later revealed to be a special investigator for the very same Youngstown prosecutor who filed the Obstruction of Justice charge against him, and who also won a conviction that got Muhammad six months in jail.

After Muhammad had been sentenced, the Youngstown prosecutor asked me to come to his office to discuss a few things. My wife, our newborn baby Benita, and our niece Yoshica were banned from the meeting. The prosecutor said that the Muhammads had again claimed that they were taking over the rackets with the assistance I was providing them. The prosecutor put his finger in my face and told me that no one was taking over "his" territory. I was told that I'd better pick the winning side or stay out of the turf war completely. Just for good measure, I was told that the Youngstown prosecutor's office could stack charges on me until I buckled from the weight. I was told that a very beneficial opportunity was coming my way. If I were a smart boy, I'd take advantage of that opportunity, he explained. My wife and any other witnesses had been banned from our "sit-down," but I had heeded the advice of Lying Johnny, and I carried a micro recorder to the meeting. After that, I carried the micro recorder everywhere I went. I recorded any and everybody. Taping all of my telephone calls became an absolute must. Sometimes paranoia can be a survival skill.

The opportunity that the Youngstown prosecutor spoke of presented itself through the Hubbard policeman called the Pitbull. One day in late September of 1980, the Pitbull called me at my mother's home when I was in the bathtub. When I got out of the tub, I got out my micro recorder and put in a new cassette cartridge and new batteries. I called the Pitbull to see what he had to say. Almost immediately, he started crying about his money problems, since his wife had divorced him and he had to move in with his mother. I suspected he was taping our conversation, just as I was, but both of us assured the other that no taping was going on. The Pitbull told me that the problems between us were caused by a lack of communication. He claimed to have permission from the Trumbull County prosecutor, J. Walter Dragelevich, to make a deal with me in which everyone would prosper. He emphasized that he could put an end to all of my problems, and that he was in a position to offer me more than anyone else had offered so far. Arrangements were made to meet him at Perkin's Pancake House in Hubbard, the next day, September 28, 1980, at 8:00 p.m.

When I met the Pitbull, I was searched immediately, because of my reputation for recording all of my conversations. The deal was simple: lie low for a while and let the lawsuit lapse because I would not have shown up at any of the hearings. The police felt particularly vulnerable to the lawsuit and the publicity because they had looted many other homes without cause, and never returned the looted property. The property taken from my home was of considerable worth, and no justification was ever given for the indiscriminant looting. The Pitbull revealed that the property was gone and that there was no way that the police could recover it. Furthermore, the police didn't want to give their other victims the encouragement to file some type of action to recover their looted property. Federal officials were investigating some of the activities of the Hubbard Police Department and those under suspicion didn't want the extra attention. According to the deal, after the court dropped the lawsuit because I failed to show up at the hearings, the Hubbard Police would drop the arson charges against me and I could still collect the insurance money to rebuild my home. We were to meet again at midnight to cement the deal with the Trumbull Prosecutor himself, J. Walter Dragelevich.

I cursed myself for not spending the five hundred dollars for the wireless microphone that looked like an ink pen. It would have been perfect for this situation. I told my closest friends and relatives about the proposed deal. Those who supported the deal and those who opposed it were split down the middle, fifty-fifty. I had been made another proposal earlier in the week, when my Progressive Insurance agent, Edwin M. Dickey, told me that the witness and the case against me were not credible, and that for a ten thousand dollar reduction in my claim, he could assure me that my claim would be honored by his company. At the time, I was insulted by the suggestion. Looking back on it now, it was the deal of a lifetime. My lawyer's fee alone was going to be more than that; in addition, my attorney wanted one-third of my settlement to sue the insurance company. Progressive Insurance assured me that anytime I decided to present my evidence to prove my innocence, they would be delighted to pay the claim. I later found that they decided to hide behind the statute of limitations for honoring claims, even though I could prove my innocence. At a future date, Progressive Insurance authorities had no problem admitting that they had to fire Edwin M. Dickey for suspected criminal behavior in processing insurance claims in which he was a party to the suspected insurance fraud. He was also suspected of "shaking down" the insured if they wanted their claims honored. Since then, I have found out about one case in particular, in which Dickey extorted money from an individual to process his claim that his Jaguar XKE was accidentally burned. I met Dickey through the individual involved, and sat in on the negotiations over the split of the insurance money. Dickey never knew who I was. He told the other individual how much he wanted from the deal, and the insured reluctantly complied. That individual is available and willing to testify today about the corrupt policies of Edwin M. Dickey, while at

Progressive Insurance. The individual mentioned has several other insured who wish to reveal the true nature of their relationship with Edwin M. Dickey and the insurance company he represented.

I met the Pitbull at Perkin's Pancake House at midnight. As I sat in the parking lot, he approached my car and rapped on the window. The Pitbull claimed that the person in the other car was in fact the Trumbull County Prosecutor, J. Walter Dragelevich, and the deal was solid. I never could see if the individual in the other car was the prosecutor or not. When I left the parking lot, I hit my bright lights to try to get a better look at the person in the car, but that person ducked down in anticipation of my attempt. The Pitbull had already told me that some Hubbard police were irate over my accusations and my lawsuit. He said that some of them couldn't be restrained and that it was difficult to predict their actions. The Youngstown prosecutor did indeed attempt to stack charges on top of me. An employee of his went to college with me at Youngstown State University. That old friend warned me that the prosecutor was thinking about charging me with Obstruction of Justice because I was an associate of the Muhammad brothers, and a stretch of the facts might insinuate that the Muhammads acted on my behalf in contacting the confidential informant. The Muhammads had already denied that I had any part in their phone call to my parts chaser. Oddly enough, the Muhammads revealed that the Youngstown prosecutor had promised to give them less time if they admitted that I had something to do with the highjack of a truckload of steel pipes, that ended up in the South, for sale at an auction. I never made the connection. I had no idea why the Youngstown prosecutor wanted to implicate me in the highjack and sale of a truckload of stolen pipes that were only suited for underground sewage systems.

I couldn't believe my ears and eyes when I saw my picture being flashed on television, with the statement that I was the leader of the Italian mob, the Hispanic mob, and the black mob. These groups were always at constant war over somebody's "turf."

Neither the United Nations nor the Pope could have negotiated any type of mutual compromise between these traditional enemies; yet I was credited with being the head of all three. The caption on the television screen said that I was armed and extremely dangerous. Policemen were instructed to shoot me on sight. So much for our deal. The double-cross had started already. It was time to go, but I had to go the right way. I had to be dead, or at least make it look like I was. I had studied crime scenes with some private detective friends, and I knew enough about blood splatter and gunshot residue to stage my own murder. I chose an abandoned warehouse in a remote part of town. I parked my car in the drive and tossed food about the front seat. I used a syringe to draw four vials of my blood to be sprayed from a highpressured spray gun with a modified tip the diameter of a .38 caliber revolver.

As I sprayed the shirt-covered board, I also fired a gun through the two open front windows of my car. The mixture of the blood splatter and the gunshot residue, along with my own bloody fingerprints, painted a convincing picture that I went to meet someone, and was shot while eating in my car. My smeared fingerprints on the outside of the car gave the impression that I was carried away after the shooting. I left the car running with the keys in the ignition. I walked to a payphone to signal a friend to pick me up. The date was September 28, 1980; trick-or-treat had come early that year.

CHAPTER 3

A Few Miles from Home

One of my closest friends, and also a member of our private hot rod clubhouse, came to pick me up just five minutes after I called him from the payphone. He lived and worked in Lorain, Ohio, just a few miles from Youngstown, but his girlfriend lived in Youngstown. He was one of the ones who voted not to trust the deal with the Hubbard policemen. We went to his place in Lorain, Ohio, in less than an hour's time, where I was surprised at how clean the town was in comparison to Youngstown and Hubbard. There also seemed to be a mutual respect between the races that was obviously absent in Youngstown and Hubbard. Larry from Lorain introduced me as his cousin, when we bumped into some of his associates at the local grocery store. Larry did mention that there were a few Youngstowners who worked there in Lorain. He pointed them out to me and showed me where they lived. One of the Youngstowners attended Youngstown State University at the same time that I did. We knew each other well and often attended the same drag strips and fraternity functions. We used to lift weights together in the Youngstown University gym. I'd have to keep out of his sight because he could recognize me very easily. I knew that he had been an intravenous drug user and had received the treatment, but it was rumored that he was still "using." Most users had reputations as snitches and informants. I will identify this individual by the same nickname he used in college: Muscles. Muscles worked in the same steel mill as Larry did, but they worked different shifts. Larry warned me often that Muscles was bad news.

When I walked away from my mother's home, where everybody I loved lived, I didn't even say goodbye. It was approximately 1:00 a.m. when I left there. By the time Larry and I got to Lorain, it was about 2:00 am. After hitting the grocery store, Larry suggested that we stop at his favorite bar. I knew that it was Sunday and that no bars were open on Sunday.

Larry took me to an after-hours joint that was as illegal as Al Capone. The first thing that I thought about was the police raiding this illegal after-hours joint and accidentally stumbling into me. Larry assured me that this place was "cool" because the owner "paid off" to the right people. I pulled my cap down over my eyes and then sat in the back of the place, in the dark. Sitting in the dark, I noticed how pink my hands were. Most of my color had come back into my face, but the rest of my body was pink like an albino. My body was covered with clothing, but my pink hands drew too much attention. Larry noticed it too and gave me his driving gloves to hide my hands with. I wore gloves like that for another six months, until the color came back into my hands. My usual excuse for wearing the gloves was that I had a motorcycle parked outside and I was tired of misplacing my gloves, so I kept them on. It was an incredibly stupid reply but no one questioned me any further.

Larry was well known at the after-hours club. It was obvious that he spent a lot of time there. Everyone there rushed to buy him drinks; and all of them knew what he drank. Two butterscotch-colored strippers were rubbing their naked bodies against each other, when Larry approached their dancing cage, which was elevated above the floor of the club. Their gyrations ceased momentarily as they recognized Larry and waved at him. When they had finished their dance number, they came over to sit with Larry and me, in the back, in the dark.

Larry introduced me as his cousin and the dancers seemed impressed that I was related to him. Larry made a point of emphasizing that they give me the same treatment as they gave him. The two girls replied that they would be glad to do so. One of the girls sat on my lap as the other went back to her cage to perform a solo dance number. These were two of the most perfect females I had ever seen. I later found out that they were sisters, but they looked more like twins. They claimed that they had started stripping to pay their way through college and got hooked on the big money. Their rationale was that they were making more money by stripping than they would have ever made from a straight job after graduating from college.

Above all of the noise in that bar, and there was a lot of noise, I heard the distinct howling laughter that reminded me of a jackal. Didn't I used to know someone who laughed like that? I sure did. Who was it that made such a ridiculous sound when they laughed? I turned in the direction of the bar, with the beautiful dancer still sitting on my lap. Larry stopped me from turning all the way around to see the person doing the jackal laugh. Larry was looking into the face of that jackal and waving to him. That jackal came over to our table and talked to Larry for a few minutes. I recognized the voice but couldn't place it. In an effort to hide my face, I whispered something into the ear of the dancer who was sitting on my lap. I don't even know what I said but she seemed to be pleased and interested. I kept whispering in her ear until the jackal left. When he had left, Larry asked, "So you know who that was, right? That was your old friend Muscles. Don't worry, he left the building. He's so drunk that he wouldn't recognize you anyway."

The dancer sitting on my lap said, "Honey, your heart is about to jump out of your chest. It's good to know that I still have that effect on a man."

Larry and I laughed and ordered some more drinks. I didn't want any more beer, I needed a very serious stiff drink of liquor, and Larry needed two. A week later, Muscles got fired for being drunk on the job. He went back to Youngstown and I never saw him or anyone else whom I knew from Youngstown again, for the entire time that I stayed in Lorain, Ohio.

I stashed myself at Larry's place from September 1980 to February 1981. I never left the house until Larry came home, and I never talked on the telephone. I missed my wife, my kids, my mother, and my cars. Even now, as I write about that time, the pain of being away from them makes a tear swell up in my eye. I spent much of my day attempting to distract my attention from my pain and problems by watching the "Playboy Channel" or reading. After I had read every magazine that Larry owned, I looked for a book to read. The only book Larry owned was the King James Version of the Bible. I always meant to read the whole thing, now I had the opportunity. Life was much freer after Muscles got fired from the steel mill and he had to move back to Youngstown. Every weekend, Larry went to Youngstown to see his girlfriend. Around Valentine's Day of 1981, I had him contact a friend of ours who was a Youngstown police officer and a distant relative to my wife, Addie. The officer relayed the message that Larry wanted to meet her somewhere. It was agreed that they would meet in the parking lot of Yoshica's elementary school one evening, while Addie was attending a PTA meeting there. Larry told her that everything was all right and that I would be moving to the clubhouse near Youngstown University a little later in the year. What he didn't tell her was that the clubhouse was a stone's throw away from the Youngstown Police Department's private bar and club. Usually, there were more policemen present at the policeman's club than there were at the annual policeman's ball. Youngstown State University's football team practiced next to our hot rod clubhouse, and the policemen were always at the practice field when the football team was doing its practice drills. Nonetheless, that was where our clubhouse was and we had never had any trouble from the police. We tolerated them and they tolerated us. Often the policemen acted so ridiculously that we wished that we could have called the police on them. But the question is, "Who polices the police?"

In Lorain, I spent the day absorbed by the Bible. Everything I read in it lead me to ask more questions. I found myself going to the library to find Bible reference books and other scholarly works on Bible interpretation. A rabbi that I met in a Lorain library told me about the Hebrew to English translation of the Bible that was a lot more accurate than the King James Version. Unfortunately, that particular Hebrew version was never on the shelves of any of the Lorain libraries. I made myself content to read the King James Version over many times. I'd always write down the questions I had about a particular passage of scripture. Before I knew it, I had several notebooks filled with unanswered questions about the Bible. From my conversations with the local preachers, rabbis, and priests, I surmised that they didn't know any more about the accurate interpretation of scripture than I did. They were essentially blind shepherds leading blind sheep. Trusting souls were leaving their salvation up to men who didn't even know what they were talking about. How many lost souls got even more lost because they settled for the inaccurate interpretations of men who were too lazy to seek out legitimate and reliable sources of Bible interpretations?

My own dire situation mandated that I get the correct meaning of the scriptures, if I intended to let them guide me, now, in my most critical time of need. I was particularly inspired by the story of David hiding in the wilderness from King Saul, but always believing that the Creator would reward him for his perseverance and faith. I felt that I had to maintain my faith in the Creator, even when my future looked its darkest. Larry got to the point that he teased me about my Bible reading, and started calling me "The Deacon." The nickname stuck and everyone in Lorain started calling me "The Deacon." Larry told me about a homeless person that he met outside of the after-hour joint, who fit my description. For a few drinks and a few dollars, the man could be persuaded to give up his ID, report it lost, and get some new ID. The perfect thing about using this man's ID was the fact that he didn't have a job, so he didn't pay taxes or Social Security, he didn't drive or have insurance, he didn't have a police record anywhere, and he didn't have any relatives or next of kin looking for him. He could use the new ID and I could use the old ID. Since there were no records or "trails" that could be used to trace his activities or whereabouts, we could have been in the same town or on opposite sides of the world, and no one would ever know that two people were sharing the same identity. So long as neither one of us got arrested and fingerprinted, we could get away with this. Larry called this method of procuring ID "double entry," because two people were entered into one identity. Actually, several people could have used the same identity.

So long as the original ID was not called in stolen, the double-entry system worked fine. If the original owner of the ID said that the ID were destroyed in the washing machine, then he was promptly issued another. If he said that the ID were lost, he'd probably get another one quickly. If he said that the ID were stolen, then the authorities would initiate some type of investigation, because many unscrupulous types were always stealing someone else's ID. There has always been big money in legally registered alternate identification, and there still is. I started to listen to the Bible interpreters on the radio and the television. Some of them seemed to have some idea of what they were talking about; others didn't seem to have a clue. I wanted to be sure about the correct interpretation of scripture and often found that the same scripture was being interpreted by the same "expert," differently each time he or she interpreted it. If I hadn't been keeping notes, I would never have caught on to this inconsistency. I'll bet that most of the listening audience didn't catch these inconsistencies.

The word came from friends in Youngstown that the police had called the FBI in on my case. Everyone I knew was being threatened with taking lie detector tests. The police and the FBI walked into my mother's home as if it were the local department store. Most of the time, warrants weren't shown or issued. I was the oldest of five brothers. Four of us fit the same description. Any time one of the four was at my mother's home or in the neighborhood, the police would detain him and fingerprint him to see if he were me. I had tall cousins who lived in the neighborhood and were always at my mother's home. They suffered the same fate as my brothers. My brothers had tall friends who were also detained and fingerprinted for being in the vicinity of my mother's home. We have a tall female cousin who likes to wear baseball caps. She was stopped one day by the authorities because she had just left my mother's home. They thought that she was me. Needless to say, few friends or relatives wanted to visit my mother's home. My mother got to the point where she kept the curtains drawn in her home. Her bright and sunny home took on an air of darkness, and despair.

By now, talk of my taping several individuals was pervasive in Youngstown, Ohio.

Everyone was trying to think of what we talked about when we last conversed. It is reasonable to say that most of Youngstown was worried that they had compromised themselves on my micro recorder. There were several rumors that politicians, policemen, and mobsters thought it best if my recordings and I never surfaced. In Lorain, I was still playing the role of the religious bookworm, ever seeking answers to the questions I had compiled in my three note-books. In the evenings and the early morning hours, I accompanied Larry to the local after-hours joint. One evening, in the middle of February 1981, we saw the owner of the place being threatened by the person we assumed the owner paid for protection from raids.

The conversation got loud enough that someone turned off the music, while everyone in the packed place paid full attention to the confrontation. The thick, muscular man in the black suit was mak-ing a point of letting everyone know that he was in a position to do anything he wanted to the owner of the club. He grabbed the owner by the collar and was leading him to one of the back storage rooms. Larry did something that I know he should have known better than to do—he interfered. Larry walked up to the thick, burly man in the black suit and asked him if there was a problem. The man ignored Larry as he continued to dictate terms to the owner of the club. Larry made matters worse by tapping the burly man on his shoulder.

The big man turned toward Larry in a very slow deliberate fash-ion that let everyone know that he was mad as hell. He stared at Larry for a long time, with eyes that looked like blue ice. It was the coldest, deadest pair of eyes I have ever seen. Again Larry asked if there were a problem. The thick, burly man replied, "Nigger, are you trying to impress the ladies or what?" Larry answered that he just didn't want to see anyone get hurt. To that the burly man yelled, "Nigger, are you saying that you're going to hurt me?"

"No, sir," Larry said in his most humbled tone.

The burly man thought that he saw a sign of weakness in Larry and decided to teach this nigger a lesson for interfering in white folks' business. The big man released the petite owner of the club from his vise-like grip and gave Larry his undivided attention. I was thinking, "This is the very reason why I shouldn't be in a place like this." Didn't I know better than to be here in the first place? When the big, burly man swung a wild and deadly punch at Larry, Larry blocked the punch and kicked the man in the groin. The big bully doubled over in pain and started to spit up his lunch. The barmaid gave the big bully some napkins to wipe his mouth and he was led to an exit door. The owner of the club assured the bully that the payments would be brought up to date very soon. The bully grunted something and staggered out of the door. Larry was the hero of the hour. Everyone bought him double shots of the most expensive liquors that the club sold. The finest women in the club whispered sweet promises in his ears. While Larry reaped the rewards of being a hero for a day, I asked the owner of the club about the dangerous-looking man and the people he represented.

The owner revealed that the burly man worked for a small band of thugs who had connections with the local politicians and the police. For a fee, the owner of the club was permitted to run his place the way he wanted, but when the Feds were in town, the order to shut down for a while had to be strictly adhered to. The petite owner of the club obeyed orders and was making enough money to buy an impressive home in the suburbs and he was sending three daughters to college. For him, crime was paying. The owner of the club was glad to add that the small-time thugs in Lorain were taking orders from the big shots in Akron, Cleveland, and Youngstown. He specifically mentioned the last names of several of Youngstown's top mob figures. As small as this place was, as out of the way as it was, and as clean and robust as this town seemed to be, it was still a "connected" town. According to the owner, every now and then, someone would drop in from Akron, Cleveland, or Youngstown, just to make sure that everything was going smoothly. A great uneasiness overcame me when I thought about Youngstown mobsters coming to this club to check it out.

I realized that it was about time to accept one of those drinks that Larry's fan club was buying.

As I sat at the table, in the back, in the dark, with Larry, I noticed that there were two new dancing girls at the club, and there was a new doorman on duty. Larry and I ordered double shots of Scotch and fish sandwiches. Larry was explaining for the one hundredth time that he had been a martial arts instructor for the Green

Beret during his time in Vietnam. He was actually showing barmaids and dancing girls how to perform simple acts of self-defense.

I was impressed with Larry's knowledge of the arts of self-defense, and I had seen him in action several times. Larry delighted in holding these pretty girls closely, as he instructed them in their deadly maneuvers. One small delicate-looking young lady proudly proclaimed that she had a black belt in karate. She was more than anxious to get into this display of exhibitionism with Larry and his crew of would-be female assassins. Larry and his deadly females were going through a series of punches and kicks for the audience that had gathered around them. This lightweight exhibition of martial arts skills was actually stealing attention away from the new dancing girls, who were really showing their best assets.

The attention of the club patrons was divided between the new dancing girts and Larry's karate demonstration. The new doorman wasn't very good at his job and got caught up in watching the two shows instead of watching the door. The club owner had stepped into the back room for a minute to check on his supply of liquor. No one paid any attention to the massive figure that lumbered into the club. No one paid any attention as he looked around the club until he found his target. No one paid any attention as he reached inside of his trench coat and pulled out the Uzi machine pistol. Standing in the middle of the club, flashing the Uzi, was the burly man, and he had bad intentions on his mind. He aimed the Uzi directly at Larry and froze him as if he were deep frozen. Larry was paralyzed with fright. He no longer thought of karate and hand-to-hand combat. All that Larry or anyone else in the club thought about was death or flight. The burly man aimed the Uzi toward the ceiling and fired off a burst of ammunition. Then he lowered the gun to the floor and kicked off another burst of bullets.

Glass and wooden splinters were flying everywhere, as the patrons of the club ran over each other like rats in a bucket. The Uzi was talking to me and it was saying, "Get the hell out of the way." Everyone ran out of the bar and down the street. I think some are still running today.

When I finally stopped running, I must have been two miles away from the club. My heart was pounding out of my chest. Larry was nowhere to be found. Groups of people were talking about their escape from death. No one had the nerve to go back to the club to see if Larry and the owner were all right. I was sure that the burly man was only interested in making a show of force to keep the locals in line, after Larry embarrassed him, but you never know what crazies will do. I walked to a pay phone and called the club to see what was going on.

The owner of the club answered the phone and told me that the burly man had left and that Larry ran out of the club when the rest of the patrons fled. No one was hit by the gunfire and according to the owner, this is how the burly gunman got people's attention when he wanted to make a point. Well, he got my attention and he made his point. I bummed a ride back to Larry's apartment just to find him laughing about the whole thing. He had the nerve to tell me that he was never worried about the shooter actually hitting anyone with the gunfire. According to Larry, the shooter was just a lot of mouth and hot air. It was then that I realized that Larry was a little too bold and too high profile for me to be trying to hide out with. I'd be noticed for simply being with him. My whole objective was to not be seen—to be invisible.

I was still scared. I was shaking like a flag on a pole on the fourth of July. I also had been fighting the loneliness of being without my devoted wife, my new baby, my niece, and my mother. Larry found out that my niece had gone back to live with her mother and father. Her mother had made a miraculous recovery from leukemia and she was expected to live a normal life span. Larry had told our friends in Youngstown to spread rumors that I had gone to California, Brazil, Mexico, and Canada. I was being sought after everywhere but in Youngstown, Ohio. I had planned to slip back into Youngstown and hide out at the old clubhouse. None of my friends would tell and the police weren't even aware of my association with the place. Lorain was a sweet old girl, but I had to let her go. This was not a place to hide out in and Larry was the last person to hide out with. I could have died in that club, just a few miles away from home, and no one would ever know who the stranger was with the false ID. Friends on the police force said that Youngstown was the last place anyone expected me.

Larry had also told our friends to spread rumors that I had extensive plastic surgery and that he didn't recognize me himself. My old race car buddies were glad to spread the misinformation for me. One thing I had learned from the thousands of old cowboy movies that I was addicted to as a child was to always backtrack when the pursuers least expected you to do so. Enough time had lapsed and my friends had done a good job of spreading rumors of where I was and what I looked like. I knew that I could slip into Youngstown by night and never be discovered at the old clubhouse. Maybe I could see my gorgeous wife and my new baby. It would be wonderful to hold my better half in my arms again and to tell her how much I missed her. I really missed seeing my only child grow, walk, and talk. What I had learned from my Bible reading was that if my cause were just, then the Creator would provide a way for me to overcome all of these obstacles and I could still live a long and productive life with my family. I simply had to believe that the Creator was in control. The thought occurred to me that I had been married for five years and I hadn't been a husband to my wife for the past five months. Maybe she was tired of waiting for me and found someone else. Then again, I was talking about my wife, Addie; my soul mate, the woman that the Creator sent to me to be my partner for life, until death do us part. My faith in her and the Creator made me believe that she would give me more time to straighten out this mess. Goodbye, Lorain, I'm going home.

Though Lorain was just a few miles from home, it just did not offer the comforts, the memories, or the loved ones that I left in Youngstown. It bothered me that I never even got a chance to say goodbye to my loved ones and I knew that they would be fighting mad. I expected them to hug and kiss me first, then I expected them to tear me apart.

Hiding in Plain Sight

B ack in Youngstown, next door to the Youngstown State football practice field, a stone's through away from the policemen's bar and club, sat our little hot rod clubhouse. Larry and I arrived there at night. There were only eight members there. These were "The Knights of the Round Table," they would die for each other. I was bombarded with questions and answers at the same time. Someone was reporting on my brothers, my mother, my wife, and my child. Someone else was asking me about Lorain and the Uzi. What really got my attention was someone mentioning something about altering my appearance. From the time that I had been admitted to the Akron Burn Hospital, I had grown a beard because my skin was too sensitive to shave. I had always been clean-shaven before the fire and everyone assumed that my face was so badly burned that I hid the bums with my beard.

I had worn glasses all of my life and no one had ever seen me without glasses. My skin had been lightened considerably by the fire, and I was actually told that I had the black burned off me. My hair was long enough to comb over my eyes to conceal my forehead. After much debate, trial, and error, my buddies came up with a disguise for me that my mother wouldn't be able to see through. At this point, I'd like to say that if it weren't for the expertise of my friends, I would have been caught and possibly murdered a long time ago. I became a product of my friends' wits. Everything I learned, I learned from them. I was trained by them to survive. They all contributed to my survival skills, then they prayed for me, and sent me on my way.

Before the fire, my skin color was the same as Michael Jordan's. After the fire my skin was white, then pink, and then red. In Lorain, my skin darkened to the color of Denzel Washington's. That alone aided me considerably in disguising myself. I shaved my beard and mustache off; then I got a pair of hazel-brown contact lenses. I combed my hair over my forehead and just above my eyes. I didn't recognize the Puerto Rican standing in front of the clubhouse mirror. I practiced disguising my voice by using a tape recorder to listen to the changes. After satisfying myself with several new voices, I decided that a noticeable limp would be a nice touch. It was time to try this disguise out on someone who knew me very well. It was time to go home to my family. Larry left his car at the clubhouse and we had the other members drive us to my mother's home in a van. It was close to midnight when I rang the doorbell at my mother's home. One of my brothers was still living there at the time and he answered the door. "Yes, may I help you? Who are you looking for?"

I replied, "I'm looking for you."

My brother took a deep breath and stared at me very closely, "Ben, is that you?"

If I hadn't spoken in my normal voice, he would never have known who I was. Larry stepped from around the comer of the porch and said, "If you had seen me, you probably would have guessed who he was." We went on into the house while the van waited on the other side of the street, as if they were visiting someone else.

My wife was still living with my mother. My brother called her down the steps and she sleepily staggered on down. My mother had heard the doorbell when we first rang it and she arrived in the living room at the same time that Addie reached it from the upstairs bedroom. "Hi, Larry, who's your friend?" my mother asked.

Larry replied through his laughter, "Don't you recognize your own son, Mom? Don't you recognize your own husband, Addie?"

Both of them had to sit down. I suspect that they were both about to faint. After a long pause the two of them showered me with hugs and kisses. I heard a noise behind me and I turned to see my eight-month-old daughter, Benita. She looked like a miniature of her mother, Addie. It pained me not to have been there when she spoke her first word or took her first step. The worst thing about it all was that I still couldn't stay with them. I held my baby in my arms as I told everyone about my Lorain adventures. I hugged and kissed everyone and told them that I'd be staying at the clubhouse for a while. Addie followed me outside the house for a few private moments. She held me so tight and kissed me so hard that I still remember the kiss to this day. I loved the way her lips felt on mine and I was mad that I had to leave those lips. I didn't expect any promises from Addie because I didn't have any control over my own fate, but she told me, "I will forever be your wife and you will forever be my husband. There will never be anyone else for me but you, until death do us part." That was all the reassurance I needed.

Before Larry and I slipped back out to the van, Addie told me that she preferred my old color, but that this color was all right for the time being. "You know I'm not very big on brown men," she said as I left. Those very words would have a profound effect on my life later on.

Valentine's Day had just passed and this was the first time since I'd met Addie that I hadn't gotten her something for that day. Many holidays and special occasions would pass with neither one of us knowing whether the other was alive or dead. I could only hope for the best and put my total and complete trust in the Creator. I was glad to hear that Addie was still a staunch churchgoer, and that she was serious about the accurate interpretation of scripture.

After a few days, I got settled in at the clubhouse and Larry went back to Lorain. There was a telephone in the clubhouse, but I never used it. A prearranged signal was agreed upon, in case someone needed to reach me. My wife and daughter came to visit me often at the clubhouse; as did my brothers, my mother, and my father. It was agreed by all that if my lawsuit against the Hubbard Police were dropped and they still didn't drop the arson charges against me, it might be better to find some other permanent place to live, instead of trying to fight the bogus case in court. No one believed that I could win the case against the racists in Trumbull County. The prosecutor and the judge in the case had made personal comments to the media, in an attempt to paint me as a mad dog who needed to be put out of his misery.

I thought of going to the FBI with the tapes I had of the crooked Hubbard policemen, but then I discovered that Cleveland FBI agents were actually paid money to release confidential information to the subject of one of their own organized crime investigations. The FBI took a bribe from the mob to reveal how much the FBI had on the mob. Shortly after that, one of the heads of the Cleveland FBI actually became the chief of police in Youngstown, Ohio, and it was rumored that he was on the payroll of the local mob boss. This same former FBI agent was known to operate a bar owned by that local mob boss. The Cleveland FBI office actually had to investigate this former colleague of theirs. Naturally they gave one of their own a clean bill of health. So much for going to the FBI for a fair roll of the dice. It looked more and more like I would have to make running a way of life. If I could get my hands on enough money and the right ID, I could relocate and send for my wife and child. I could grow old and prosperous somewhere other than Youngstown, Ohio.

After the novelty of my presence at the clubhouse wore off, the members slacked up on dropping by. I was usually at the clubhouse by myself all day long, until Addie or one of the members dropped by after dark. Addie and I tried to map some future out of this ball of confusion. The best we could come up with was for me to go somewhere to generate enough income to relocate to another country. I had just the place in mind and they didn't honor American extradition. I was already conversant in the language and I was determined to speak it like a native very soon. When I wasn't perfecting my language skills, I was reading scripture. The clubhouse formerly belonged to an elderly preacher. He died and left volumes of Bibles and biblical history books. His library was replete with books on anthropology, archaeology, and Black history. I only watched the television for the news. Usually I was absorbed in one of the books from the late preacher's library. No one else was ever interested in that library, not even after I revealed what a treasure it was. Now it was my library.

I often sent Addie or one of the club members to the Youngstown Public Library to get the Hebrew-to-English interpretation of the scriptures. Even though I could see the library from the clubhouse,

I didn't dare venture out of my hiding spot in the daytime or go to a public spot. To keep the police from paying any attention to the cars visiting the clubhouse, everyone visiting me parked a block or two away from the club and walked to the house. The lights, music, and noise at the clubhouse were kept to a minimum to avoid attention.

The Hebrew-to-English interpretation of the scriptures made sense of the confusing wording and meanings of the King James Version of the Bible. The scriptures took on a whole new meaning. Soon I was able to answer the questions I had accumulated in my three notebooks. One of the most important bits of information I got from the Hebrew-to-English interpretations was the name of the Creator and his son. According to the scriptures, there is power in the actual name of the Creator. That name was used to heal the sick and to perform miracles in the old days. That same name had power in it for all time. In times of trouble and danger, one was advised to call on the only name that saves: Yahweh (Yah-way). Yahweh means "I am" or "I exist." The son's name honors the father by mentioning the father's name and his function. The son's name is Yahshua. It means, "Yahweh is salvation." To mention or call upon the son's name is also to call upon the father's name, because the father's name is included in the son's. I called on the father's and the son's names so much that I thought that they probably got tired of me pestering them. In a short time, I was to find out that they were not pestered but pleased. I would soon reap the benefits of calling on them by their names.

Up to June of 1981 I had not had any medical problems that required a doctor. On my daughter's birthday, June 8, a wisdom tooth started to hurt very badly. By my wife's birthday, June 20, my face was swollen and the pain was killing me. I thought about pulling the wisdom tooth with pliers or vise grips, but the pain was too intense to even touch the tooth. I eventually had to do what I didn't want to do. I had to go to a doctor. I used a false ID to go to a dentist in Akron, Ohio, less than an hour away. When I signed in at the registration desk, I triple-checked to make sure that I didn't use my real name or Social Security number. After having the tooth filled, I was so groggy that I wondered if I had given myself away by saying something I shouldn't have, while I was anesthetized. Addie signed me out of the clinic because I was still having a bad reaction to the drugs the dentist gave me, which left me very groggy. I went back to the club-house to let my gums heal. That night I had the first of many bad dreams about signing my real name and Social Security number on the forms at the doctor's office. The dream worried me so much that I decided to erase my real Social Security number from my mind. The danger that my real Social Security number posed to me was more than enough to force me to hypnotize myself into believing that the fake ID was who I really was. In the years to come, I would actually have trouble remembering my original Social Security number, and I would actually wonder if I knew anyone by the name of Ben.

Addie had dropped me off a couple of blocks from the club-house and I walked the two blocks to my hideout. If it weren't for the toothache pain, it would have been nice to go to dinner and a movie with my gorgeous wife, while we were away in Akron. Even being out of Youngstown with her for a couple of hours was a treat for me, and it made me dare to think that we could be together somewhere other than Youngstown, Ohio. After I got inside the clubhouse, I waited for the familiar three rings of the telephone to let me know that she had made it home. I bit my nails as I waited another two hours for the phone call. We had returned from Akron under the cover of darkness, and I was worried that something had happened to her while she was running around this dangerous town at night. I summoned the nerve to venture out past the policeman's club, across the Youngstown University Campus, and up the street to the corner store, to use the pay telephone.

My mother answered the telephone and told me that my brother would be by to see me in a few minutes. I rushed back to the clubhouse and waited for him to show up. Ten minutes after I reached the club, my brother came through the back door. He revealed that the FBI had been to my mother's house while Addie and I were in Akron. They were still staking out our block when Addie returned home. The FBI swarmed her when she pulled into the driveway, with their red lights flashing and their alarms scream-ing. Addie was pulled out of the car at gunpoint and her vehicle was searched. Nothing was found and they had the nerve to apologize and then to tell her to have a nice day. It wasn't wise of me to have involved her as much as I did. The pain of being away from her had made me careless to the point of being stupid. I would have to fight the loneliness of being away from my better half until it was much safer to be with her. The danger she endured for me was nerve-racking for both of us. I had Larry tell her that I had gone to Cleveland because it was no longer safe here.

That was at the end of June 1981. Actually, I didn't leave Youngstown until October 31 of that year, on the second anniversary of the bombing of my home, and the courts still hadn't dismissed my civil lawsuit against the Hubbard Police Department.

I killed time at the clubhouse by sharpening my foreign language skills and reading the late preacher's books. I felt that the knowledge I had stumbled across in the library of the clubhouse should be shared with others. This knowledge wasn't being taught in the churches or the schools. It was at this time that I first thought of writing a book that interpreted Bible scripture for the common man. Other authors had made the same attempt, but I felt that they had fallen short of the mark. I had read their books and I always felt that they didn't offer enough proof of their claims about the accuracy of scripture. I wanted access to the original scriptures, or the closest thing to them. The *Dead Sea Scrolls* and the Hebrew-to-English Bible turned out to be the next best things. It would be some years before I got my hands on a copy of the *Dead Sea Scrolls*. I had led Addie and my family to believe that I had already moved to Cleveland while I was still staying at the clubhouse. Often members of our clubhouse would take me for a nighttime ride in the van, just to get a breath of fresh air and a change of scenery. Once they took me for a daytime ride to see Addie's softball team compete for a tournament. Her team was made up of her General Motors coworkers.

Addie played first base extremely well. Benita was there also, cheering her mother's team on to victory. I wanted to go to both of them, but realized the foolishness of that move. I saw several of her coworkers whom I knew very well. Some of them had been very good friends of mine. Two brown-skinned males were vying for Addie's attention, and she was giving them plenty of it. I was surprised at the flirtatiousness of her actions toward them.

They were hugging and grabbing each other as if they were accustomed to doing it all of the time. I saw several other girls come over to the trio and joined in their horseplay. I knew most of these people, and all of them were married, yet all of them were grabbing, hugging, and wrestling with someone other than their spouses. "True blue" Addie had no trouble at all doing what the rest of them were doing. She fit right in with this crowd of grabbing exhibitionists. I had been away from my wife for only a short time and she was already giving me reasons to doubt her. After winning the tournament, Addie's team went to a bar a few blocks away to celebrate; we followed. I had a good view from my seat in the van, into the large glass windows of the bar. The two brown-skinned men, whom Addie had been horsing around with earlier, were taking turns slow dancing with her, in a deliberately slow, sexual manner; and she was enjoying it as much as they were. After dancing with both of them, they joined the rest of their crowd in drinking several beers. Addie drank four beers. I had never known her to finish one beer. Benita was playing in a section of the bar that was designed for the children of the baseball players. Her mother was enjoying herself so much that she only checked on Benita one time. I knew the two men with whom she had spent so much time that day.

I had seen enough. I had Larry ask my brother, who worked with Addie and the two men, if anything was going on between them. My brother replied that rumors abounded about the three of them, but that he nor anyone else believed the rumors. Besides that, "Addie never was very fond of brown-skinned men." I remember Addie telling me that many times before. She even said it to me when my skin had lightened from the fire. These men that she was flirting with were the same color as I was after the fire changed my skin color. One rumor was that the two married men's wives had actually had words with Addie about their husbands, and Addie assured the women that they were all just good friends and coworkers. I saw a loneliness in Addie; she craved male attention. Whether she was missing me or just men in general was difficult to figure out. I wondered how long would it be before she decided to turn one of these friendships into something more romantic—or had she already? I had to hurry up and do something about my situation or my wife would be someone else's wife. I could see the handwriting on the wall. My next move would have to improve my lot substantially.

I had my brother ask my wife about the rumors concerning her and the two brownskinned men. She told him to tell me that she was just having fun with some friends and that it meant nothing. There would never be anyone for her but me. She told my brother to tell me that I should do whatever I had to do. She would always be waiting for me. I half-heartedly believed her declarations because I had seen her actions myself. Addie had changed on me already. The thought crossed my mind, "What would happen if I had to do three to five years in jail?" I had been on the run for less than a year, and I already had doubts about her fidelity. My fellow club members were as curious about Addie as I was, and they reported her comings and goings to me on a regular basis. Baseball season was over and she was not seeing either of the two men except on the job, and then only sparingly. For the moment, my suspicions were allayed. Over beer and pretzels my motley crew often discussed where I could go to make enough money to relocate my family. Every one of the club-house members had a friend or a relative who lived out of town, and who would provide some type of under-the-table employment to help me get on my feet. There were offers from New York to Los Angeles, but I was only interested in jobs in the state of Ohio. Years ago, I had heard of a fugitive on the run who never left the state he was wanted in. After years on the run, he gave himself up to the authorities, who had already discovered the real perpetrator, and then they dismissed all charges against the innocent man. The "flight to avoid prosecution" charge was dropped because the man was able to prove that he had never crossed the state line. An attorney verified that in many cases of "flight to avoid prosecution" or cases of "fugitives from justice," judges usually are more lenient if the accused never crossed the state line.

This was just the excuse I needed to stay in close proximity to my family. I was a family man who loved his wife and child. I was not a rolling stone who was anxious for new adventures around the world. One of my club members told me about an uncle who had a body shop in Cleveland that specialized in rebuilding wrecked cars to near-new condition.

The cars were then sold for a few thousand dollars less than at the regular car lots, and the uncle's shop was making a fortune. The flaw in the operation was that they didn't have a good mechanic for the operation. A young man with a master's degree in engineering, like I had, would be a valuable asset to his uncle's business. The necessary phone calls and arrangements were made and I prepared to go to Cleveland, Ohio. Addie and my family thought I had already moved to Cleveland several months ago. The second anniversary of the bombing of my home was coming up in a few days, on October 31, 1981. Believe it or not, Halloween was here again; it was time for me to be extra cautious. Lying Johnny, Larry, and the rest of the "Knights of the Round Table" gathered to give me some final words of advice.

All of them realized that this may very well be the last time that they ever saw me. Even though I was only moving to Cleveland, all of us knew that I would be a lot more exposed than I had ever been since I started running. Everything imaginable was brought up as they brainstormed possible scenarios I might find myself in. These men were my brothers; they cared what happened to me; each felt a part of themselves was going with me. I know that they loved me and that they would look after my family as best as they could.

I was given several IDs, one thousand dollars, a stun gun, a lock pick, several phone cards, a false bottom trunk that had hidden compartments, a money belt, handcuff keys, and a new copy of the Hebrew-to-English interpretation of the scriptures. Several of the club members attempted to lighten the mood by cracking jokes about me getting caught by wild women in Cleveland before the police caught me. Many cracks were made about venereal diseases and the use of condoms. Then Larry uttered one of his favorite mottos from his Vietnam days, "Praise God and pass the ammunition." Larry had always been teaching me the martial arts. Now that I was about to really step out on the fugitive's path, he went over everything that he had ever taught me, plus a little extra. "Get serious, this can save your life," he constantly admonished me. After Larry had finished with me, he turned me over to Lying Johnny, the former Vietnam intelligence officer.

The first thing John did was to give me a reversible jacket and a reversible cap. These items were successfully used by him on several occasions when he wanted to lose someone who was following him. Now they were mine. John pulled out a blood pressure gauge and made me swear to never reveal his technique for beating the lie detector test. After several failed attempts, I finally got the hang of the technique. Lying Johnny's final advice, after giving me the blood pressure gauge, was, "Practice, brother, practice! Rome wasn't built in a day, you know."

The brothers from the clubhouse loaded my junk into the van and we took our time driving to Cleveland. It was dark outside and the children lined the streets wearing their Halloween costumes. The goblins, ghouls, and ghosts reminded me of my walk out of the ball of fire that used to be my home. I thought about the Halloween of two years before, when I almost became a ghost. An eerie feeling came over me and I felt chills for just a moment. Praise Father Yahweh for his mercy. Someone mentioned something about a costume party in Cleveland. I remember making a very poor joke about the party, "Maybe I can go to the party disguised as a free man." No one laughed at the joke. I didn't think it was funny either.

After that, we rode in total silence. Only the hum of the van's motor and the sound of the tires on the road were heard. Each of us was lost in thought about what the future held for me.

CHAPTER 5

Cleveland's Peaches

When we finally stopped driving, we were so far out in the country that the only living creatures we saw were cows. We had stopped in front of a six-car, red-brick garage that had a large sign displayed on top of the building that said, "Peaches' Place." I remember thinking to myself, "I guess this must be Peaches' garage."

Nelson's uncle was standing in the doorway with a double-barreled shotgun. "Nelson, that you?" came a gravelly voice out of the night.

"Yes sir, Uncle Peaches, it's me," answered his nephew, Nelson.

We were all introduced to Peaches and his shotgun. It was obvious why the old gentleman had picked up that nickname. Peaches was a very light-skinned black man, whose skin was awfully close to the color of peaches. The nickname fit the man and he had it for a longtime. Peaches was very sympathetic to young men on the run, because he had been on the run himself for thirty years. Peaches had been married to a white woman while they were living in Mississippi.

When a crowd of Klansmen attempted to lynch him, he defended himself by shooting the leader through the heart. When the remaining Klansmen scattered, Peaches took off running, and he had been running ever since. When I met Peaches, he was sixty years old, but he looked fifty years old. He wore shoulder-length hair that was often in a ponytail when he was working on cars at his garage. Peaches was a tall thin man, who probably could have been a model in his earlier years. The only thing Southern about Peaches was his accent, which was as country as country could be. He didn't seem to be very hard to get along with.

I was given the guided tour of the garage by Peaches and some of my future coworkers. The garage was extremely clean; there weren't even any cigarette butts on the floor. Peaches didn't allow any smoking in his garage. The front and back halves of several new Lincoln Continentals and Cadillacs filled the six stalls of Peaches's garage. These cars were beautiful, even in their wrecked and unfinished conditions. There was no doubt that these cars would fetch some handsome money when they were completely refurbished.

Peaches decided to put my mechanic's skills to the test. "I hear that you build racing engines," he growled out in his gravelly Southern voice.

"Yes, sir, I build all types of engines," I replied.

Peaches went on to explain that he had to have an engine rebuilt for one of the Lincoln Continentals, but after the engine specialist had finished, the engine was still knocking. I asked Peaches if the engine rebuilder had replaced or reconditioned the rod that had gone out in the engine. Peaches revealed that the engine rebuilder had not. I put a mechanic's stethoscope on the engine while it was running and I was able to locate the knocking sound. "Number six rod is out of round and needs replacing or reconditioning," I explained.

"Can you do it?" Peaches asked.

"Sure I can," I replied.

We were finished with shop talk for the moment. I knew that tomorrow my mechanic's skills would be tested, but I had no problem with that. I made the type of repairs that the Lincoln needed all of the time. I literally could have repaired the Lincoln with my eyes closed. Peaches showed me a bedroom over the top of the garage, where I could store my belongings. "If I decide to keep you, this will be your room," Peaches growled. The bedroom had a perfect view of everything up and down the road for ten miles, but there was nothing to see but cows, grass, and trees. I knew that there were other buildings in the area because we had passed them on the way to "Peaches' Place," but I felt that I was sitting right in the middle of nowhere. As if he were reading my mind, Peaches said, "The middle of nowhere is the perfect place to be when you're on the run, son." Peaches was right. This was the perfect setup for me. I would make good money here and I'd have plenty of privacy to study in peace.

The club members saw that I was comfortable in this place and decided that it was time to get back to Youngstown; they had jobs to go to the next day. Lying Johnny, the old sage of the group, gave me some final words of wisdom to live by. "Don't look these suckers in the eyes because that's when they really see you. Forget about wearing flashy clothes and driving flashy cars like we used to do. Try to flirt with the women as little as possible. You don't want to be noticed by anyone, for any reason. You don't want to be seen. You want to be invisible. Get used to it; you're no longer an Ohio player, you are now 'The Invisible Man.'"

My friends hugged me and shook my hand as they walked out of the door of Peaches's garage. I was saddened to see them leave because they had always been such a large part of my life. In some ways it was the same as parting with my mother or my wife and daughter. Peaches put a hand on my shoulder and said, "Cheer up, they'll probably be back tomorrow. You couldn't pay them to keep away from you."

I watched the van disappear over the hill and thought, "There go my last ties to Youngstown and my family. Yahweh, give me strength."

Peaches told me that he was headed to his twenty-five-year-old girlfriend's house and that I was welcome to anything in Peaches' Place. All of the other workers had already left for the day and Peaches was getting into a black Lincoln Continental to drive to the young lady's apartment. I made sure that all of the doors were locked and went out to the kitchen for a sandwich and a beer. I thought about the large amount of money that Peaches said I'd be making there at his shop. Maybe I could invest some of my earnings in the business and earn some of those large profits that Peaches and a few of his workers were earning. Maybe there would be enough to send some to my wife and baby. It would be great to be able to help her in any way that I could. Since I couldn't be there with her, maybe it would help to send some cash. I tried to calculate how long it would take to earn enough money to relocate my family to another country. By my calculations, I would be able to make the move in less than a year. I went to bed that night thinking of my wife and wondering how long it would be before I kissed those soft lips again and felt her body next to mine.

It seemed like I had just dozed off to sleep when Peaches rushed into my room to tell me that it was time to get up. It was 7:00 a.m. "Early bird gets the worm," he said.

I replied, "That's fine if you like worms for breakfast, but I prefer bacon and eggs."

Peaches laughed and told me to hurry and get dressed. He was taking me to town. In fifteen minutes we were riding the big black Lincoln down the country roads past the cows, the trees, and the grass. It took us only another fifteen minutes before we hit the freeway. After a half an hour on the freeway we exited onto a downtown street. Peaches parked the Lincoln in front of Heidi's Tattoo Parlor. He got out of the car on the driver's side and motioned for me to follow him.

Inside of the tattoo parlor, a fat, blond, biker-type chick was busy tattooing a client's forearm. "Hey! What's shaking?" Heidi yelled out.

"What's up, baby?" Peaches replied. "I came by to see if you could put some black back into this brother's hands."

Heidi glanced up from the job she was doing on the client's forearm to get a look at my hands. She then raised her shirt sleeve to reveal a brown snake tattooed on her arm. "Sure thing, I've got that color right here," she responded.

I had forgotten that I still had a few quarter-sized pink spots on the backsides of my hands. I called the spots my mementos from the house fire. Ten minutes later she was finished with the client and I was next.

Heidi blended a mixture of red, black, yellow, and brown colors until she had my exact skin tone. The device she used to tattoo the quarter-sized pink spots hurt like you'd expect needles to hurt. I wondered how some people stood the pain of having their breasts and faces tattooed. Heidi was done in less than an hour but it seemed like forever to me. I actually felt the pulsating of the needles on the back of my hands several hours after she had finished.

This was not something I would have gone for if it had not been for the fact that my spotted hands were a very noticeable give-away. Heidi wiped some Vaseline on my hands after she had finished the tattooing job. Except for the wrinkles I had on the back of my hands after the fire, my hands looked much like they had before the fire. The color did much to normalize the appearance of my hands, and the wrinkles on the backsides of my hands were now common among carpenters, mechanics, and even boxers. The covering of the spots on my hands did much to help me blend in with everyone else; to become invisible.

Peaches paid Heidi and we followed her into the back room of the tattoo parlor. Heidi pulled out a bag of what appeared to be flour. Peaches asked her if it was as good as the last batch and she assured him that it was better. Peaches pulled out a wad of one hundred bills, told her thank-you, and we left Heidi's Tattoo Parlor.

"You didn't see a thing, right?" he said to me.

"Right, Peaches, I didn't see a thing," was my reply. A half an hour's ride on the freeway and we were parking in front of Peaches's twenty-five-year-old girlfriend's apartment. Peaches blew the horn and she opened the front door. Rachael was very beautiful and her long pigtails made her look even younger than her twenty-five years.

I wondered what a sixty-year-old man could do with a young thing like this. I wondered how often she almost gave Peaches a heart attack while they were in the bed. She too must have been able to read my mind because she said, "Don't let his age fool you. That old man tries to kill me when we're in the sack." By that I assumed that Peaches must have been some kind of stud in bed.

We went into Rachael's apartment, where I was overwhelmed by the chrome, glass, and mirrored decorations in her place. This place was exquisitely furnished; no price was spared. The chrome, glass, and mirrored scheme reminded me of the home that Addie and I had in Hubbard before the fire. Rachael's bar was stocked with every type of liquor known to mankind, and most of them were quite expensive. Rachael had a beautiful red Doberman pinscher that looked like he should have been in a dog show. His posture was magnificent. Her dog was named after Peaches. "They're both sons of bitches, aren't they?" Rachael was quick to comment when asked about the naming of her dog. I was given a beer by Peaches and told to relax and watch some television while Peaches and Rachael discussed some business. From their spot in the back bedroom I could faintly hear them talking about the price and quality of the cocaine, and the amount of money they made off of the last batch. When they came back to the living room where I was, they kissed and Peaches and I headed for the door. I told her that it was nice to meet her and she told me to come again. Peaches was very quick to interject, "Not without me, he can't!" I got the message. Don't get overly friendly with Peaches's woman. Little or nothing to say to her was the only way to stay on the good side of Peaches, my new boss.

When we got back to the garage, Peaches gave me a pair of surgeon's white rubber gloves and said, "Put some more Vaseline on the back of your hands, then put these gloves on. You don't want to get any dirt or grease into those fresh sores from the tattoos." I did as I was told and started to work on the engine of the Lincoln that had the bad rod in it. Peaches's shop and tools were magnificent. His power tools made my old manual tools look like something out of the stone age. In two hours' time, I had the engine out of the car and torn apart. We took the rod, which was out of round and causing the knocking sound, to the machine shop, where they heated it and reshaped it in two hours. We then took the rod and some new rod bearings back to Peaches's garage and reassembled the engine from the Lincoln. In two hours' time, the engine was started up and everyone waited to hear the knocking sound again. To everyone's amazement the engine purred like a kitten. Peaches got into the car and spun the tires as he floored the gas pedal of the car and shot out of the garage. When Peaches got the car to the street, he floored it again and took off down the street like a tornado. Five minutes passed before Peaches returned to the garage. He pulled the car back into the garage and no one could hear any knocking in the motor. Peaches jumped out of the car before it had even come to a complete stop.

"That's my nigger, right there, right there." The skinny yellow old man picked me up in his arms as though I were a baby. I wondered if the coke made this weak-looking old man that strong. I was the man of the hour and it felt good.

When we worked at Peaches's garage, we really worked hard. Now was a time for celebration. The weak link in Peaches's auto operation was replaced with a strong link. For some reason, excellent mechanics and machinists were very hard to find in Cleveland.

Scores of Mercedes and Jaguars lined auto repair garages because the cost of repairing foreign luxury cars was too expensive or no one knew how to repair them. Peaches's investments in repairing Cadillacs and Lincolns was a much smarter proposition because General Motors and Ford-Lincoln-Mercury products had been the lifeblood of the auto industry for so long that most mechanics knew how to repair them and the parts were not as expensive as the Mercedes and Jaguar parts. I sat and enjoyed my beer and sandwich, while my coworkers celebrated with a shot of some type of liquor. Peaches slapped me on the back and said once again, "That's my nigger!" This time he put two one-hundred-dollar bills in my shirt pocket. "Stick around for a while. There's more where that came from," Peaches said in his gravelly voice. This was the first time I had ever been paid for a job audition. I liked Peaches's style. I could get used to this.

As time moved on, I went from being the engineering mechanic to actually learning the body work and painting aspects of the business. I had assisted body men and painters at my own garage back in Youngstown, but now I had progressed to the point where I could do the hardest jobs myself. I learned to straighten the frames on wrecked cars and eventually I even learned the appraisal aspect of the job. Peaches saw in me a person who had successfully run his own business and who could run Peaches's business, while Peaches took care of his cocaine trade. In a year's time, I was running the garage full time and Peaches only dropped in to see what changes I had made or how quickly we could repair and sell his cars. I learned to buy the wrecked cars at the car auctions and to buy the replacement parts at the most reasonable prices. Peaches was very satisfied in the way I managed the garage. Peaches was very fond of asking me if I had turned one of the Cadillacs or Lincolns into a hot rod.

By the end of 1982, Peaches dressed like a Wall Street executive. He was always attired in an expensive business suit, a dress hat, and Stacy Adams shoes that you could see your face in. Rachael had blossomed into an adult businesswoman. She now wore her hair on top of her head, and like Peaches, always wore some elegant business suit. They drove a different one of the Cadillacs and Lincolns from the shop every day. They claimed to be test-driving the finished product, but I found out that they were actually using the various cars to make "dope runs" out of town. The businessman and the secretary disguises were part of their "fronts" or cover stories. I don't know how much money Peaches made from the cocaine business, but it must have been substantial. He constantly talked of giving me the garage when he retired to Rio de Janeiro, Rachael's home. After expenses and wages, the garage cleared two hundred thousand dollars a year, and Peaches and Rachael called that sum "chump change."

Cleveland was a very large city compared to Youngstown or Hubbard, Ohio. I have heard that Cleveland is the tenth largest city in the United States. Downtown Cleveland is filled with tall black men who look just like me. For the first time in my life, being a stereotype was paying off. All I had to do was to wear a pair of jeans, a tee-shirt, tennis shoes, a pair of sunglasses, and a baseball cap; that made me look like thousands of other tall, black males.

A clean shave with no mustache made it difficult to determine my age. Often I was mistaken for some basketball player from Cleveland State University. Some people thought that I was still a teenager. My face was now so smooth after the fire that many people didn't believe that I had to shave, even though I had worn a very thick and heavy beard, after the house fire and up to the time the clubhouse members decided to disguise me. My old club members only came to visit me at Peaches's garage when they had something to report, and that wasn't often. Everyone was spooked since the FBI started to give my friends lie detector tests. My family was especially spooked when the FBI pulled Addie over one night and searched her car. No one wanted to take any unnecessary chances. In Youngstown, my folks didn't even mention my name anymore. I was referred to by friends and family as "that boy" or "Boy" or "Boyd."

News from home was often six months late. I didn't know that Vincent, one of our luxury car members of the CYP club, had been shot in the head and left for dead in 1981. It was rumored that the crooked Hubbard police and my old car parts chaser had something to do with the attempt on Vincent's life. Vincent survived the shot and walked to a nearby home for help. He wouldn't formally identify his assailant, but he told my friends that the "hit man" who botched the job told him who ordered it done. Vincent sent word to me that he was attacked because he was a friend of mine. Other friends had received threats. I thought that someone should have told me that my lawsuit against the Hubbard Police Department was finally dropped by the Civil Courts in 1982, but no one saw the need to tell me that, since warrants for my arrest were still pending. It had been two months since the lawsuit had been dropped and it was obvious that the police and the prosecutor were not going to honor the deal we made on that dark midnight in September 1980. Literally, I still had a target on my back; I was still a wanted man. I had to remain an invisible man. I wondered how long I could be invisible when Peaches was attracting so much attention as a big-time cocaine dealer.

Peaches was wanted on an old murder charge and he was supposed to be inconspicuous and even more invisible than I was. Yet, Peaches and Rachael were living the high life, in more ways than one. Peaches spared no expense for himself or Rachael when it came to keeping up with the "Joneses," who in most cases were fellow cocaine dealers.

Peaches and Rachael had abandoned the two-bedroom apartment that she formerly rented. Now they leased some old, rich, rubber producer's mansion in the very best part of town. I wondered if the police or the highway patrol had gotten suspicious of Peaches's dope runs in the various cars he was driving. Racial profiling had gotten to the point where policemen and highway patrolmen were stopping any and every black man and woman who drove a nice car. It was hard to believe that Peaches and Rachael had not been noticed and stopped by these racist goons, even in a racially diverse community like Cleveland. I wondered if all of us were being watched and about to be raided. It crossed my mind that Peaches and a few other fellow desperadoes thought they were doing me a favor by letting me live and work here, but I realized that I had a bigger chance of being caught by my pursuers because I was around them. Most of them were wanted for crimes much more serious than the crimes I was accused of, snitching was a way of life for many fugitives. It was common to snitch to get leniency for oneself. I needed to pay more attention to who was paying attention to me. I needed to pay more attention to the driver behind me on the freeway. Lying Johnny's words bounced around inside my head like a Super Ball, "Sometimes paranoia can be a survival skill."

Cleveland had a lot more money circulating around than Youngstown did. In July 1982, motorcycles, hot rods, and SUVs were on the city streets in abundance. No one seemed to care about the price of gasoline or the price of mechanical parts. Back in Youngstown, a near depression was going on. The steel mills and General Motors were laying people off by the hundreds, only to be told that they might never be called back to work. In Cleveland, concerts and tours were being attended in record numbers. Very many well dressed men were sporting the latest fashions and they didn't seem to be the least bit concerned about the cost of those fashions. The motorcycle and automobile fanatics hung very closely with the strippers, the hookers, and the drug dealers. Their underground economy was often the only thing that kept many of the Ohio cities from going broke. The police were taking bribes at an all-time high rate. Even the FBI was revealed by several newspapers for being on the take. Smart drug dealers who had a lot of cash often paid off Highway Patrolmen so that they would allow truckloads of drugs to travel unmolested by the authorities. Peaches was one of those smart drug dealers who had enough cash to buy an occasional policeman or patrolman.

I couldn't figure out why Peaches and Rachael sponsored motorcycle treks from state to state as often as they did. It got to be quite common to see motorcyclists hanging out at the garage. They always serviced their own bikes and never needed any assistance or tools.

The membership of this motorcycle club consisted of all black men and their girlfriends. It was mandatory that the girlfriends be white. The bikers would depart from Peaches' Place to different parts of the country, usually no further than a state or two away. These bikers carried large quantities of various drugs from state to state. Peaches sponsored these bikers when he thought that his cars were too well known on the highways. For a few dollars paid to the right officers, the bikers were allowed to travel unhampered by the authorities. Once, a biker was pulled over by a policeman while the biker was carrying a large amount of cocaine in his saddlebags. His fellow bikers were about to reach for their weapons when the officer told the biker, "Why don't you put on a helmet before you spill this pretty bike and crack that thick skull of yours?" The biker complied immediately and they completed their trek unencumbered.

After the dope run, Peaches warned the bikers not to disrespect the police just because he was paying them off. Some violations were so flagrant that the officers had to act on them.

Peaches was famous for his after-the-drug-run parties. I attended one of these parties just to see what everyone was so excited about. I had been to the front porch of Peaches's mansion several times, but I had never been inside. On this particular night, the front parking lot was full of motorcycles, SUVs, and luxury cars. I had driven to the mansion in one of the Cadillacs that we were working on at the shop. I was the test-driver this particular night. In Youngstown, parties always started late. In fact, it was considered stylish to appear at a party late. I was surprised to find out that these party animals had been at it since 6:00 p.m., and it was now midnight. I looked all over the huge mansion for Peaches, but he was nowhere to be found. I had a lot of fun looking for him, since I had to wade through hundreds of beautiful women to find him. Several women asked me to dance with them, and many others wanted to know if I'd like to do something more intimate. Everyone in the place was as high as a kite. This must have really been some "monster" dope that they brought back from this trip.

The mansion had the same chrome, glass, and mirrored scheme that Rachael's apartment had, but on a much grander scale. I saw several five-pound sugar bowls filled to the top with cocaine. Everyone's nose was white with powder and running. All partakers were sniffling as if they had very bad colds. Champagne, cognac, and your liquor of choice were all proudly displayed on the thirty-foot-long bar that just seemed to pop up in the middle of the place. Pizza, shrimp, chicken, cakes, muffins, donuts, and coffee were set out in a smorgasbord style on seven tables. I delighted in the splendor of so much obvious wealth. I amused myself by wondering how much money did Peaches actually have. I continued to wade through the food, the drinks, and the women until I finally found Rachael. Her nose was also snow-white from snorting the powder. She was dancing by herself because no one dared to dance with Peaches's woman. When I spoke to her, she asked me if I cared to dance with her. I replied, "I'd love to, right now, but tomorrow when Peaches cuts off my legs, I will probably regret it." She laughed and tried to grab me around the waist, as if to dance with me in spite of my protests. I pulled away from her very quickly and told her, "I'm as serious as a heart attack."

She replied, "So am I. I know what I want when I see it. I'm told that you look a lot like Peaches did when he was younger."

So that was it. Not only did Peaches see himself in me, but his woman saw him in me as well. I had to be very particular around Rachael because she had become a little too bold about voicing her desires in public. The last thing that I needed was for my benefactor to feel any type of threat from me. When I finally found Peaches, he was in the backyard of the mansion, in the dog house with Peaches the Doberman pinscher. They were both howling at the moon. Peaches never noticed that I was calling him, even though I was screaming at the top of my lungs. Someone touched me on the shoulder and I almost jumped out of my skin. It was Rachael. She had followed me to the backyard. "When he gets like this, it might take a few days before he comes down again. By that time, you and I could become very good friends." This woman was so seductive that she scared me. I scared myself when I allowed the thought of being with her pass through my mind for a split second. Peaches was like a brother to me, or an uncle; better yet, he was like a father to me. Tempted though

I was, I am glad that I didn't succumb to this temptress in the silver see-through evening gown. When I left the party, Peaches was still in the dog house howling at the moon. Yes, these must have been some "monster" drugs that they brought back this time.

CHAPTER 6

Surprise! Surprise!

P eaches was really accumulating some wealth. He started several other businesses in someone else's name, usually Rachael's. The taxi service was a booming success, and so was Peaches's farm. Peaches had left Mississippi a very long time ago, but he still had a lot of country boy left in him. Peaches grew hogs and cows on his farm; then he became his own best customer by opening several barbeque joints and then buying the meat from his own farm. Peaches had nearly a hundred people working for him. One hundred possible snitches were enough to make anyone a little paranoid, and Peaches was getting paranoid. Rachael said that the cocaine was affecting his mind. Rachael had contacts in the music industry and she and Peaches started providing live entertainment on their farmland, for the motorcyclists and the auto fans. Every other week a Woodstock type concert and barbeque took place on the huge farm. Peaches often had jazz artists perform there as well. Everything was looking very prosperous for Peaches, Rachael, and their employees. The motorcycle trek was a clever way to transport drugs, but the out-of-town motorcycle outing was fun in itself. I went on several of the local bike trips and discovered the benefit of a motorcycle helmet and the shield that goes with it. The helmet and shield were the perfect disguise. I actually rode to Youngstown several times on a Kawasaki motorcycle. The first few times I rode the bike to Youngstown, I rode with several other bikers. Eventually, I slipped into Youngstown on my own to surprise some of my friends at the clubhouse, who brought me up to date on the news.

My old buddies were still leery about coming to Peaches's garage in Cleveland because they were worried about being followed. So far the authorities had no idea where I was and everyone tried their best to keep it that way. I had been saving some money and sending some to Addie and my mother. Addie was making plans to buy a home soon and my mother wanted to remodel her own home. I was thinking about sneaking to my mother's house to visit her, Addie, and my daughter Benita, when Nelson asked me if my brother had told me what Addie wanted to do. I had no idea what Nelson was talking about. My brother hadn't mentioned any question that Addie wanted him to ask me. Nelson revealed that the male coaches on Addie's baseball team and some of the men from her job were always asking her to go out on friendly dates. Their claim was that since they were friends, it wouldn't be like a real, romantic date, just some movies, dancing, and dinner between friends.

Addie wanted my permission to do this. She wanted me to believe that these men were just like female friends to her except that they had penises. No romance or sex was even being considered by her or them, so she said. I told Nelson that if Addie had gotten to the point that she needed male companionship so badly that she would actually ask and expect my permission, and then want me to believe that there really wasn't anything going on with her and these male friends, then I suspected that our marriage had already been broken by the strain of my situation. I told the club members that Addie was going to do what she wanted to do, and she did. I never gave my consent and I didn't contact her then, but I did watch her leave one of her baseball games with a male friend. I did see her stop at a restaurant with him for a quick bite to eat, and yes, I did see her kissing him on the lips in the parking lot, before they went their separate ways. Not only was my wife cheating on me, she was cheating on me with one of the brown-skinned men that she claimed she didn't like because of his color. This man was also very, very married. The motorcycle helmet and shield that I was wearing to conceal my identity also hid the tears that were running down my face. Addie was no longer mine. "Until death do us part" was forgotten by her two years after I started running. She was very convincing when she told me she'd wait for me forever.

Lying Johnny had a bit of news as well. Two members of the Muhammad gang had moved into the house next door to my mother and Addie. They asked about me often.

Several times they even asked my two-and-a-half-year-old daughter if she had seen me. The Muhammads were stashing stolen Jaguars in the garage of the house, then they would trade the cars in New York for cocaine and firearms. They still planned to take the rackets away from the Italian mob. John also reminded me that the mercury vapor light outside of my home in Hubbard always distorted the colors of the cars in my driveway. The car seen by the trick-or-treaters on that Halloween night when my home blew up was not pink or lavender but cranapple to burgundy in color. The car had been identified by "Mike the Arab," owner of the local grocery store. He too had seen the car when he came to my place to get his truck fixed. Mike identified the driver of the car as my parts chaser, who was also the state's confidential informant when arson charges were brought against me. Surprise! Surprise! I was in a state of shock. What was this all about? This was even more upsetting than seeing my wife kiss another man. Did the parts chaser have a role in blowing up my home? The day's revelations left me numb, as the Kawasaki and I limped back to Cleveland, to my home.

I stayed busy at the shop. It was my therapy. It was a lot cheaper than giving a shrink twenty-five dollars an hour. I became a workaholic. I actually believed that I could accumulate enough money to relocate my entire family, not just Addie and Benita. The Muhammad gang members living next door to my mother's home was much more than a coincidence. I used my leisure time to continue my studies of the old dead preacher's books and my foreign language. When I finished the last of the preacher's books, I started haunting the local libraries. I became obsessed with finding more accurate Bible history and Bible interpretation sources. I actually began buying books that I couldn't find in the local libraries. Soon I had accumulated a collection that rivaled the dead preacher's library from our old clubhouse in Youngstown. Peaches and Rachael had their usual fabulous

Halloween and Christmas parties, but my depression over my legal situation and my wife's infidelity was only eased by my obsession with uncovering true Bible knowledge, including genealogies and the whereabouts of the present-day descendants of Bible figures.

Peaches's parties were starting to attract many out-of-towners, including Youngstowners. I knew that if I frequented the party scene, it would just be a matter of time before I bumped into someone I knew from home. Several new and popular malls had been built in Cleveland, and many Youngstowners shopped there on the weekends. Once in a while, I slipped into the malls of Cleveland, during the late evenings on weekdays, during the winter snows. These were the times when Youngstowners were least likely to visit the Cleveland malls. I took some security in knowing that most of the people who knew me in Youngstown wouldn't recognize me anyway. But one never knows anything for sure. When big-named artists came to Cleveland's State Theater, the Palace, the Front Row, or "the Blossom Music Festival, I was always tempted to check out the show. I was trying to be invisible in the sense that I didn't want to be noticed, but I'd really have to be invisible to attend any of the concert halls in Cleveland. Youngstowners attended these functions as frequently as the Clevelanders did, and more often than the visiting audiences from Akron. I really passed up some unforgettable concerts in Cleveland, but my plan was simple; I had to find a way to accumulate a great deal of money, at a faster rate than I was currently. I remembered that Peaches had said that I could invest my money in one of his businesses. Maybe that was the best way to attain my goals. Maybe I could eventually start my own business as well.

Peaches's drug habit was showing on his face. Peaches was only sixty-two years old but he looked eighty. His smooth facial skin had uneven dark spots in it. His eyes bulged in their sockets and he had the blackest circles around his eyes. Peaches was a corpse looking for a grave, and he looked long overdue for one. Rachael was her usual exquisite self; she actually looked better every time I saw her. "Hey, Sandy," Peaches growled out to me in his gravelly voice. Calling me Sandy was a private joke. Peaches had hooked me up with the identification papers of Sandobal Reyes, a Dominican Republican painter who had worked for Peaches. Reyes decided to return to his native land to be with his family and sold the ID to me for four hundred dollars. The long-standing joke between Peaches and me was the fact that Reyes was a Black Spaniard; I didn't even speak Spanish. Other than that fact the ID fit me perfectly, and there was no risk of him calling it in stolen as so many other sellers of IDs had done in the past I could use this ID indefinitely. I could actually be Sandobal Reyes.

I had bought several IDs from homeless men who got the money and then reported the ID stolen so that they could get another to sell again. For some of the homeless, ID sells were their only way of eating. It felt good to have an ID that I could use for a while; I had already been six different people. Peaches told me that I should go into a business that was totally different from working on cars. The authorities were issuing memos that stated that I was expected to seek work of some type that related to automobiles. Since I didn't have the nerves to transport or sell drugs, Peaches proposed that I start a mail order business. He already had several options to choose from. A treatment for baldness was just hitting the U.S. markets. Peaches had a connection in the Philippines that sold minoxidil (Rogaine) for a fraction of what it cost here in pharmacies. For some of the money I had made at the garage, I could order a supply of the treatment, advertise it in local and national publications, and then wait for the money orders to come pouring in. Rachael got me a post office box address in her name. I named my company after the middle initials of Addie's, Benita's, and my mother's names: D.D. & D.

In three months' time, I replaced my greasy and dusty tools from the garage, with envelopes, stamps, and small cardboard boxes. Hunting season came up and Peaches revealed a source of stainless steel hunting knives from India. These excellently handcrafted knives featured pure reindeer antler on the handles of the knives. These knives were so beautiful that many people bought them for the novelty and never intended to go hunting. The only problems I ever had in the mail order business were finding reasonably priced advertising that drew a large number of orders, and in finding a photographer who could get the type of visual effect I needed of the hunting knives and the before and after shots of the users of my bald scalp treatments. Trial and error revealed the professionals who had the skills I required. Because the hunting knives sale was a seasonal venture, I constantly sought other mail order possibilities. I sold tall men's clothing, adult videos, and sexual aids and accessories. I was aware of the problem of having space to store inventory; then I fell upon the idea of not having to keep inventory or supplies—just paper. I would sell paper. I remembered the blueprints of the silencer that I had redrawn for the Muhammad brothers. I made several copies of the blueprints and sent them to some popular gun and hunting magazines to see if they would permit me to sell such how-to instructions in their publications. After finding the magazines that pulled the greatest number of orders for the amount of money I spent on advertising with them, I was on my way. I was selling white and black paper for green paper.

The only thing I didn't like about the mail order racket was having the post office box and the company's bank account in Rachael's name. It was estimated that Peaches had a net worth of five million dollars, and all of it was in Rachael's name because Peaches and I weren't quite legal. We had the necessary paperwork to pass a cursory inspection but we lacked credit histories and job histories in the fake names that would get us the Visa Gold Card or the Mastercard. The Sandobal Reyes ID I was using was listed by the immigration department as a temporary resident with an application for permanent residency. I had a green card. Peaches often joked about me being deported to the Dominican Republic before I relocated my family to another country I had chosen. Peaches even filed taxes on his shop in Rachael's name, and so did I. The more money Peaches made, the more he partied with his big shot buddies, and they really knew how to party. I suspect that all of Peaches's new playmates had considerably more money than he did. These big shots had large investments in cruise lines and the stock market. They wouldn't be caught dead in a Cadillac or a Lincoln. Peaches leased his mansion, but his big shot friends owned theirs. Peaches was not a gambler. Nonetheless, he let his new acquaintances sucker him into ridiculous bets that cost him huge sums of money. Peaches got to the point where he actually thought that he was supposed to make sucker bets and lose large sums of money to impress his rich friends. I think the cocaine was causing him to make poor decisions. Peaches was strung out.

Rachael saw what was happening; the drugs and Peaches's new friends were playing him for a clown and he didn't even see it. Rachael discussed it with me many times but I always thought that Peaches would snap out of this condition he was in. He didn't; he just got worse. He used even more cocaine and he made even dumber bets and investments.

Peaches was losing money much faster than he had made it. His latest favorite saying was, "That's what money is for, to spend it." Those words scared everyone around Peaches. His former favorite saying had been "Make money, make money for you." Rachael decided that it was time to bring in the second string quarterback—her. Over the next few months Peaches had less and less to do with any business at all. Peaches only wanted to get high and ride his motorcycle. Rachael claimed that she was doing everything possible to save everyone's money who had invested with Peaches. Many investors thought they were on a sinking ship and wanted to desert. They demanded their money even before deals were completed and profits materialized. The investors wanted their money before it was available.

Rachael held a meeting of the investors at the mansion. I knew most of these people, but there were a few that I didn't know at all. Rachael told all of us that withdrawing our money now would cause certain transactions to fall short of their profit potential; we would be losing money. She promised that we would all be more than satisfied with the bonus she would give any of us who showed confidence in her leadership in this time of financial confusion. Rachael flashed that million-dollar smile of hers and convinced all of us that she knew what she was doing. If she hadn't been so gorgeous, I really don't think her speech would have had any effect on calming this untrusting lot. I laughed at the way this temptress had all of these vultures eating out of her hand—including me. Rachael explained that she had something in the works that would guarantee everyone's investment and provide substantial bonuses for the faithful. It would take a few days to put the deal together, but she promised results by

the end of the week, and it was already Tuesday. The meeting con-
cluded, and as the crowd thinned out, Rachael signaled for me to
follow her to the backyard where Peaches the dog was.

"Do you have enough money to hold you over until the end of
the week?" Rachael asked me. I told her that I was running a little
short and that I had been expecting to get paid much earlier than
this. Rachael put a roll of one hundred dollar bills in my hand and
asked, "Do you think that will hold you over until pay day?"

I laughed at her as I looked at the wad of bills. "Yes, I think this
will keep me in gas money for a while," I replied. Peaches the dog
barked a few times and I went over to his doghouse to pat his head.
I guess he just wanted a little attention.

Rachael looked at the dog and said, "I told you that both of
them are sons of bitches, didn't I?"

"Yes Rachael, you told me several times," I answered. I put the
wad of bills in my pocket, said goodbye, and headed for my car. As
I walked away, I couldn't help but notice how big a bulge the roll of
money made in my pants pocket. I wondered how she could have
concealed a wad of money this big in that skin-tight dress she was
wearing. She didn't have any pockets and she wasn't carrying a purse.
Rachael was a very mysterious woman.

One of the new painters caught up to me in the parking
lot and asked if he could get a ride back to the garage. We talked
about Peaches's drug habit and Rachael's plan to save the investors.
Inevitably, we ended up talking about that tight dress Rachael was
wearing. Stevie Wonder would have noticed the way that dress was
fitting her perfect form. We were still laughing about Rachael's dress
when a police cruiser pulled up behind me with his lights flashing
and his siren blasting. I knew that I hadn't been speeding. Did I have
a tail light out or something? I knew that the ID I was using was still
a good one and I wasn't really concerned about being stopped by
these racist police, who believed that every expensive car driven by
a black man must be stolen, or that the driver is transporting drugs.
Once before I had been stopped in Cleveland for nothing more than
"racial profiling." Police stop blacks because they claim that we make
up such a large percentage of criminals that we merit constant moni-

toring. Generally, the officer will check your ID, search your car, and check to see if you have any outstanding warrants. If you are clean, then you are sent on your way.

This officer didn't even approach the car. He stayed in his car and we stayed in our car. Two additional cruisers appeared on the scene, one in front of us and the other on the side of us. Now the first policeman, who had parked behind us, exited his car and walked toward my car. "Y'all having a nice day?" the huge officer bellowed. He looked like he should have been playing the tackle position for some professional football team. He asked for my driver's license and for some form of ID from my passenger. I knew that it was very unusual for three cruisers to stop one traffic offender, even in cases of racial profiling. I knew that it was unheard of to ask a passenger for identification, unless the police had reason to believe that the passenger was involved in some crime. What did these police suspect us of? Not once did any of the officers place his hand on or near his firearm. That told me that these officers were fishing for something and didn't really have a reason to stop us. The three cruisers were intended to intimidate us. As I suspected, the first officer came back from his car and reported that our IDs and the car had checked out, but he wanted us to follow them to the station for questioning about a robbery in which a white Lincoln was involved. We allegedly fit the descriptions of the two suspects in that robbery. I wasn't concerned about being a suspect in a robbery. I knew that was a bogus excuse to get us downtown to question us about Peaches's and Rachael's businesses. What concerned me was the possibility of their fingerprinting me and discovering who I really was. I tried to look relaxed and unperplexed by all of this, but I wondered if the officers could hear the way my heart was pounding out of my chest. The painter from the garage looked as if he could care less about being rousted by this goon squad. He looked as if he were used to this type of thing.

At the station, we were seated in the middle of six police officers, who ran rapid-fire questions at us to see if they could catch us in some inconsistency. We didn't know anything about a robbery and they knew that. We were there because they wanted to find something on Peaches; everyone in the room knew that. Pretending to be dissatisfied with our truthfulness, the first officer who stopped us insisted on giving us a lie detector test. I could have insisted on seeing a lawyer or I could have demanded my constitutional rights, but I was very concerned about the possibility of these clowns fingerprinting me. I was convinced that the best option was to go along with the lie detector test; in fact, I insisted on it. I asked the officers if they could speed it up because I had to go to work. The painter was the first to be tested. I wasn't permitted to view his actual testing, but after a while I was told that he had passed the test and it was now my tum. I remembered Lying Johnny's instructions about beating the lie detector. I asked to go to the bathroom and I was followed to its entrance. After relieving myself, I complained about the hard back chair they wanted me to sit in for the test. I told them that I had been receiving therapy for chronic back pain. I asked to be tested in the cushioned recliner that one of the officers had at his desk. The chair was very comfortable and I was so relaxed that I almost dozed off.

After the lie detector was actually attached, I went into my "semi-somma" state of consciousness; a nearly unconscious state of bliss, that borders on self-hypnosis. I was consciously lowering my blood pressure, my heart rate, and my breathing rate. The questions came and I answered them. I didn't know anything about a robbery and they knew that.

Finally they focused on what they really wanted to know. I was asked if Peaches used any stolen cars or stolen car parts in his auto rebuilding business. I was asked if I knew about his cocaine business, and they asked about the role the motorcyclists played in that business.

Even after the testing, I was still so downed out from the semi-somma state that I actually staggered when I got up from the chair. I blamed the stagger on my bad back. The officers told me that even though the test revealed that I was being truthful, they wanted me to watch myself around Peaches and his playmates because I was going to get busted for being there with them, even though I didn't have any idea what was going on there. I thanked them for the advice, rushed the painter into the Lincoln, and tried to look calm as we slid away.

When we pulled up to the garage in the big Lincoln, several employees ran out to us to tell about the raid on the garage. Inspectors went up under each of the cars, looking for altered of replaced serial numbers on the cars' bodies, engines, transmissions, and rear ends. No stolen cars or stolen car parts were found and the inspectors had the gall to say, "Have a nice day," when they finally left. Peaches was nowhere to be found and neither was Rachael. I went to their mansion to report the day's events, but when I got there, I could see that someone had gotten there before me. The lawn of the mansion had deep tire tracks all over it.

None of Peaches's acquaintances would dare to drive on his lawn. Only the authorities were so arrogant as to intentionally destroy a black man's property out of spite and jealousy. Peaches's mansion must have been raided also. I went through the huge front doors and on into the sitting parlor. Peaches was turning a bottle of bourbon up to his lips when I found him. "Is everything all right?" I asked him.

"They didn't find a thing," Peaches said. Peaches went on to say that he wasn't concerned about the police tearing things up a bit, but he was really worried that he hadn't seen or heard anything from Rachael. I told him about the investor's meeting Rachael chaired earlier in the day, and about my experience at the police station. He already knew about the raid on the garage. He said that someone had been to the farm and the taxi service as well. Everything was fine. He didn't even mind the police taking a look around.

What was really driving Peaches crazy was the fact that Rachael was missing.

Peaches couldn't find her anywhere in the mansion. Peaches shook his head violently, in an effort to clear his mind of the bourbon and cocaine hangover. "The last time I saw Rachael, she was headed for our secret safe in the basement, when the raid first started," Peaches said to himself out loud. When we got to the basement, Peaches pulled back the thick rug on the floor behind the bar. Peaches hurried through the numbers of the safe and flung the door open. The safe was empty. There wasn't even a speck of dust left in the safe. Everybody's money was gone and Rachael was gone. None of us ever saw or heard of Rachael again.

Peaches's woman had slipped out of the mansion while the raid was going on, with more than five million dollars. We looked everywhere for her until the weekend came, and we still hadn't seen Rachael. It was rumored that she had bought a place in her native land of Rio de Janeiro. Peaches was so outraged at being outfoxed by Rachael that he shot Peaches the dog. He said that the dog barked too much anyway since Rachael left.

CHAPTER 7

Akron's Pigmeat

Peaches suspected that Rachael had actually phoned in enough information to the authorities to cause the raids on his businesses as a diversion while she looted the safe. I sympathized with Peaches, not so much because the money was stolen, but because he had been disappointed by someone that he loved very much. I was reminded of the pain I felt when I realized that my wife Addie was seeing one of her coworkers. Peaches was pained more by the lack of Rachael's love than he was by the lack of his money. Truthfully speaking, he probably would have given her the money if she had just agreed to stay with him. The only money Peaches had left was the pocket money he had on him. That was close to five thousand dollars. That money was used to finish the Lincolns and Cadillacs at his garage. The farm was still producing money and the taxi service was still productive. Peaches had no legitimate front man and ended up putting the businesses in his cousin "Pigmeat's" name. Pigmeat lived a short distance away in Akron, Ohio. He had a mechanic's garage there, and only periodically rebuilt wrecked cars. There was always good money in rebuilding wrecks, but Pigmeat never seemed to have enough investment capital to get the ball rolling. He was forced to do simple mechanic work to make ends meet. Peaches had several death threats from the investors who had lost money when Rachael absconded with the funds, but no one actually made a move on Peaches. They knew that he would pay them back as soon as he got the ball rolling again. It didn't take him long either. After a few cross-country trips, he had money again.

Since Peaches's garage had been raided, it was obvious that we were being watched.

It was decided by Peaches that I should go to work in Pigmeat's garage in Akron. I visited Peaches in Cleveland once in a while, at night, but I never made a habit of hanging around the mansion or the garage again after the raids. I always knew that I ran a great risk of being discovered there because of the company I was keeping. Peaches personally took me to Akron and showed me the town and Pigmeat's garage. The town was much smaller than Cleveland and the cars were not as new or as expensive. Akron reminded me of the1960's hippie movement, in the sense that everyone was into helping everyone else, and there was no real interest in making money. Free love, partying, and self-expression were encouraged. Proficiency in the arts and crafts was considered desirable. Any type of creativity was highly lauded. Classic and custom show cars and motorcycles were the talk of the town. Common blue-collar workers worked for years to save enough to buy a GTO or a Harley Davidson motorcycle. Akron was definitely reminiscent of the 1960's hippie movement.

Pigmeat's garage was half the size of Peaches's garage, and it was a pigsty. I later learned that Pigmeat was called by that nickname because he had an intense craving for any part of the pig. He loved barbeque, hot dogs, pork roast, pig feet, pig tails, and chitterlings. It was always a safe bet that whatever he was eating, it had to come from a pig. Pigmeat actually looked something like a pig. He was a short man with a protruding stomach. He had a very wide nose that reminded one of a pig's snout, and he was the color of a light-skinned pig. Even though his mother and Peaches's mother were sisters, the only physical similarity Pigmeat had to Peaches was his light skin. He too was nearly the color of canned peaches.

Pigmeat hung around his old shop long enough to show me the ropes and to introduce me to his helpers, then he took off for Cleveland with Peaches, as Peaches's new front man. Pigmeat wasn't a very smart man, but he was family and Peaches trusted him. Pigmeat's good reputation and clean legal record were all that Peaches needed to set him up as the owner of several of Peaches's businesses. Peaches became a recluse and confined himself to the mansion, or he hid his face under a motorcycle helmet and shield, while he darted around Cleveland on his Harley Davidson. Peaches had to learn all over again to be invisible.

I had the run of Pigmeat's shop. We went from doing regular oil changes and minor mechanical work, to specializing in custom and classic auto work. We also repaired motorcycles; we did everything. The money was never very good because no one in that area had very much money. Hippies are not very big on making or spending money. Most of our trade came our way by word-of-mouth advertising, since we were located in the remote suburbs. My job consisted of managing the shop, troubleshooting problems, and then assigning a mechanic to fix a problem. I was very seldom in the front of the shop or on the lot out front, in case a familiar face from Youngstown rode by that could identify me. I was still confident that my disguise would pass inspection by the average Youngstowner who knew me. Peaches had repaid the ten thousand dollars of mine that Rachael had run off with. I sent half home to my family and used the other half to improve Pigmeat's garage. It eventually became mine, except for the licensing and the ownership of the building. Pigmeat was in the big-time with Peaches in Cleveland, and they very seldomly visited the small-time circus I was in.

Peaches let me keep one of the Lincolns to drive and I had my choice of his power tools.

Jobs weren't very plentiful in the area and money was not circulating as freely in Akron as it was in Cleveland. I barely made ends meet at the garage. I literally had to run as fast as I could just to stand still and not slide backward. Now I knew why Pigmeat had never made much headway at this shop. Occasionally, I made enough money at the garage to buy a wrecked car at the auction to rebuild. That was the only way that I got ahead at Pigmeat's garage. Once I got the wrecked car, it usually took me a month to get the car together enough to make a decent profit. At Peaches's garage, we used to remake a wrecked car in two weeks and we often had the car sold before it was finished. In the part of Akron that my garage was situated in, luxury cars were not the hot item. Classic cars and collector's items were the hot ticket. Most of the cars we reconditioned, we found in old barns or abandoned garages. Once in a while we would actually find something worth rebuilding from the classified section of the newspaper. If these collector's items were rebuilt with original factory parts, then the car was worth more. If we had to use whatever was available, then we generally got much less for the finished product. My dream of relocating my family was on hold for a while. It seemed impossible to get ahead enough to make the kind of move I had been working toward while I was at Peaches's garage. Peaches and Pigmeat were on a roll, but I didn't dare approach them or even appear with them in public. I was an engineer, not a drug dealer. I didn't need the attention or the headache. The drug money was plentiful but so was the prison time that went with it. I knew that sooner or later I would be in a position to make my move.

Stuck in a rut at the shop, I made life bearable by losing myself in a foreign language, researching Bible genealogies, and by occasional visits with my wife and daughter. Time flew by and before I knew it, the year 1986 was here. I was existing, not progressing. Some people would actually say that being alive and free was progress enough, but I had responsibilities to my family. They still seemed to believe that we could be alive and free together. My "fugitive from justice" warrant was rumored to be dropped in 1985 and I recall thinking that maybe the Hubbard Police would honor their original proposal. I hoped it but I didn't expect it. I received news that Addie had to have neck and spinal surgery to repair bone that had been damaged in an old car wreck. The surgery was potentially life-threatening. I immediately gathered my few belongings and headed for Youngstown, Ohio. Addie had gotten the surgery by the time I got to town. She had to wear a metal head brace that was secured to her skull by metal screws. The device was called a "halo" and it was also secured to the neck and shoulders by what appeared to be shoulder pads and straps. Bone was taken from her hip and placed in the areas of the neck and spine where the bone had deteriorated. She had to remain motionless from the waist to the head for several months.

I nursed her the way she had nursed me when I came home from the Akron Burn Center in 1979. When one of us pained, the other felt it. It had always been that way. I especially noticed it when she was pregnant with our daughter Benita. I actually had morning sickness and stomach pains when she did. My photographs hidden behind my mirror in the apartment over Pigmeat's garage were a constant reminder that she could have died from that surgery and I would not have been there for her. I was glad that I took the chance and went to her side. It felt good to be a husband and a father again. I knew better than to be photographed with Addie and Benita, but I wanted something to remind me of the life I was missing with them. I guarded the photographs as if they were gold. They are still in pristine condition today. Even though I knew that she was seeing "male friends," I let her believe that I believed that she was still waiting for me, and I guess in a way that she really was. She just wasn't sitting at home knitting in the meantime. One of her bosses at General Motors had also been one of her softball team coaches. He was one of the light-skinned men that she claimed she wasn't attracted to, but later revealed just the opposite. Ronnie came by my mother's house to visit Addie while she was recuperating from the neck surgery. He had no way of knowing that I was there. He laughed and talked about what was going on at work, and he often told her how much her coworkers missed her. When it was time for Ronnie to leave, he often kissed Addie on the cheek before he left. After several visits, when my mother was not present, Ronnie would kiss Addie on the corner of the mouth, instead of the cheek.

When I asked her about it, she constantly claimed that it didn't mean anything. This boss of hers was one of the gentlemen Addie was rumored to be seeing behind his wife's back. It was also rumored that his wife had voiced dissatisfaction to the level that Addie's and Ronnie's relationship had developed. I was giving Addie the benefit of the doubt when she said that they were just friends, until I heard her tell him that there was nothing she'd prefer to do in life besides talking to him. She later told me that she was just playing with him when she said it. Not being able to be there for her caused me to be less critical of her actions than I normally would have been, and she took full advantage of that fact. I felt bad about not being able to fulfill the promises I had made her earlier in life, but realistically, I was barely surviving myself.

I had to find a way to change my condition. I had too many people waiting for me to straighten out this mess. Every one of my family members was suffering because they felt my suffering; they felt my pain.

Back in Akron, I sold a 1955 Chevy that I had been working on for a few months. That money was enough for me to get started in the mail order business again. Advertising prices had gone up and the number of people purchasing from mail order had gone down. Money was tight and everyone was trying to save for a rainy day. These were not good conditions for the mail order business. The small amount of income I eked out of the mail order business helped me to get better equipment for the garage. The money from the garage helped me to purchase wrecked cars to rebuild. I was still running as fast as I could, just to stand still and to not slide backward. The hunting knives sold well during hunting season, but hardly sold at all at other times. The tall-man series of clothing didn't sell very well, but some recipes that I advertised in the backs of some cooking magazines showed real promise. I sold my mother's recipes for potato salad, sweet potato pie, and low-sodium barbeque sauce. Some organizations against television violence spread their influence to the gun and ammo magazines and asked those magazines not to accept advertising for the sales of how-to books that dealt with knockout drops, explosives, and silencers. The ban on advertising such items lasted for five years in some magazines.

The recipe sales venture provided better equipment for the garage and an occasional car or motorcycle to restore. There was no danger of my getting rich or relocating at this pace. I operated my mail order business through a post office box for Pigmeat's garage. I also filed taxes for the mail order business with Pigmeat's garage's income taxes. In later years, Addie rented a post office box for me to operate D.D.&D. Enterprises. I filed the business along with her regular income taxes from 1989–1995. In 1988, Addie decided to move away from my mother's home and into her own home. She was able to purchase a seventy-thousand-dollar home for thirty-five thousand dollars because the owner was in need of funds to settle some type of family inheritance dispute after the mother had died. I was proud that Addie was able to come up with the down payment and the financing for the home. By the time I got to Youngstown, she had already completed the real estate deal and had moved into the house. The place needed a lot of work, and I did it all. I had some money stashed that was supposed to be for our relocation expenses, but we recognized that the house could be an investment from which we could reap a forty-thousand-dollar profit, after the necessary repairs were made.

This was a much better proposition than the occasional classic car I was restoring at Pigmeat's garage. The outside of the home was brick and required no repairs. The inside of the home was gutted and completely redone. I sanded and restored the hardwood floors. The walls were patched, sanded, and painted. Carpeting was installed in several rooms and in the basement. I did such a good job of installing ceiling tile and wall paneling in the basement that the basement actually rivaled the living room in comfort and beauty. I rebuilt the furnace, the washing machine, and the dryer. From June to December of 1988, I remade 2252 Coronado Avenue. The very first day that I was in the house, I made a secret six-foot-square crawl space in one of the closets of the home. I hid in this crawl space when company came to our house. Everyone who visited the home wanted to go on the grand tour of the place, and all who saw the home thought that a professional interior decorator had done the work. When our house was first finished, the traffic from the spectators was phenomenal. I ran to my secret hiding space several times a day, and oftentimes I had to hide in the cramped space for two hours. Addie's relatives never seemed to want to go home. Benita's schoolmates came to the house very often; many spent the night. When I eventually revealed my presence to the kids, Benita and Addie introduced me to the children as "Uncle Bobby." For the next twelve years, those same children interacted with me and believed that I was Benita's "Uncle Bobby." They too called me Uncle Bobby.

I often went to Addie and Benita's home for extended stays. They often went to movies, steak houses, and shopping centers with me in Akron. This was the closest facsimile to family life that we had. At the end of the day or the week, I had to go home or they had to go home. The strain on all of us was tremendous. Poor little Benita couldn't even call me "Daddy," except in very private and remote locations. My daughter had to be content with calling her father "Boy" or "Uncle Bobby." Back in Akron, I again ran across an article in which a fugitive had remained within the borders of the state and was given leniency by the judge for not fleeing into another state. I decided to document each and every event in my life. If I went to a doctor, I saved the receipt and any other documentation. I made sure that all of the anniversary, birthday, Christmas, and Father's Day cards that I received were signed and dated by the person giving them to me. This established a record of my presence within the state of Ohio. I needed some secret place to keep all of this information, and I ended up stashing it in the secret crawl space I had built in the closet of Addie's new home. When I was forced to hide in the crawl space, I used the bundles of information as pillows. I have much of that information today. I have become addicted to statistics and the preservation of all types of information. I often filed my junk in a box labeled "Trivial Pursuit."

In1989 I strained myself while I was attempting to slide a motor across the garage floor. I later found out that the acute pain I was suffering came from a small hernia that I had tom into a larger hernia. Immediate surgery was necessary. The doctors told me that I would not be able to work in my garage for a while until the stomach muscles had mended quite a bit. I would need nursing and care. That sounded like a good excuse to go back to Addie's and Benita's house to recuperate. Addie got a money order from her bank and made it out to the Hernia Center. Ten minutes after giving them the money order, I was semiconscious on the operating table. The large hernia turned out to be several small ones. I got a much larger incision than the doctors had originally planned. That meant that my recuperating time would be even longer than previously estimated. In the past, I had nightmares about going under anesthesia and revealing my true identity. I no longer had that problem. I spent my recuperation time at Addie's home reading my Bible interpretation guides and studying my foreign language. I put a lot of time into perfecting the artwork for my mail order advertising.

I spent much of my time tutoring Benita in her school work. I wanted her to be all that she could be. For several months, I stood daily on the front porch as Benita walked one block down the street to catch the school bus. On one occasion several stray dogs chased her while she was waiting for the bus. After that, I stood on the porch each morning with a rifle that had a scope. I told Benita to never run from the wild dogs; just lie down and I'd nick them on the butts to run them off. Once I had the rifle on the porch, I never saw the dogs again, but I kept the rifle handy while I watched her board the school bus, just in case some two-legged dogs decided to bother my baby. Child molesters were quite prominent at the time. On one occasion, a van slid off the icy road, jumped the curb, and followed a fleeing Benita up into one of the neighbor's yards. I actually ran down to my child to see if she was hurt. She was scared to death but she was not hit by the sliding van. No one paid any attention to me as I walked back to Benita's front porch. The school bus finally arrived and carried Benita to school that day and the two of us laughed about the event for many years afterward.

I came to Youngstown more often after that. While I was busy operating the mail order business out of Addie's house, I left assignments for the mechanics and painters at Pigmeat's garage. I was back and forth between Youngstown and Akron constantly. In the early 1990s I perceived that the system of corruption in the Youngtown-Hubbard-Campbell area was beginning to fall apart. In Hubbard, in 1988, Allan Frost II fled to New Mexico to escape Hubbard's Chief of Police, John Karlovic. Karlovic was convicted of assaulting Frost when a drug deal with Karlovic's niece went sour. In 1990 Frost sued Karlovic and other Hubbard officials and won an undisclosed amount from the lawsuit. FBI agents advised Frost to leave the area since Karlovic had threatened his life. Luann Nicolaou also filed charges against Karlovic, stating that he beat her repeatedly during their extramarital affair.

She stated that she could never get any help from the local police or lawyers because Karlovic was a police chief. Around Christmas of 1990, a Youngstown reporter revealed that McDonald's restaurants had complained that the Hubbard Township Police Department had so abused McDonald's long-standing policy of serving free food and drinks to the police that the fast food chain wrote a letter of complaint to the new chief of police. The letter claimed that the amount of food the officers took from McDonald's was extremely excessive and abusive. They could not possibly have eaten all of the food they took. Hubbard Police Chief, Howard Bradley, resigned from his position after claiming that his life had been threatened by one of Hubbard's Township Trustees. Sandra Choppa, a police dispatcher, removed twenty-two police reports from the department files. She was suspended for eight days with pay, and any record of the incident has been purged.

Also in1990, a federal judge ruled that Trumbull County Sheriff, Richard Jakmas, distrusted black deputies to the point that he discriminated against them. Jakmas's own highranking officers testified against him. Jakmas made a practice of telling white deputies to keep secrets from black deputies about the department's plans for raids. Jakmas was also found to be racially biased when he knowingly tolerated the making of derogatory comments about blacks by members of his staff, and has made such derogatory comments himself. It was also demonstrated that Jakmas refused to promote qualified blacks to the lieutenant's position but readily promoted lesser qualified whites to that position. A federal affidavit revealed the widespread interaction of mobsters, politicians, attorneys, and judges in the Mahoning Valley gambling rackets. Charges, indictments, plea bargains, and convictions revealed that the aforementioned parties operated a network of gambling, drug dealing, and bribery rackets.

Many of the top mobsters, politicians, attorneys, and judges agreed to inform on others in return for more lenient sentences. Lawrence "Jeep" Garano was revealed to be the local boss of the Hubbard area, where the Hubbard Police Department resides.

Mayors, commissioners, and many other politicians have been exposed for receiving political contributions from alleged operators of an illegal gambling ring. The corruption runs across many counties, cities, and states. The Ohio-Pennsylvania area was particularly targeted by authorities because of the pervasive complicity in that area. High-stakes poker and crap games in the Youngstown-

Campbell area were reported to have rivaled those in Las Vegas. One gambling house in that area was reported to have fountains, chandeliers, and other furnishings that were facsimiles of those in Vegas. I never thought that I would see the time when the local newspapers revealed the connections between the mobsters and the good citizens of the Youngstown-Hubbard-Campbell area. This current flood of information reminded me of the time that I saw a former FBI agent, who had become a Youngstown policeman, standing behind the top local mobster's bar, selling cocaine and stolen leather jackets like they were Sno-Kones. Everybody in the bar knew who he was, and he acted as if he had a license to do what he was doing. Rumor has it that he was handpicked by the local crime boss to become Youngstown's chief of police.

It looked like the media were finally doing their jobs by exposing corruption on all levels of society. As mobsters turned informants to get lenient sentences, some other mobsters decided to make takeover moves on territories they had eyed for a long time. Some mobsters had also decided to put an end to the recent popularity of informing to the police to avoid doing time. This was a very unmanly thing to do for a "made man." No one is sure who or what precipitated the hit on local crime boss, Joey Naples, in 1991. He was gunned down at the new home he was building in the suburbs outside of the Youngstown area he operated in.

My daughter, Benita, was a student at St. Anthony of Padua! Parochial School. Joey Naples was a member of that church. Father DeMarinas, pastor of St. Anthony, held Naples's funeral at his church. Father DeMarinas stated that he was aware of "Little Joey's" reputation, but the good father insisted that Naples was a good Christian Samaritan who did much for many in the community. DeMarinas went on to say that Naples came to church often and that the priest knew that Naples was polite to women. The priest mentioned that Naples often gave huge donations to the church. DeMarinas was joined by local attorney, Don Hanni, when they stated that they never heard "Little Joey" Naples curse.

Mayor Pat Ungaro stated that he wondered if Joey's death signaled a shake-up in the mob. Ungaro feared what was next to come from the local and out-of-town mobsters. Ungaro feared a turf war. A federal government informant stated that he had attended meetings at which members of Naples's faction talked about taking over the local operations from Naples.

The informant said that he believed that Naples's associates backstabbed Naples, but that outside factions may have been responsible for the hit. I was surprised to hear that Eddie Truelove, manager of Dee's Lounge, had died of a heart attack, when his heart literally exploded during a cocaine snorting contest. With the Hubbard Police on the defense and their department headed by someone other than Karlovic, I wondered if it was time to pop back up in the Youngstown-Hubbard area. I didn't think that I had to worry about any of Eddie's friends bugging me about working for them, since he was dead. The only faction that I was still concerned about was the Muhammad gang. Some of them still occupied the house next to my mother's home, and they still claimed that they intended to take over the local mob action.

I was concerned about the Muhammad gang but I didn't fear them. I no longer thought of getting enough money to leave the country. Now I thought in terms of getting enough money to hire an attorney outside of the influence of the "system in the Youngstown-Hubbard area I had spent most of my money on the home Addie had bought and on the hernia operation. I knew that it would take time to accumulate enough money for a good attorney. I was confident that I could win my case and be free to love my family publicly. I didn't want to relive the pain of not being there for my loved ones when they were sick or dying. My brother Carnell died of cancer in 1992, and I was not free to attend his funeral. I had spent several months with him at Addie's home before he finally died. It was wonderful hanging with Carnell after so many years. He had been a jet mechanic for the Air Force in Utah. We shared passions for racing cars and hunting. Carnell was a regular at my home in Hubbard before the fire. Addie loved Carnell as much as I did. Benita saw Carnell as a younger version of me. My grandmother on my mother's side also died while I was hiding out. She was the glue that held several families together. When she died, our families seemed to fragment and drift apart to indifference. All that I could do for my mother was to sit and talk to her about the good old days with my grandmother. My brothers had the job of comforting my mother at the funerals because I wasn't in a position to fulfill my responsibilities as her oldest son.

Addie went to several banks in an attempt to get a loan on her home so that I might hire an attorney to look into my case. The banks told her that her home needed some more improvements before it was worth its potential seventy thousand dollars. As it was, it was only appraised at fifty thousand dollars. She had financed it for thirty-five thousand dollars and took out a second mortgage for about fifteen thousand dollars. She couldn't borrow a penny on the house until she made more improvements on it. I had spent all of my money and I couldn't think of any place to get a loan but from Peaches and his cousin Pigmeat. If I could get enough from them to rebuild a few wrecks from the auction, I'd be in good enough shape to hire an attorney and to make more improvements in our home so that it would be appraised at its potential value. Maybe I could invest some of the loan into my mail order business and generate some income that way. I had not hit Peaches or Pigmeat for any favors or loans for a long time. I guessed that I was overdue and I knew that they would be more than glad to help me. I told Addie not to worry, I had a solution to all of our problems. It was time to go to Cleveland. The thought of walking into that web and getting caught made me paranoid. I knew what Peaches and Pigmeat were doing in Cleveland.

Peaches was playing the invisible role, but Pigmeat was playing the front man role.

I had heard about Pigmeat's drug parties and the number of beautiful women he kept around him. The flashy cars he drove were enough to draw plenty of attention to him.

Pigmeat played the master at the mansion now; Peaches was seldomly there, his role was not as obvious. As I lay in the bed with my wife, I thought of how wonderful it would be to take a stroll with Addie and Benita through the mall. I pushed back the dread of being caught in Cleveland with well-known drug dealers. It was likely that I would be stopped and questioned for even visiting the mansion. I knew that it had to be under constant surveillance. Even Peaches only periodically sneaked into the place at night. He generally resided in the old apartment that Rachael used to have. I was definitely going but I had to do it right; I had to anticipate any possibility. It would be nice if the "Invisible Man" were really invisible.

CHAPTER 8

Pulling a Houdini

D riving to Cleveland on New Year's Eve of 1993, I thought of how packed the mansion would be. I decided to take a detour to Akron to pick up a few things and to check on the garage. The mechanics at Pigmeat's garage told me about several strangers who had inquired about the garage and its owner. The mechanics had told these strangers that the owner was on an extended vacation, but that the manager would be in any day. The mechanics thought that the inquirers were concerned about purchasing the business. The improvements I had made to the building projected the image of prosperity to any who passed Pigmeat's garage. It was no surprise that anyone would be interested in taking over the business, but what if that was not the reason for the inquiries? What if someone was interested in the place because it was in Pigmeat's name, and Pigmeat was drawing attention to himself in Cleveland as a big-time drug dealer? What if they were interested in the manager of Pigmeat's garage; after all, I was Pigmeat's front man? I hurried upstairs to my old apartment over the garage. I gathered my few belongings, including my collection of pictures of Addie, Benita, and me. I knew that I had to slip into Cleveland as if my life depended on it because it probably did. I had waited too long and hoped too hard to let this opportunity to straighten out my life pass me by. Pigmeat's and Peaches's money seemed like the only viable options. I just had to get to them and away from them as safely as possible. Talking to them on the telephone was definitely out of the question.

It seemed like the ride from Akron to Cleveland lasted forever, even though it only took forty-five minutes. I went directly to Rachael's old apartment to see Peaches. No one answered the door and I assumed that he would be at the mansion since this was New Year's Eve. I parked the car several blocks away from the mansion and walked the rest of the way. Cars were jammed and double-parked for several blocks in any direction. I had never seen this many cars at any of the parties Peaches used to give. Pigmeat definitely believed in overkill. Pigmeat's Mercedes was parked in its spot in front of the garage of the mansion.

Several other Mercedeses were in the driveway. I wondered if Peaches had gotten himself a Mercedes also. Security guards walked the premises and communicated by means of radios. All of this was costing someone a bundle of money. Music blasted out of the house and I could tell by the announcing of each song that a live band had been hired to perform for New Years. I recognized very few of the people I saw at the many tables in the mansion and very few of them recognized me; maybe the scraggly beard I had grown at Addie's house, while I was recuperating from surgery, was disguising me a bit. Maybe the afro-styled hair I was wearing confused my old acquaintants a little. Maybe wearing eyeglasses instead of my contacts threw a few people off as well. I looked just like the person the police had been looking for all of those years. I looked just like Benjamin Robert Holmes Jr.

As I waded through the usual crowds of women, food, liquor, and confetti, I wondered what Addie and Benita were doing at that moment. It would have been nice to have been home with them for New Year's. Someone grabbed my arm and spun me around. Before I realized what was going on, someone had me in a bear hug and had lifted me off of my feet.

'Who the hell you trying to fool with that disguise," Peaches blurted out in his drunken voice. I had gained twenty pounds since he first snatched me off my feet ten years ago, and he had just done it again; this time it seemed even easier for him than it had been in earlier days. I told him that he probably scared ten years off my life. He laughed and said that he was glad that someone else was getting old besides him. He said, "I didn't expect you to show up tonight, especially with the type of traffic coming through this time of the year. I really hadn't planned on coming here tonight myself, but Pigmeat pestered me until he changed my mind." Peaches told me that he didn't plan on staying very long because he had a new woman waiting for him back at the apartment. I told him that I had been by the apartment but no one answered the door. Peaches told me that she was not allowed to answer the door. He told me that he was satisfied with being a behind-the-scenes partner with Pigmeat.

Peaches said he wanted to be just like me—invisible. Both of us agreed that we had no business being at the mansion on this particular night. Peaches was there out of nostalgic curiosity and I was there out of desperation. I explained my problem to Peaches; I told him that now was the right time to take my case to court. All that I needed was a little investment capital so that I could make enough money to take care of a few things. We waded through the crowd until we found Pigmeat sitting at the end of an enormously long dining table. Just as I had heard, Pigmeat had a set of exquisite twins seated with him. He called them Joy and Toy. I couldn't tell them apart. Both girls were about five feet and eight inches tall. Their hair was in a ball on top of their heads. Both girls wore white fox fur capes over white gowns. The stiletto heeled shoes made them appear taller than they were. They looked like they may have been related to Halle Berry, except that their hair was much longer. I wondered if they got in the bed with Pigmeat at the same time or if they took turns. Pigmeat was a prime candidate for a heart attack with all of the pork he consumed. A few minutes in the sack with these gorgeous and fit specimens would guarantee him an early grave. At least he'd die happy.

Peaches motioned for Pigmeat to follow us to the study in the back of the mansion. Pigmeat hugged me and asked about the hernia operation. After five minutes of catching up on the latest events, we got down to discussing what I needed to get myself together.

Peaches sent Pigmeat down to the basement floor safe, behind the bar, to get ten thousand dollars for me. More was offered but I was sure that I could make this amount work. Even though the two of

and mention his middle name. She went on to explain that he had been asking her out on dates even when he was married. She further explained that she was interested in him teaching her to play tennis and to golf. His valuable lessons would also benefit Benita's play on the high school tennis team. I privately asked Benita if this was an excuse for Crawley and Addie to be together. Benita suspected that to be Crawley's true intention, but she believed her mother to be gullible enough to believe that Crawley was only interested in playing tennis with her. Several times when Addie and Benita were playing tennis at the park, Crawley and a male friend popped up to keep Addie company, and not to play tennis. Benita relayed that information to me and she also revealed that her mother had told Crawley that she would be there. Shortly after that, Addie constantly complained that her car was giving her trouble. She eventually had to call a friend for a ride, who lived in our neighborhood and who also happened to work the same shift in the same place Addie worked at General Motors. Addie called James Henry Crawley Jr. to give her a ride to work, on a regular basis. They never came straight home, and she was always overly impressed with his Cadillac Seville. As in the past, she assured me that she was not attracted to him because of his light coloring. She again swore that she never did like men of that color.

I recalled how similar Crawley looked to the man Addie had kissed in the parking lot of the restaurant after the softball game a number of years ago. I knew Crawley through his younger brother who used to race cars with my club. I knew Crawley wasn't the man I had seen years ago, but he certainly could have passed for his kin. Addie lied about being interested in that softball coach years ago and I suspected that she was lying now. She attempted to sidetrack my suspicions by making fun of the gap in Crawley's teeth and by criticizing his big stomach and little legs. My suspicions increased and were not allayed, because she talked about him so much, even when she was criticizing him. Addie bought a new car and claimed that she hardly ever saw Crawley anymore because she didn't need a ride. Benita assured me that they still associated on many occasions, but it was just a friendly relationship. I believed my daughter because she had never lied to me before and I didn't want to believe that she would now. Addie, I wasn't so sure about.

She had a radical hysterectomy around about that time and claimed that the pain from sex could only be lessened by using heavy vaginal lubrication like Vaseline. Use of the Vaseline was the only thing I found different about our sex lives after the operation, except sex was less frequent. I often wondered if the daily lunches she had with Crawley on the job had anything to do with that. Again, I nursed her as she had nursed me every time I had been ill. I had medical problems of my own at that time. Years of standing on the cement and concrete floors of the garages I had worked in caused my arches to drop. This caused me very severe foot pain. At one time my doctor talked of surgery, but I was able to correct the problem with specially made foot arches. I had to get the custom foot arches several times over the next two years to correct the problem. The special arches cost five hundred dollars a pair. I dealt with a doctor in Champion, Ohio, twenty miles away. This was the closest to home I had ever visited a doctor. On one occasion when I was picking up a pair of custom arches, I saw a girl who looked very familiar. I was sure that I knew her and her family. I walked out of the office as soon as I saw her, and I sent Addie and Benita back to pick up the arches. When I got to Addie's house I looked in my old yearbook and found a picture of Gwen Patterson. She graduated with me from Rayen High School in 1969. I never went to that doctor's office again; I ended all contact with them.

Even though Addie earned sixty-five thousand dollars a year on her job, she suddenly developed serious money problems. All of her credit cards were overdrawn because she was using them for cash advances. Was she buying drugs? Was she giving it to her family? Was she giving it to some man? I had no idea. Even the little money I had accumulated for a lawyer, she went through like a hot knife through butter. She borrowed two thousand dollars at a time from my mother and my brother, without my knowledge. She told them that she had some outstanding medical bills of mine to clear up. At other times she claimed that she needed the money to help pay Benita's tuition to parochial school. None of this was true. I snooped around the house every day while she was at work and Benita was in high school. After several months I found a stash of lottery slip receipts that amounted to two hundred dollars a week. That did not include the extra fifteen dollars a week she played with her coworkers in a lottery pool. I later found out that she and her cousin Carolyn went to Pennsylvania every Sunday after church to play the famous Pennsylvania Sunday lottery.

Addie was throwing away a total of 230 dollars a week on the lottery. She admitted she had a slight gambling problem, but since she didn't drink, use drugs, or mess around with other men, she really didn't see why I was so concerned about a simple vice like playing the lottery. I could not get her to understand that 230 dollars a week was 920 dollars a month flushed down the toilet. She hardly ever hit the number, and when she did, she only hit for forty dollars, but she didn't really care about hitting, she got enjoyment from playing. She voiced a desire to go to Vegas to drop a few thousand dollars on the slot machines, poker tables, and the crap tables. I couldn't believe my ears. Little church-girl Addie had a serious gambling habit. How could I have missed it all this time? We were broke and she thought it was my fault because I wasn't working a regular job to match her income. She constantly stated that I was in no position to criticize her gambling, and I had no say in what she did with her money. She chose to forget how much I had put into our home and into her pockets. Just as I pulled a Houdini disappearing act during the raid of Pigmeat's New Year's party, so had our savings done a Houdini. They had disappeared; they were gone. I wasn't sure about Addie's and Crawley's relationship, but I was damn sure about her love affair with her latest beau. His name was "Mr. Ohio Lottery." He was her lover and her pimp; she gave him all of her money and mine. She didn't care if her daughter had food to eat or if the bills got paid. She was hooked; she was strung out on something every bit as strong as drugs. Her pimp wanted money and she had to comply. Abracadabra, your money is gone; now you see it, now you don't.

CHAPTER 9

Revelations

I t was a bad time to have money problems. The most opportune time to present my case was on May of 1997, when the long-awaited expose on the connection between organized crime and politicians was revealed in the *Youngstown Vindicator*. An emphasis was placed on the role the mob had made for black drug dealers in the "New Mafia." The recent shortcomings of the traditional Italian mobsters left shortages of manpower and cash. Black drug dealers had both. The old Muhammad gang died when the two heads of it died. The remnant of the gang joined the "Ready-Rock" cocaine dealers to make up a new and improved black mob. The weakened traditional Italian mob saw this new black alliance as a force to be reckoned with. Rather than have a turf war that the Italians couldn't win, the Italians made room for their black cohorts and included them in all aspects of organized crime, including the payoff and extortion rackets. Prostitution and gambling were the lifeblood moneymakers of the traditional mob, who wanted black drug dealers to invest their bountiful crack cocaine profits in those enterprises.

The May 9, 1997 article in the *Youngstown Vindicator* mentioned that aging mobsters, Bernie "The Jew" Altshuler and Lenine "Lenny" Strollo, conspired to murder a rival, Ernest A. Biondillo Jr. Biondlllo died June 3, 1996, from two shotgun blasts on the East Side in a thirty-five-thousand-dollar murder-for-hire scheme engineered by Altshuler, the FBI said. An informant mentioned that black shooters were recruited by the mob for the hit, and that they had earned positions in the mob by investing their drug profits into the gambling rackets. George Wilkins III, Jeffrey Riddle, Lavance Turnage, Cleveland Blair, and Rasheed Brown were the black defendants accused of committing the hit for the mob. Biondillo had tried to take over parts of Strollo's turf and Biondillo paid off politicians without informing Strollo or splitting the benefits of those payoffs, an FBI informant said. Biondillo had installed poker machines in private clubs that were in Strollo's territory. Biondillo had been aligned with the Joey Naples faction of the mob and lost clout when Naples was killed earlier. A Strollo-Biondillo power struggle ensued. Biondillo took to wearing a bulletproof vest and took alternative routes to work. Biondillo was to inherit the Naples faction of the mob when Naples retired in August of 1991, but Naples was killed before the reins of power were turned over. Strollo thought Naples would take over his territory after Strollo started serving time in late 1990 for violation of the RICO statute against organized crime. There was always a great deal of friction between the two factions.

FBI documents revealed a three-year investigation of extortion, loan sharking, robbery, gambling, drug trafficking, and payoffs to politicians in the area. A deputy and a local police chief were suspected of taking payoffs from the mob. Another expose went on to reveal that a weakened mob may have had Joey Naples knocked off because he was against bringing in the black drug dealers to fatten the mob back up with their cash. The *Youngstown Vindicator* article of June 8, 1997, emphasized the connection between the black drug dealers who hit Biondillo and the new boss, Lenny Strollo. Black gangsters and Italian gangsters were now in business together. The turf war even seemed to spread to the political arena. Mahoning County Prosecutor Paul Gains said that his predecessor, James Philomena, hired a hit man for 30,000 dollars to kill him. Jeff Riddle, one of the black shooters accused in the Biondillo hit, was accused of accompanying another black man and a white man, when they shot and tried to kill Gains after he defeated Philomena in the Democratic primary. FBI wiretaps of local mobsters revealed most of the details. Gains was shot by a white man, in the kitchen of his home, while the two black men waited outside.

Another *Vindicator* article of 7/31/97 reveals that Edward Flask, director of Mahoning Valley Sanitary District, pressured James Fiorenze, a Trumbull County engineer, to give work to Flask's choices in exchange for a part of the firm's fee. Fiorenzo is said to have informed the Mahoning County Fraud Task Force of the kickback scheme. A *Vindicator* article of 6/27/98 revealed that Andrew Rauzan Jr. and Gerald Keish, two retired detective sergeants from the small town of Campbell, pleaded guilty to conspiracy to obstruct the enforcement of state and local gambling laws between 1990 and 1997. Rauzan and Keish were promoted in 1996 when Strollo supplied the Campbell law director with a list of five men he wanted to be detective sergeants. Charles Xenakis, retired Campbell police chief, and Lawrence "Jeep" Garano, of Hubbard, were coconspirators in the plot. The police were to provide protection for the illegal gambling operations in Campbell. Not since the O.J. Simpson Trial and the Rodney King Trial had police and government corruption been so vividly exposed. Evidence had been destroyed, payoffs had been made, and conspiracies to hide the truth abounded.

The Simpson and the King cases put the authorities under the magnifying glass and made them accountable for their actions. In that same vein, the local *Vindicator* exposed corruption on a daily basis. This was the time to present my case—if I had some money.

I had some old steel pennies from World War II that I had been saving for a rainy day.

I guess this was that rainy day. A collector had been seeking the three pennies that I had been saving ever since I had a paper route in the early sixties. When I tried to make contact with the seeker of my coins, I discovered that he had died and passed the collection on in his will. It took another two years before probate awarded the coin collection to his heirs and they again sought my three coins to complete their collection. I held onto the coins until that time. Meanwhile, I tried to get Addie to stop sinking us further in the hole with her incessant gambling. She had added sports betting to her list of gambling vices. Someone got her hooked on it from work. She was still blowing more than two hundred dollars a week on her habit. Little by little, I was able to accumulate a little cash, only to have

Addie claim that the money was needed for some dire emergency. The money was never replaced when she got paid.

Addie's credit cards were all overdrawn and her creditors asked her to stop using the cards.

Corruption in the sheriff's department was exposed when a June 28, 1998 article appeared in the *Youngstown Vindicator* mentioning that the sheriff planted real and fake drugs to stage a scene for news cameras in the Youngstown area. Large amounts of drugs were placed on tables in front of television news cameras to exaggerate the size of the haul from a drug raid. After the cameras were gone, the prop drugs were ordered back to the department's Major Crimes Unit. Jeff Chance, Sheriff Phil Chance's brother, orchestrated the planting of the prop drugs, that often turned out to be flour. Small-time drug dealers were indicted for major crimes as a result of the planted drugs. Jeff Chance was indicted for a number of charges, including stealing money allocated to him to buy drugs while undercover.

It was June of 1998, and my daughter Benita was about to graduate from high school. It was a very happy time for me, but I was saddened a bit because I wasn't free to attend the graduation ceremonies with her and the rest of the family. Friends and family came from out of town for the event. All of Benita's school friends and cousins were in attendance at the graduation ceremony and at the after-graduation party. A very large number of Addie's church members and coworkers from G.M. were in attendance at the party. Several of the male coaches that I had suspected her of being too attracted to were also in attendance. Some of her female friends that I had not heard anything about for a long time were at the party. I had no way of knowing what went on at the party until I was told by family members after the event. I hid out at my mother's house while out-of-town company stayed at Addie's house.

When I was told that James Crawley accompanied Irma Wesley to the party, I wondered why Irma was in many photographs and Crawley was in none of them. There were way too many photos of Addie and way too few of Benita, who was supposed to be the one honored at the event. Who was the photographer who made Addie the object of his focus and left Benita to relative obscurity? The only person that I did not see in any of the photographs was James Crawley. I asked Benita who took the pictures and she revealed that Crawley had been the photographer. He escorted Addie around the hall the entire time that the event took place. He ate with her, he sat with her, and most people asked if he were her husband or boyfriend. Addie quickly denied any involvement with Crawley, but her constant and playful chatter with him made many people very suspicious of their relationship. Irma, the girl he came there with, hardly spoke a word to Crawley or Addie during the entire celebration.

Startling revelations came almost on a daily basis. Not only was there evidence that the mob was involved with crooked policemen, there was also evidence that the police were involved in planting evidence and setting people up. Most significant to me was the revelation that the mob had courted and married some of the same local black talent that they had been at war with for decades. The mob's use of blacks made me wonder what my drinking buddies at Dee's Lounge had in mind for me back in the 1970s. The infusion of black drug dealers' money pumped the mob back up to its former strength. Bribes and payoffs got healthier and more politicians compromised themselves with corrupt deals. Local newspapers reported the latest mob activities on an almost daily basis. Rumors circulated that one could "buy a murder case for a two-hundred-thousand-dollar bribe to a local judge. Members of the prosecutor's office were rumored to be shaking down the accused for all that they could get. The judges and prosecutors mentioned in the rumors countered by saying that they would clear their names of the unsubstantiated accusations. None of them were ever able to do that.

My daughter, Benita, was hired on the summer intern program at General Motors because her mother had an excellent work record there. The very first day on her new job, Benita came home upset over the pervasive rumor that Addie and James Crawley had been lovers for a long time and were now engaged to marry soon. Addie denied the rumor and arranged a meeting with Crawley to convince Benita that they were not lovers or engaged.

Benita was not buying their denials because she observed them having lunch together too often and she noticed their habits of touching each other too much and of whispering in each other's ears a little too often. Most of all, Benita noticed the coldness Addie began to show me on a regular basis. I first noticed Addie's "iceberg treatment" of me on New Year's Day of 1998. Instead of spending that time with me, she chose to visit Pilgrim's Baptist Church for their midnight celebration of the arrival of the new year. At a later date, I found a church program that was dated for May of that year. Addie had attended the church a few days before Benita had graduated from high school.

Addie was a member of a "sanctified" church, and they never attended Baptist churches. When I asked her about visiting the Baptist church, she denied having attended it, and she told me that "sanctified churchgoers" don't attend Baptist churches. She told me that whoever told me that she had been to Pilgrim's Baptist Church was a liar. I pulled the program out of her personal Bible and pointed out her own handwriting on the program. She couldn't account for the handwriting or the program. She simply left our home to have dinner with some family members. This was the first time that Benita had ever refused to accompany her mother. Benita said something very strange that I didn't understand for another two years, "I don't particularly care to eat dinner with whom she's having dinner." When I asked Benita what was the problem with going to dinner with Addie's family, Benita looked at me, shook her head, and walked away. I was totally dumbfounded. Benita later told me that James Crawley was a member of Pilgrim's Baptist Church, and that Addie had met him there. I assumed that he was also attending the family dinner that day. I later learned that Crawley had been at our home to meet Addie's out-of-town family members when they came to Benita's graduation, while I was hiding at my mother's home, down the street. When Benita went through her gifts and the money-containing cards from the graduation party, she found a few $20 bills, many $50 bills, and only one $100 bill. The card accompanying the $100 bill was signed by James Henry Crawley Jr. I knew then that Addie was "seeing" this man.

Later that year, Benita answered the telephone, only to have someone hang up on her several times. After the third hang-up,

Addie answered the phone at the same time that Benita did. Benita said "Hello" several times but the caller hung on without saying anything. After a long pause, Addie told Benita to hang up the phone because it was for Addie. I was with Benita when the first calls came in. I was also with her when she and Addie answered the phone at the same time. When Addie told Benita to hang up the phone, I placed my hand over the mouthpiece of the telephone and hit the button as if the phone were placed on its pedestal. Convinced that Benita had hung up the telephone, Addie and the man felt free to converse.

The man was named Bill Bland. He was a red-headed white boy who worked in the battery department at General Motors. Addie told him that it was all right to call her anytime at work, but that she had told him before not to call her at home. He told her that he was about to go to Florida to take care of some business, but that he'd be back in a few days. He expected the two of them to get together when he got back home.

He went on to say that he had been after her even before he got his divorce. He mentioned that their "friendship" had started back in 1986, just before she got the neck surgery and had to wear the "halo." Now that his divorce was finalized, he didn't feel like hiding their "friendship" anymore. She told him that her situation still hadn't changed; that she wasn't satisfied with whom she was with, but they were still together. She was looking forward to a change so that she could see him openly. Bill Bland asked her to promise him that she would think about the two of them in the bed together until he got back from Florida. She promised him that she would. He told her that he loved her and she said, "Okay."

After they hung up their telephones, Benita asked her mother whom she had been talking to. Addie told Benita and me that she had been talking to her cousin, Carolyn, about doing Carolyn's income taxes. I asked Addie if she had to lie in the bed with Carolyn to do her taxes. Then Addie knew that I had listened to her telephone conversation with Bill Bland. She pretended to be offended that I had violated her right to privacy by listening in on the phone call.

I laughed at her pretense and asked her, "Is that the best that your mammy taught you to lie?"

Aware of my suspicions about her activities when I was away, she made a futile effort to allay those suspicions. She said, "I just like to flirt to see if I'm still attractive to other men, since I'm approaching fifty years of age."

Then it hit me. She was only thirty years old when I disappeared. Almost twenty years had passed, and I was still struggling to be free. She and Benita had been prisoners as much as I had. All of us had been living incomplete lives. The stress was maddening.

In the autumn of 1998, a title to a Cadillac came to the house in the mail. The car was titled to Benita Holmes. When I asked Benita and Addie about the title, they both told me that they had no clue about what was going on. Benita did mention that a boy she was seeing had recently bought such a car. I asked her how a twenty-year-old could afford a Cadillac while working as a busboy. Two weeks later Sianni's mother called Benita in the middle of the night to tell her that her son had been arrested by the police for suspicion of burglary. His car was registered in Benita's name and Sianni's mother needed the title to get the car out of the police impound. Benita claimed that it was the first time that she was ever told that the title she had received in the mail was for Sianni's car. I knew that if she had been riding in his car on a regular basis, she had to know that the title was for his car. Benita's mother placed the blame on Sianni, and denied that Benita had any involvement in putting the car in her name.

In the state of Ohio, you must show proof of insurance when you purchase an automobile. Often when a young man could afford a car, but not the insurance, he would put the car in the name of someone who had insurance to circumnavigate the stipulation. Whether Benita put Sianni's car in her name or not was never known to me. Sianni's mother had Benita transfer the title to the mother's name; then she sold the boy's car. He blamed Benita for turning the car over to his mother, instead of safekeeping it until he got out of jail.

After a few days of jail on the suspicion charge, Sianni was released. I had met him earlier in the year when he came to the house to visit Benita. I tried to get him to lift weights with me. I was introduced to him as "Uncle Bobby," the name I also used when I met Benita's classmates: Troy Dubose, Jason Johns, Meredith Manning,

DiOuana Bridges, Shifon Ballard, Renee Orroyo, and Benita's prom date Derrick Page. I also met the young man she lost her virginity to, Kenneth Green. The fact that she shared that information with me, and not with her mother, shows the trust my daughter had in me. I was the one who told her mother about Kenny; Addie still believed Benita was a virgin. Some of Benita's female classmates told me about the inequities in the female and male athletic programs at their school. Male athletes were treated like gods by the faculty and the female athletes didn't have adequate facilities or equipment. I sent a letter to the ACLU of Cleveland, Ohio, complaining about the discrimination. They promptly responded with a list of organizations, lawyers, and documents that would aid me in launching legal action against the offenders. Their response was addressed to Robert Holmes of 2252 Coronado Avenue. I have saved the response as I have saved most other documents that verify my presence in the state of Ohio.

In November of 1998, my brother, the real "Uncle Bobby," sent Benita a car as her graduation gift. The car was a stick shift, and I had to teach her how to drive it. I had taught Addie to drive some of the stick shift racing cars I had in the past, but she was a little rusty now. The neighbors, Dave and Cindy Morrison, often laughed when Benita and I were practicing driving the stick shift car. I was introduced by Addie and Benita to these neighbors as "Uncle Bobby." Before this young couple moved into their home, it was occupied by Jim and Debbie Maughn. Jim had been a teacher at Ursuline High School when Benita was a student there. Jim and Debbie were introduced to "Uncle Bobby" while I was making the mechanical repairs to Addie's and Benita's cars. The Maughns often saw me when I used the power saw in the backyard to cut down some small trees. It seems that every time I had to replace the outside nightlight on the garage, Jim and Debbie were in their backyard window, waving at me. I was good enough to shovel another neighbor's snow one year. For the next few years, the elderly neighbor, Mrs. Fitzgerald, asked Benita or Addie if I could shovel her snow again. I was outside the house in the backyard all of the time, but I didn't dare show myself in the front of the house, where the street traffic was fairly heavy.

I had no idea that Sianni was a member of the Ready Rock Crew, crack cocaine dealers. Seven members of his crew took turns threatening Addie and Benita on the telephone. It got so bad that Addie had the phone number changed. Benita was afraid to venture away from the house. One night, I had Addie and Benita show me where these drug dealers hung out. I could easily see from the street into the windows of the house, where seven of them were passed out on their drugs. I had Benita call them on her cell phone as we sat on the street, looking at them through the window. When one of them answered the phone, I had Benita hand me the phone. I identified myself as Benita's "Uncle Bobby," and told them that I was outside looking at them at that very moment. I told them that it would be no problem at all to part each of their scalps before they got out of their seats. I told them to let this be the end of harassing Benita or I would be back to part those scalps. I was met with a chorus of "okays" and "yes sirs." Benita never had any more trouble out of the Ready Rock Crew.

Benita got on with her life after that. She was accepted into the National Honors Society and she received a scholarship to Kent State University. I overheard Addie tell one of her relatives that she was going to get herself a boyfriend when Benita went away to college. I asked her if she meant to get another boyfriend besides the ones she had, or if she planned on dumping the ones she had and starting over again. She had the look of total bewilderment when she realized that I had heard her make the comment on the telephone. I knew that my wife was not very trustworthy. If I couldn't trust her with my heart, how could I trust her with my freedom, safety, or my life? We were planning on getting enough money to present my case and win my freedom, so that we could live the rest of our lives in peace. Besides that, I planned on writing my book, and then explaining it to the world. I had not planned on hiding out for another eighteen years. Even though she told me that she was just kidding on the phone, I wondered what her real plans for the future were, and I wondered that every day afterward.

My father was admitted to an Alzheimer's clinic, after he suddenly lost himself in his own basement. He came to Addie's house every day to visit me before he got ill, and I was there most of 1998. I was sorry that I couldn't visit him at the clinic. Even in his mental state, he had the presence of mind to keep calling me "Boy," when he asked about me. Addie and Benita entertained their family and friends at their home just before Christmas arrived. I went to my mother's home while their guests partied with them. I only expected to be at my mother's place for a few days, but Addie's brother, Calvin, surprised her when he came to town from Oregon. Addie, Benita, and Calvin went to Virginia for Christmas to visit relatives. When they all returned to Youngstown, Calvin decided to stick around for another two weeks. I ended up at my mother's home for almost a month. Addie did not visit me at my mother's home any of the time that her brother was in town; Benita visited me there often.

New Year's Eve was upon us and Addie told Benita to tell me that she was going to her church that night to observe the arrival of the new year. At the turn of the new year she called me at my mother's home to tell me Happy New Year. I could hear some man telling her to hurry up and to get off of her cell phone so that they could go to the party. He asked her who was she talking to anyway. I had not seen my wife during the entire Christmas and New Year's season. She used her out-of-town relatives as the excuse, but they were often across town at other relatives' homes, at the shopping malls, or out of Youngstown visiting. Addie was with them only fifty percent of the time, according to Benita. Where she was the other fifty percent, I had no idea and Benita would only say that wherever she was, she had her cell phone turned off; something that she never did when she was away from home.

Around the Christmas season I received a copy of the Hebrew-to-English interpretation of the Bible from my brother, Darnell, a minister in Los Angeles. This was the source of information I had been looking for the last eighteen years. It had the original Hebrew translations, and many of the translations didn't even remotely resemble the King James Version of the Bible. Yahweh, the true name of our Creator, was mentioned several times on most of the pages of the Hebrew-to-English Bible. This was the missing ingredient I had been looking for to write the type of book I was interested in. This version of the Bible was undiluted; nothing was lost in interpretation. I understood passages that had been a mystery to me beforehand. This Bible explained everything to me. This was indeed a revelation.

CHAPTER 10

Lying Addie

I got to the task of reading the voluminous Hebrew-to-English Bible. It was the only thing I read, once my brother sent it to me. The knowledge in it was addictive. The more I read, the more I had to read. The questions about scripture that I had for eighteen years were answered every time I opened the book. The mail order business had become relatively nonproductive compared to the high cost of the advertising. I discontinued that business for a time. Obsessed with the Hebrew Bible, and determined to get my book written before I turned myself in to the authorities and presented my case, I often spent sixteen hours a day reading the Hebrew Bible.

Valentine's Day arrived, and I had Benita pick up some roses and a card for my wife Addie. On the card, I promised her that I would write my book and straighten out our lives this year. She responded with an unconvinced "Uh-huh" and walked away. She did not bother to thank me for the flowers or to place them on the mantle of the fireplace, as she had done in the past when I gave her roses. Benita looked at her, then she looked at me, shrugged her shoulders, threw up her hands, and also walked away.

I wondered if my empty promises of straightening out my life sounded that insincere or if Addie just didn't care anymore. Addie and Benita stayed gone away from the house whenever Addie was not working and Benita was not at Kent State University. They claimed to be at relatives' homes or shopping at the mall. It was very strange that they always left in two separate cars and then returned at different times. It was obvious that they were not together all of the time that they were gone—if they were together at all. I kept busy reading the Hebrew Bible and making notes that would form the basis of my outline for the book I would write. As I read and made my outline, I wondered how far had Addie gotten into the relationship she obviously was having with someone. Even though she and Benita swore by Yahweh's holy name that she was not having an affair, I could tell by her coldness toward me that something was going on. Benita was obviously trying to hide the truth from me; I could always read her like a book. Benita was in a lot of torment from having to lie to me. I prayed that Addie had not fallen hopelessly in love with someone, and that I could salvage our relationship when I finished my book and cleared my name.

When Benita was away at school, Addie stayed in the streets even more than she had when Benita was at home. Addie claimed to be at her relatives' homes, but the very ones she claimed to be visiting called our home many times a day and left messages on the answering machine asking why they couldn't reach her at home or on her cell phone. Addie made a habit of coming home every evening at 11:30 p.m. on the nose. Benita began to openly voice dissatisfaction in the fact that Addie was never where she had told us she would be. I often saw Addie clearing her calls from her cell phone while she sat in the garage, before coming into the house for the night. I had to clear my mind of that drama if I intended to concentrate *on* the outline for my book. Yahweh must have given me the strength to put this nonsense out of my mind because I really don't think I had the strength to do it on my own. I lost myself in my work, and did not think about Addie's and Benita's lies, until I took a break or had finished for the day. Compiling data for the book and then actually typing it became a form of therapy for me. The more scripture I read, the more convinced I was that Father Yahweh would provide solutions to all of my problems. I just had to concentrate on the work at hand and have more faith in my Heavenly Father.

I finally made contact with the coin collectors who wanted to buy the 1943 "steel" pennies to complete their set. They offered three thousand to nine thousand dollars for each coin, depending on the condition of the coins. I only got nine thousand dollars for all three coins. I kept the selling of the coins to myself because Addie was spending money like she had a money tree. Her gambling was totally out of control. She continued her usual habit of spending 230 dollars or more on the lottery and sports betting. She began to have trouble keeping her bills paid. She oftentimes had her telephone, cable television, electricity, and home gas turned off because her checks were bouncing. "Insufficient funds" was as frequently found on a check as her name was. I was surprised to find out that while Addie was spending 230 dollars a week on gambling, Benita had to live off twenty dollars a week at Kent State University. The more I complained about Addie's habit, the more she spent. Soon all of her credit cards were ordered deactivated.

An article in the 'Youngstown Vindicator, dated February 4, 1999, reported that Mahoning County Sheriff, Phil Chance, was scheduled to appear in U.S. District Court in Cleveland, after being indicted on federal racketeering charges. The six-count indictment had been a secret indictment against the sheriff. Chance was accused of violating the RICO statute against organized crime, conspiracy to extort money from businesses, extorting money from illegal gambling enterprises, and of obstructing local law enforcement with intent to facilitate an illegal gambling business. This scandal that involved the sheriff reminded many of the 1982 allegations that Sheriff Jim Traficant was in bed with the mob on gambling and political corruption enterprises. In 1999, mob boss, Lenny Strollo, entered into a plea agreement with the federal government and agreed to lay out the Mafia's operation in the Youngstown-Hubbard-Campbell area. He also agreed to cooperate in the investigation of the hit on Joey Naples, who many believe was killed because he refused to allow black drug dealers who were aligned with Strollo to join the mob's operations. Some of those black drug dealers have been charged with killing Naples's associate Ernie Biondillo.

Former Mahoning County prosecutor, James Philomena, was suspected, but not charged, with the hiring of a hit man to kill newly elected prosecutor, Paul Gains. Mobsters allegedly wanted to keep Philomena as prosecutor because he allowed them to get violent felony cases fixed for a price. It has been rumored that two hundred thousand dollars would fix a murder case. An article in the *Vindicator*, dated May 6, 1999, states that an investigator for Prosecutor James Philomena extorted money from an osteopath who was accused of illegally distributing diet pills. In addition to that charge, the investigator was charged with fixing DUI cases, theft by deception, money laundering, bribery with intent to corrupt a public servant, and attempted bribery. Hubbard-based mob figure, Jeep Garano, was sentenced to fifty-seven months in prison after Judge O'Malley heard how his cooperation helped to dismantle the Strollo enterprise. Garano was noted for his casino-style gambling operations in the area. Garano, the hardened criminal, was seen visibly weeping when Judge Kathleen O'Malley sentenced him. FBI tapes revealed in March of 1999 that millions of dollars' worth of paving, garbage, and waterline contracts went to the people Strollo wanted. Mostly, Strollo snitched on his black scapegoats.

On March 2, 1999, after Addie's sister and brother-in-law left for home, I returned to Addie's home from my mother's home to resume work on my book. I needed to compare the wording in two of the Bibles that I had with the wording in Addie's personal Bible that she always carried to church. No sooner had I opened her Bible, then a church program fell from between the pages of her Bible. The program was from Pilgrim's Baptist Church. It was dated for that day. A section of the Bible had been highlighted with a magic marker and cut from the pages. It was the scripture of John 8:7–11 that told of the adulterous woman being forgiven by Jesus, only because she agreed to go in peace and to sin no more. Jesus had told the crowd that was waiting to stone her for adultery, "He who is without sin, cast the first stone." Addie had only highlighted the portion that stated that no one could judge the adulterous woman unless they had not sinned themselves. Addie got so much relief and vindication from this scripture that she had actually mutilated the Bible that her dead aunt had given her before she passed away. Addie took this scripture as a license to commit adultery. She didn't pay any attention to the portion that said that the adulterous woman was forgiven after she agreed to sin no more. Her misuse of scripture was one of the reasons why I wrote my book.

Within the program from Pilgrim's Baptist Church was a sheet of paper from Crawley's station at work. It had some Bible verses written in his handwriting and Addie's. One comment on the paper was circled, "The worst sin in the world is to only think of yourself." I wondered how Addie and Crawley could be so hypocritical as to sit in church sinning and then have the nerve to circle scripture about selfishness. Apparently, they didn't care what their adulterous relationship was doing to Benita or me. Naturally Addie lied about the program from Pilgrim's Baptist Church. She claimed that someone from her church had given her the program. I pointed out her handwriting and James's on the piece of paper from James's station at General Motors. Addie stared in amazement, with her mouth hanging open, for nearly five minutes. Then she said that she had taken her relatives there to break the monotony of going to her church every time they came to Youngstown. The truth was that she had taken them there to see her boyfriend again. Again, I put her lies aside. I had to finish my book and present my case while the time was right. If I could salvage my relationship with Addie, that would be fine, but it looked to me as if she was already in love and committed to Crawley. She was a very poor liar, but that didn't stop her from lying. She got much better with practice, and she practiced often. It got to be amusing to see her lie and get caught, only to tell an even poorer lie to support the first lie. Nothing Addie said was believable. Lying Johnny often lied for entertainment's sake, but Addie was a serious and malicious liar. Addie had taken the title that John had taken a lifetime to earn. "Lying Addie" was the new sovereign of lies. Long live "Lying Addie."

On April 13, 1999, Lying Addie was hit head-on by a drunk driver. She was carried from her car on a stretcher. She sustained serious back, neck, and head injuries. After being released from emergency, her relatives brought her home. Her car was towed to one of the local tow yards, pending investigation by the authorities. Addie could barely walk when her relatives brought her home. Benita was called at school and she met her mother at home.

We put Addie in a hot tub of water to see if it helped her any. She was in such bad shape that she made Benita cry, and I also wiped away a tear. Many people had heard about the car accident, and a few of them called her while she was in the tub. As she talked on the telephone, she remained in a prone position because sitting up caused her too much pain. One particular phone call caused her to sit at attention almost immediately, in spite of the pain she was in. She put forth her most pleasant manner and pushed aside the pain and drug induced haze she had been in. She talked to this person for a half an hour, which was remarkable, since she only talked to her sister for five minutes because of the pain she was in. I asked her who was so important to her that they merited her sitting at attention when she talked to them. She claimed that it was just some friends from work. I went down to the basement where I had attached a recording device to the telephone for just such occasions.

Addie had given me ample reason in the past not to trust what she said at this point in time.

I heard a man's voice that I was not familiar with, say, "I worry about you all of the time. Pretty soon I'll be able to look after you the way you should be looked after. You know I love you don't you?" Addie replied that she knew, but that she couldn't talk right then. Addie then called a doctor and made arrangements to see him the next day to further check out her injuries. When Addie got out of the bathtub, she asked me to massage her back—something I had been doing for years. I ended up massaging her back for two hours. When she felt better, she asked me to get her something to eat, then she went to sleep. The next day she was in even more pain, and I had to put her in the tub of hot water and massage her back again.

Benita had gone to a tire dealer to get some new tires for her car. She was to meet her mother there after Addie's doctor's appointment. My mother came to our house to take Addie to the appointment. Addie had told us that her cousin would pick her up from the doctor's office when she was done there. Addie's cousin did not pick her up because Addie had not called her. Addie had called Crawley on her cell phone, from the doctor's office. Crawley picked her up there and took her to meet Benita at the tire dealer's shop. My brother Jerry was there also, and Addie told him that Crawley had taken his mother to the same doctor and that he was good enough to give

Addie a ride to the shop. Crawley's mother was nowhere to be seen, and Addie and Crawley were several hours late, after leaving the doctor's office.

When I got word of all of this, I asked Addie where she and Crawley had disappeared to for two hours, and she claimed that they had gone to the tow yard to retrieve some of her belongings from her wrecked car. She showed me a book bag full of things from her car. I knew she was lying but pretended to believe her for the time being. Later, when she was in the bathtub again, I called the doctor's office to see if Crawley's mother had an appointment that day. She did not. She wasn't even a patient of any doctor at that office. I examined the contents of the book bag that Addie had brought home from her car. A jar of Vaseline was in the bag and so was a Valentine's card from a year before. Addie never used Vaseline on her hair or her skin. She only used exotic hair dressings and expensive body lotions. Addie only used Vaseline as a sexual lubricant because of the sensitivity of her vagina, since she had gotten a hysterectomy a few years earlier. The Valentine's Day card was dated from 1998, a year earlier. It was from James Crawley and he was thanking her for what she had given him. He wanted her to remember the hotel room number, 459, as their lucky number. I had been wondering what the significance of that number was for a year, when I looked at her lottery slip receipts. Now I knew. I later found out that the 6849 was Crawley's address, 8052 was his license plate number, 2793 was his department phone number, and 555 was his brother's address. Addie also replaced my birthdate number with Crawley's birthdate number.

I found several number books that interpreted dreams and gave a designated number for certain dreams. Addie had become a serious number player. Most revealing was a voodoo ordering catalog, which offered tips on playing the number, but it also offered potions to get rid of old lovers and husbands, love potions to get a new man interested in you, and potions to make someone sick. There were advertisements for lucky lottery candles, of which Addie had many, but I didn't know what they were until I read the voodoo catalog. Church girl Addie had become a committed believer in numerology, spell casting, and potion usage.

Addie had become a devil worshipper, in addition to being a liar and an adulterer.

I found receipts around the house from a loan company called Cash Advance. Addie would borrow five hundred dollars from them for two weeks and then she had to repay them 575 dollars.

She had been doing that for some time. I had no idea how bad off she was financially, and she continued to play the lottery and to spend too much time in the shopping malls.

Father's Day fell on Addie's birthday in 1999. On June 20, I told Addie happy birthday and happy anniversary. We were married on her birthday and we always celebrated both at the same time. Now that Father's Day fell on that same day, I thought that we might go to Akron to celebrate. She and Benita never told me Happy Father's Day or Happy Anniversary, and they had already planned a big party for Addie's Uncle "Bernard." Addie's cell phone records later revealed that she had called Crawley four times that day to wish him a Happy Father's Day.

When I tried to hug Addie and wish her a happy birthday and a happy anniversary, she said, "Why wish for something you can't have? A father isn't just the one who makes the baby, it's the one who provides for the baby. The next man I sleep with will have enough for me and my baby."

I asked her if the man she was sleeping with now had enough money for her and Benita. She swore that she wasn't sleeping with anyone. I asked her why her panties were often filled with Vaseline, even when we had not had sex? I asked her why she carried the Vaseline in her car? I asked her if she really thought that she fooled me when she came in for the night and took off her clothes in the basement, and then put her clothes in the washing machine? Did she really think that I was fooled when she continuously claimed that she had accidentally dropped her dirty panties into the bathtub and had to wash them out?

Again, she could only stare in amazement that I had paid that much attention to her actions. She actually had thought that I didn't pay any attention to her charades. Lying Addie thought that she had me fooled and she was surprised to see that I wasn't as gullible as she had thought. I had made an appointment with a chiropractor to see if the crippling back pain Addie was experiencing from the car wreck could be alleviated some. She was in therapy for several months; then the chiropractor put her in contact with an attorney to represent her in suing the drunk driver who hit her head-on. It was necessary for Addie to write up a summary of her physical mobility, before and after the accident. On the night that she was to write up the report, she couldn't be found by any of her relatives, Benita, or me. Her cell phone was turned off the whole while she was gone. Addie came home at 11:30 p.m. and Benita had already said that she knew where she was but that she couldn't tell me. From that statement, I knew that Benita knew all about her mother's affair and that Benita had been lying to me to conceal that affair. From the coldness Addie had been showing me, I guessed that the affair had been going on since just before Benita graduated from high school. I was sure that Addie was involved with Crawley. Benita would only admit that she too believed that the "friendship" had developed into something else, but not love; at least not on her mother's part. Benita said that her mother had told her that the relationship was one of convenience on her part. Once I realized that Benita was also lying to me, I didn't believe her any more than I believed Lying Addie. My daughter had become a strong contender to her mother's "lying" throne.

According to Benita, everywhere she and her mother went, Crawley popped up. This was by design and not by coincidence. Addie coordinated weddings for friends and relatives. She often took pictures of her arrangements or had someone take pictures of her. I picked up a recording on my listening device in the basement one day, in which Addie told Benita to pick up some photos from the shop that were of a friend's wedding that Addie had directed. She told Benita to look over the photos then hide them under the seat of an extra car we had parked in the backyard. That was their secret drop-off spot. When Benita left the house, just before Addie came home from work, I went out to the car and took a look at the pictures they didn't want me to see. The pictures were of a very fine wedding, but the pictures Addie didn't want me to see were of Crawley and her in attendance at the wedding together. James had a very firm grip around Addie, as the loving couple showed the world how happy they were to be together. I got the message. I was only there to finish my book. Addie was sneaking to see the man she wanted to spend the rest of her life with. She went through the motions with me, but I could see that her heart wasn't in it. Our lovemaking lacked passion; it was just raw sex.

At midnight, on July 9, 1999, a telephone call interrupted our passionless, raw-sex, lovemaking. Benita answered the phone and told her mother that it was "Uncle J.C." I heard Addie give a series of "yeahs" and "uh-huhs," but she didn't really say anything except that she couldn't talk then and that she would call them back tomorrow. We continued our lovemaking as I wondered who that really was on the telephone. The next morning when she was running the streets, supposedly with Benita, I listened to the tape from my hidden recording device in the basement. The man was lecturing her for not calling him back at the appointed time. He asked her if she were seeing someone else when he couldn't reach her. He told her that he had arrived at his relatives' home in Virginia, and that they all said they loved her and wanted to see her again. It was obvious to me that she had been there with him before and had met these relatives. Every time Addie went to Virginia, Benita went also. That meant that Benita was a party to this affair. My daughter was definitely lying to me. She was the one who had said that this telephone call was from "Uncle J.C." I guess J.C. stood for James Crawley in this case. When they had finished talking, Crawley told Addie that he loved her more than he ever had before. She simply said "Okay" and hung up the telephone. When I asked her about the taped conversation, she pretended to be offended that I had bugged the phone.

Finally, she claimed that he was one of her admirers who had become a pest. He told her that he loved her, but she pointed out that she never told him the same. She tried to con me by saying that there would never be another man for her but me. Lying Addie had struck again.

Addie found the listening device in the basement and took it out of the house. She didn't know that I had others, including a voice activated recorder that I hid under the seat of her car. A few days after Crawley called Addie from Virginia at midnight, I got her on tape, in her car, on the way to work, early in the morning. She told Crawley that my brother Jerry and my mother had her telephone bugged. They had heard the conversation between Crawley and Addie, then they reported that conversation to me in Detroit, and I had called her and Benita to threaten them. Crawley was told that he had to stop calling to her home and to never stop by because I might drop in at any minute. She told Crawley that she was sure that I would kill both of them if I found out about them. I was completely breathless. She easily convinced this man that he couldn't call or come to her house because my relatives were spying on her, and I might catch them on one of my occasional visits to her home. He swallowed the bait—hook, line, and sinker. At the time, he had no idea that I had been living in the house for a few years. I realized then that Addie was at his apartment when she could not be found. Her cell phone was turned off because she didn't want to be bothered by Benita or me when she was with Crawley. I knew that all of her relatives had to know about Crawley, but did they also know about me? They had stopped visiting Addie at the same time that I suspected that Addie had started seeing Crawley. All of this coincided with the greasy panties and Addie's coldness toward me.

As I proofread the first chapter of the book I was writing, my mind wandered. What did Addie, Crawley, and her relatives plan to do with me? Did they intend to kill me, turn me in, or let me finish my book and leave. I decided to ask Addie, point blank. Again she swore that Crawley was just a friend to her, and that they had never had sex. Again she swore that she was waiting for me to finish my book so that I could prove my innocence and live a happy life with her and Benita. She always tried to convince me of her sincerity by having sex with me, when I knew that she was lying. She put extra effort into the lovemaking to convince me that she loved me. She needed some more acting lessons; I had seen this act too many times before. This show was very boring and insulting to my intelligence. Lying Addie wasn't even amusing with her lies anymore; I was not being entertained by this—I only got disappointed.

By September, I had finished the fourth chapter of my book. Addie was in dire financial straits and she pushed me night and day to work faster on the book. We needed the money. She got to the point that she openly stated in front of Benita and me that Crawley had been married to several fat and ugly wives. He had bought them houses, cars, and he had sent their children to college. Addie told us that she knew that she looked a hundred times better than his ex-wives and she knew that he would be glad to give her the same things he had given his fat ex-wives. I asked her if she realized that she sounded like a whore in front of her daughter. She responded that she needed a few thousand dollars right away. She said that she couldn't borrow it from anyone, so she was considering going with Crawley for the money. I asked her why she had to pretend to need money to have sex with him when it was obvious that she had been having sex with him all of the time, he just wasn't very generous with his money, or she wouldn't be in the financial tight that she was. I told her that I could get the money from my relatives. She didn't know that the money was actually the money I had gotten from the coins I sold. She promised to repay the money when she received her settlement from the lawsuit she filed after the car wreck. The house payment was up to date, and her car payment was current. Benita was on a scholarship and the car Uncle Bobby gave her was paid for. Addie never explained what she did with the two thousand dollars. A short time later, my mother told me that Addie had borrowed another two thousand. These had to be loans to pay off gambling debts. I later found out that she had been threatened with criminal action for writing bad checks unless she made the checks good.

In the past three years, the *Vindicator* has reported FBI allegations or court testimony that involved Judges Patrick Kerrigan, Martin Emrich, and Andrew Polovischak. Also mentioned were attorneys Jack Campbell, Stuart Banks, James Philomena, Stephen Garea, Michael Rich, and Gary Van Brocklin. Some of these individuals have been charged and others have not. Some of them have pled guilty and others have cases pending.

Mahoning Valley mob boss, Lenny Strollo, has testified that he bribed Judge Emrich, used Rich to fix cases, used intermediaries to have Philomena fix cases, and financed Van Brocklin's successful 1984 campaign for county prosecutor. Judge Polovischak was observed by the FBI meeting with gamblers associated with Strollo, and many cases handled by the judge were seized by the FBI. In March, a government witness testified that money was given to the judge to let an inmate out of jail. Justice Moyer noted that the Supreme Court sanctioned 114 lawyers and judges in 1998 for misconduct. According to the April 18, 1999 *Vindicator* article, indictments or criminal charges in the coming months will involve ten to fifteen judges and lawyers. In another *Vindicator* article of May 28, 1999, George M. Alexander, a disbarred lawyer, was named as former prosecutor James Philomena's go-between bag man with Mahoning Valley mob boss Lenny Strollo. Alexander and Philomena were mentioned in FBI affidavits that were the basis of a roundup of organized crime figures, hired killers, mob lawyers, corrupt politicians, and low-level gamblers. Philomena's name has been mentioned repeatedly during federal and state trials by Strollo and Atty. Michael P. Rich, who testified that Alexander was the one who had case-fixing influence with Philomena.

The time to present my legal case was now; all that I needed was a little more money.

I suspected that a local court-appointed lawyer would be intent on doing a deal that would involve my making a plea bargain and doing some time. I preferred an out-of-town lawyer who was not owned by the local political machine, and that would take some real money. The money from my coin collection had been going fast in my attempt to save Addie from her inevitable bankruptcy. The only thing I had left to sell were the diamond rings that were cut from my hands by the paramedics after the fire at my home in 1979. I had always intended to have the two one-carat stones remounted in new settings, but I needed the money and I needed it right now. Pigmeat had always admired the two stones, and he had voiced his interest in them many times before. I knew that he would give me a fair price for the stones, but I feared making contact with him or any of his crew. They were a "bust" just waiting to happen. I put aside the uneasiness in my gut and talked myself into believing that I could do the deal with Pigmeat and get back out unscathed, but I'd have to be very alert and very quick. Trouble had a way of sneaking up on me when I was around Pigmeat. I took a few minutes from proofreading a couple of chapters I had written to make the telephone call to Pigmeat to iron out some deal for the diamonds. I would meet him in downtown Akron, Ohio, in two days. The words from some old song played over and over in my mind like a scratched record: "Back into the storm, back into the storm, back into the storm."

Back into the Storm

T wo days passed, and my daughter Benita was coming home from Kent State University, which was only forty-five minutes away. I had told her that I had a doctor's appointment in downtown Akron. She had taken me to see this doctor several times before for my chronic sinus infections. She had no idea that I was actually meeting someone who intended to buy my diamonds. There probably was no harm in telling her the truth, but I was concerned that she would tell her mother that I had some money and that the loans were not actually coming from my relatives. Addie had no sense when it came to curtailing expenses or feeding her gambling habit. I needed this money to hire an attorney who was not a part of the local corrupt political machine. I was hoping to hire an out-of-town attorney, who was not intent on selling me out to gain points with those in power who could do him a favor later. I could not afford to let Addie siphon my legal defense funds any longer. I needed to act on my legal defense right away. The political climate would never be more opportune.

Benita had called me from her cell phone to say that she was only a few blocks away from our home. She would be there to pick me up in a few minutes. The telephone rang again and the answer machine took the message. It was from the post office. They were calling to tell Addie that her post office box was so full that she needed to pick up her mail. I called back to the post office to ask if they were talking about the post office box I had in Addie's name, for the purpose of running my mail order business. They made it perfectly clear that

Addie had another post office box besides the mail order post office box, and it was a personal one at that. I made sure that the extra post office box was not for my daughter, but for Addie. Knowing that Addie was receiving personal mail at a secret post office box made me wonder what else I didn't know about. I went to another secret spot in the basement, where I had a listening device and a recorder that Addie had not yet found. I hadn't listened to this particular tape since I had been so busy writing my book.

The tape was of Benita and James Crawley. Benita was telling James that he needed to back off her mother because she already had a boyfriend whom Benita suspected she would marry. James Crawley told my baby that he knew that there was no other man in Addie's life whom she planned to marry. He further went on to tell Benita that he knew who was in her home and what had been going on there for quite a while. He assured her that whatever he did would be in Benita's and her mother's best interests. I sat there stunned beyond belief. Addie had told her boyfriend that I was living there in her home. This man felt so confident that he told my daughter that he and Addie planned on revealing their relationship and making it permanent. Benita had not mentioned this conversation to me and I wondered if she ever would. This tape was almost a month old. I wondered how long had James known that I was there in the house. Did he plan on calling the police? If that were the case, he would already have called them. He either planned on killing me or letting me finish my book and leaving on my own, as I had already told Addie. The thought crossed my mind that James had already had an infinite number of opportunities to kill me. At that moment, I decided to never again eat or drink anything that Addie brought to me that could have been tampered with or poisoned. I thought about the possibility of Addie or James shooting me to death in my sleep as I lay in my bed. I put the foolishness out of my head. They wouldn't dare kill Benita's father. Benita would never forgive them for it. I guessed that they would just let me finish my book and leave.

A few days earlier, my baby brother Darnell, who lives in Los Angeles, stopped at our home on his way to New Orleans to submit his doctoral dissertation in theology. He wanted to highlight some passages of the dissertation, but we couldn't find any highlighting markers anywhere in the house. When I looked in Addie's briefcase that she carried to work every day, instead of finding the highlighting markers, I found brochures and reservations for a seven-day cruise for two in the Bahamas. The cruise was reserved for next year, November 5, 2000. I had been gullible enough to believe that the cruise was reserved for Addie and her sister. Now that I had listened to the tape of James Crawley and Benita, and I knew that he and Addie planned to marry, I guessed that the sea cruise was actually a honeymoon cruise for James and Addie. I called the Progressive Travel Agency and found out that the reservations were for Mr. and Mrs. James Crawley's honeymoon cruise for November 5, 2000. Benita had to know about their plans, but she never spoke a word of it to me.

My brother left me several suits that were too small for him. He said that I'd need the suits to wear to court if I was serious about taking my case to court to clear myself. Whenever I talked to Benita and Addie about turning myself in, Addie would only shake her head and say, "You're going to mess everything up for me."

Darnell left some very ominous words with me when he was about to leave for New Orleans, "It's a whole year before November 5, 2000; anything could happen by that time."

I began to sleep in the daytime and to work on my book at night. I had no intention of letting Addie or James slip up on me. My mind flashed back on the cup of cappuccino that Addie brought me when I was working late one night. The cappuccino was cold as ice, and I poured it into a large mug so that I could microwave it. I found two large green bitter pills in the bottom of the cappuccino cup. I didn't know what they were and Addie couldn't explain them. I knew for a fact that the spigot that the cappuccino came out of was not large enough for these huge pills to pass through. Someone must have intentionally placed the pills in the cup after the cappuccino was poured from the spigot. When I accused Addie of trying to poison me, she stated in front of Benita, "Why would I want to do something like that?" She then took the pills from the cup, crumbled them up, and washed them down the drain. She also rinsed the cappuccino cup out and threw it in the trash, then she headed for her car. She said that she was going to the coffee shop to complain about the cappuccino machine.

She didn't realize that she had made me suspicious by destroying the evidence and then going to complain to the coffee shop. Why didn't she take the evidence with her? When she returned home, she claimed that the coffee shop was full of irate customers who were complaining about the bitter pills in their cups. According to Addie, the pills were used to clean the coffee machine and some of the pills had inadvertently ended up in the cappuccino. Again, I will state that the spigot of that machine is not large enough for the pills to pass into the cappuccino cup. Someone must have put the pills in the cup. Addie did not know that I had called the coffee shop to see if anyone else had complained about the pills in the cappuccino as Addie had claimed. As I had suspected, no one had complained to the manager about the cappuccino. The manager whom I had spoken with on the telephone knew Addie and he remembered her purchasing the coffee very early in the day. But no, she had not been back to the shop to complain about finding anything in the coffee. Addie had purchased the coffee at 4:00 p.m. and she didn't bring it to me until 10:00 p.m. Consider the possibilities. I heard Benita pulling into the driveway and I knew that it was time for us to go to Akron.

All the way to Akron, Benita kept asking me why I was so quiet; was I in pain? Yes, I was in pain, but it wasn't the kind of pain a doctor's pills would fix. I had gotten accustomed to Addie's indifference and dishonesty, but I would never get over the betrayal I felt when I heard the tape of Benita and James and I realized that Benita knew that James was aware of my presence in the house and she wouldn't warn me that he knew. When I should have been anticipating any possible scenario regarding the sale of the diamonds, I allowed myself to be distracted by my thoughts of James, Addie, and Benita. I was actually more concerned about Benita delivering me into some ambush that James had masterminded than I was concerned about Pigmeat masterminding a rip-off of the diamonds. I didn't trust Pigmeat a whole lot since he was strung out on the crack pipe again, but I didn't trust James, Addie, or Benita at all. I got the eeriest feeling as I thought that the child I had taught to ride a bicycle and whose diapers I had changed so many times might be delivering me for a well-orchestrated slaughter. I would continue to have this suspicion every time I went anywhere with Addie or Benita in the future.

Forty-five minutes later, Benita and I were pulling into downtown Akron, Ohio. Benita knew where Dr. Neiman's office was on Bowery Street. We had been there many times before. She parked in the lot and I went inside. I ducked out the side door and walked a few blocks down the street to the adult book and novelty store. Pigmeat was not in any of the cars parked around the place. I went inside the novelty shop and saw two of the mechanics from Pigmeat's garage in Akron. These two used to work for me when I managed Pigmeat's shop. They were good mechanics and body men, but they weren't serious about their work. They only used their skills to make enough money to invest in some hustle, usually drug sales. I had heard rumors that they occasionally did strong-arm work such as collections for Pigmeat or robberies of Pigmeat's competitors in the "drug game." Knowing all of this still didn't cause any alarms to go off in my head. I was still preoccupied with the information I had gathered earlier in the day. I was still allowing "other" things to distract me. I was not quick or alert; I was not my usual attentive self. I was going through the motions but I was doing it in a daze. I wanted to get the deal done and get the hell out of there in a hurry.

I walked over to the two men, who were pretending to be interested in buying some condoms. They had been pestering the manager of the place about some imported natural lambskin condoms. I walked past them to the magazine section of the store. One of them joined me and pretended to be interested in one of the magazines. While the manager was ringing up the imported condoms for the one, I told the other that I would meet them at the bar one block away from the novelty shop. I paid for the magazine and left for the bar. At the bar, I ordered a beer and waited for the two men to arrive. I had just received my beer when they stepped into the bar. One sat on either side of me; Joe to my left and Rob to my right. Rob ordered beers for the two of them and told Joe to pay for them while he and I headed for the restroom to make the exchange. Thirty years ago the two one-carat stones and the four quarter-carat stones were worth about two thousand dollars; now in late 1999, those same stones were worth more than ten thousand dollars. Pigmeat was doing me a real favor by giving me such a good price for the stones. A regular fence wouldn't have given me a quarter of their value, and a legitimate diamond exchanger wouldn't have given me any more than a third of their value.

Yes, Pigmeat felt that he owed me and this was his way of squaring things between us.

Rob made sure that no one else was in the restroom, then he asked to see the diamonds. I pulled the plastic ziplock sandwich bag containing the diamonds from my pocket and handed it to Rob. He looked at them for a split second and stuck them in his pants pocket. Next, he reached under his jacket for what I thought was going to be the ten thousand dollars.

Instead of sticking some pretty money in my face, he stuck an ugly, silencer-equipped 9 MM pistol in my face. I recognized the silencer design. They had made the silencer from the blueprints I had given them years ago when we worked at Pigmeat's garage together. This was the absolute epitome of all ironies; I was being robbed by old friends, who were using my old silencer design against me. I wondered if Pigmeat knew what was going on or if these two had decided to pull the rip-off on their own. Someone tried to enter the restroom and they were pissed off that the door was locked. Rob turned his head toward the door for a split second and I struck. With my left hand I grabbed his wrist and deflected the pistol toward the ceiling. I was very impressed with the craftsmanship of the silencer when I heard the muffled thumping sound the pistol made when Rob squeezed off a round. But he only got to squeeze off the one round. While I held his wrist with my left hand, I side-handed him in the throat with my right hand. Rob gasped deeply one time and then he dropped like a ton of bricks. I thought that he was dead, but I wasn't sticking around to find out. I took the diamonds and the money and made my exit out of the restroom window. I remember trying to look calm as I headed back to the doctor's office where Benita was waiting for me, but truthfully speaking, my heart was about to jump out of my chest. Approximately forty-five minutes had elapsed since I left Benita in the parking lot of the doctor's office. I had never been in and out of this particular doctor's office in less than an hour. Benita remarked that the doctor got finished faster this time than he usually did. Benita also remarked that the sinus flush the doctor used on me smelled like beer. I laughed at her and told her she was crazy.

I had Benita drive on to Cleveland, Ohio, where we stopped for spaghetti and beer. I didn't want to be on the road from Akron to Youngstown, in case a certain party was on the prowl. When Benita and I got home, it was dark. Addie wasn't at home, but she had left a note stating that she was at her cousin's house. Benita called that cousin only to find out that Addie hadn't been there at all that day. Benita then called her mother on her cell phone only to have Addie claim that she was shopping in the mall. She told Benita that she would have to see her the next time that she came home from school. After they hung up their cell phones, Benita told me that she was tired of this bullshit, then she hugged me and left. I understood what my daughter was trying to tell me. Addie was so busy with Crawley that she didn't even have time for her daughter anymore. I stashed the money and called Pigmeat to tell him about the attempted rip-off. I was to keep the money and mail the stones to a post office box number Pigmeat gave me. I asked Pigmeat if I had killed Rob when I struck him in the throat. Pigmeat responded, "No, you didn't kill him. They both committed suicide when they decided to rip off a friend of mine. Don't worry about it. It's being taken care of." I knew by that statement that both men would soon disappear.

I checked our mail and was pleasantly surprised to see that the insurance company had agreed to pay Addie twenty-four thousand dollars for the injuries she sustained from the car accident she was in. Her attorney was about to settle for seven thousand dollars, when I wrote a fifteen-page letter to the insurance company that described Addie's limited mobility since she was hit by the drunk driver. I also presented documented cases of settlements that were paid for similar injuries. At a later date, I found out that while I was writing up the request for a fair and equitable settlement, Addie was at Crawley's apartment. Naturally, her excuse for not being home was that she was at her cousin's house. I sat down at my desk and prepared to proof-read some of what I had written before Benita and I went to Akron. I thought about how Father Yahweh was with me in Akron. I could have been dead. I had the ten thousand dollars from the diamonds and the insurance company was sending another twenty-four thousand as a settlement for Addie's personal injuries.

As I looked at my calendar of religious "High Holy Days," I noticed that this day, September 24, 1999, was the first day of the Feast of Tabernacles, which celebrates the Messiah's one-thousand-year reign. This day is a blessing for believers and I am a believer. I put my work aside and prepared to celebrate the Feast of Tabernacles, I needed all of the blessings I could get. Scripture ran through my mind: "Put your trust in Yahweh and not in man," "The Sabbath is a covenant between Yahweh and his people," and "Yahweh is our strength."

I didn't tell Addie about the money I got from the diamonds. She was happy enough to hear about the twenty-four thousand from the insurance company. She seemed to have more confidence in me when I said that I would clear my name in the year 2000 and that we would live regular lives. The letter from the insurance company stated that she would receive a check sometime after New Years of 2000. All we had to do was to hold on until that time.

While Benita was away at college, Addie often drove past some of her coworkers' homes to give me some idea of where she wanted to live and what type of home she wanted next. She seemed to believe that I could clear my name, sell my book, and build a new home in 2000. She seemed more convinced than I was that things were about to change for the better. Addie's "iceberg nature" toward me softened considerably. She often initiated sex and was more animated during the sex act. She really got into it and she genuinely enjoyed it. It was remarkable what a difference money made in her, and she hadn't actually gotten her hands on the cash yet. I was reminded of a statement Redd Foxx made in one of his stand-up comedy routines, "Romancing without financing ain't nothing but the blues."

While waiting for the eventual arrival of the insurance settlement check, Addie spent her off-work time looking at materials to remodel our home. The plan was to remodel it one last time, get it appraised, use the equity to defend myself in court, then build a new home after my book was sold. Addie looked at new cars and promised to buy a new car for Benita as well. I did not keep track of Addie's bills and finances, and I really should have, considering the fact that she handled money very poorly and often allowed bills to go unpaid so that she could play the big shot by paying for all of her relatives' dinners after church. If anyone in her family needed money, Addie was always a sure thing, even if she had to borrow it to lend to her family. Many times her family members conveniently forgot to repay the loans they got from Addie. Student loans, car loans, real estate loans, and investment capital for her brothers' various ventures were all begged from Addie. She never told anyone of them that she didn't have it. She continued to play the big shot even when she was at the threshold of bankruptcy, and none of them ever knew what poor financial shape she was in, nor did they care. That was the way it had been before Addie met me, while she was with me, and it stayed that way even after I disappeared.

Instead of her family offering to help her for a change, they continued to use her. Someone always wanted to charge something on her credit cards and then conveniently forgot to pay off that balance. When Addie's credit cards were overdrawn to the point of being revoked, she used my mother's credit cards for herself and for her relatives. I remember one occasion when her family wanted to rent a van to attend a funeral in Virginia and no one out of fifty adults had a credit card to rent the van. My mother lent Addie her card so that Addie's relatives could attend the funeral. Addie led and supported her whole family, the members here in town, and in Virginia. She was genuinely tortured when she did not have any money to give or lend her family. Our daughter went without many things because Addie had lent some of her relatives a few thousand dollars that she should have saved for our needs. Before I disappeared, we had been meal tickets for her whole family, and nothing changed after I disappeared, except that they used her more.

I told Addie not to tell her begging-ass relatives that she had twenty-four thousand dollars coming in the next few months. She told them anyway. Addie had brothers in Alaska and Oregon who had accumulated as much as fifty thousand dollars in their savings accounts, just to blow the money on drugs, women, vacations, and many other insignificant things. These brothers never lent Addie any more than a few hundred dollars, but they always borrowed several thousand from her. One brother actually sent his daughter to Addie to raise for him because he didn't have time.

Addie enrolled his daughter in a private school that cost many thousands of dollars a year for tuition. Addie sent the child to the school for several years and never received any financial support from her brother, even when he was doing well with his legitimate businesses and with his illegitimate businesses. He sent money to any and all of his relatives but Addie. He seemed to have forgotten that his child was living with Addie free of charge, even after our home burned down and Addie moved in with my parents. Every time a relative wanted to move out of town, take a vacation, invest in a business, go to college, buy a home, get married, remodel their homes, or post bond money, they called Addie. Some of them even called her when they wanted to borrow money to invest in the drug trade.

Addie's mother died when Addie was just twelve years old. She, her brothers, and her sisters all went to different relatives to live. Addie's immediate family was spread across the country. All of the children had different fathers who did not think it was their obligation to see after their children. None of the fathers ever married Addie's mother. When Addie was old enough to get a job, she saved her money as best she could, but even then she felt responsible for providing for her family. The uncle and aunt she lived with used her for a meal ticket and she was treated like Cinderella for a long time. Her adopted family actually told her that she would always be indebted to them for taking her and a younger brother into their homes when no other relatives wanted them. This was one hell of a thing to rub in a child's face from the age of twelve to adulthood. I personally heard her aunt tell her that very thing when Addie was twenty-one years old. It was ingrained in Addie at an early age that she had to provide for her relatives as well as for herself. The more money she made, the more she needed. This eternal obligation was one of the factors that drove her to the lottery and other forms of gambling. Addie had to make a lot of money in a hurry so that she could provide for all of her lazy, shiftless relatives. Several of them had developed "crack cocaine" habits and needed Addie to save their homes, their cars, or to pay for drug treatment. Needless to say, these "crack heads" needed someone to help with their children.

Before I disappeared and became "invisible," Addie got into the habit of saying that she would do anything to keep her job at General Motors because she had to provide for her daughter and many others. Eventually she extended that statement to, "I would sell my soul to Satan to keep my job." Once I came into the knowledge of scripture, I warned her that what she regarded as simply a humorous phrase was actually an invitation to demonic possession. As I got deeper into scripture, I pointed out to her that Satan was seducing her with the promise of wealth from the lottery, while he was actually leading her to bankruptcy. Addie and most others know that gambling is not from God but from Satan. She had been in the church all of her life, and I know that she knew that gambling was a subtle seduction by Satan. This was Satan's way of preparing her for his inevitable satanic attack. That satanic attack would imperil my physical life and Addie's spiritual life as neither had ever been imperiled before.

CHAPTER 12

Attacked by Satan

S tudying Scripture every day for my book made me aware of the threat I posed to Satan. If I could point out in my book that Satan had deceived mankind into distorting the scriptures and the teachings of the original church, as taught by Christ and his disciples, then I was setting my family and myself up for some type of retaliation from Satan. If I intended to prove how Satan deceives the whole world, then I should suspect that Satan would not be happy about that revelation.

I had just finished the twelfth chapter of my book a few days before Halloween of 1999. I had one chapter left to go. I had already mentioned to Addie and Benita that there was the possibility that Satan might try to come at me through them, my family. They were in agreement that if my book revealed how Satan had tricked mankind into worshipping him instead of our "Creator," then it was probable that Satan would seek some type of retribution. I tried to strengthen myself by studying scripture, praying, and observing the Sabbaths and the High Holy Days. Naturally I tried to enlist Addie and Benita in those activities. Benita knew the truth when she read and heard it; she appeared to accept what was taught in the Hebrew-to-English Scriptures. Addie seemed very hostile toward the Hebrew-to-English text, the High Holy Days, the observance of the Sabbath, and to calling on the name of Father Yahweh. Addie adamantly stated that she would continue to worship as her pastor had taught her. Only when he changed his methods of worship would Addie change hers.

I didn't argue with her, I simply prayed for her. I was glad for what Benita had learned.

Halloween of 1999 found me proofreading a few of the chapters I had written. Benita was attending a party in town and Addie was raking leaves in the front yard so that the trick-or-treaters wouldn't slip on any of them. In another hour the trick-or-treaters would be in our neighborhood. From my desk in the basement, I could hear Addie raking the leaves in our asphalt driveway. She began coughing and choking. It seemed that she couldn't catch her breath. She and Benita seemed to catch colds all of the time, and then I'd catch a cold from them. A cold would then set off my chronic sinus problems, and before you'd know it, I'd be as sick as a dog. I'd end up spending a fortune with my sinus doctor in Akron. I tried to keep Addie and Benita healthy so that I wouldn't end up with their colds. When I heard Addie coughing and choking, I went to the door and asked her if she wanted a drink of hot tea and lemon. She replied that she would like that plus some Tylenol and some Sucrets. By the time I returned to the driveway with the things she had asked for, the first wave of trick-or-treaters had started. The next-door neighbors' kids were sporting their devils, goblins, and cowboy costumes, as Addie gave them handfuls of candy.

When they had gone, Addie asked me to get the cough syrup from our bedroom. As I climbed the stairs to the bedroom, I heard her cell phone ringing in that bedroom. The telephone number from the party making the call was illuminated on the screen of Addie's cell phone. I recognized the telephone number as one from General Motors, where Addie worked. I knew that no one was calling Addie from her job at that time of night, and I thought that the call may have been from my brother or my cousin, who both worked at General Motors also. I called the number to see who would answer the telephone. When the person who had called Addie answered the telephone, he said, "Plant 1055, James Crawley speaking." Immediately, I went outside and gave Addie the cough syrup. I also handed her the cell phone and told her that her boyfriend, James Crawley, wanted her to call him at work, in plant 1055. She looked as if I had staggered her with a blow to the head, as she took the cell phone and looked at the number glued to the screen. She "assured" me that she didn't want to be bothered with him, but she found an excuse to leave our home in a hurry; I suspect that she left to call him back on her cell phone. The "lovefest" she had been pretending that we were having was nothing but a charade. I could have slipped my voice-activated tape recorder in her car to see what she and James had to talk about, but there really wasn't any need for that. I already had some idea. Her excuse for leaving in a hurry was that she needed some more candy for the trick-or-treaters. She was back in a few minutes, and I asked her if she was able to reach her boyfriend when she called him back on the telephone. She replied, "Don't you already know? Don't you have my car bugged as well as the house and the telephone?"

"No, not this week," I answered. "I already know all that I need to know about you and Crawley." Then I walked back into the house to finish my work on my book. It was the only thing that mattered to me.

Benita went back to Kent after the party here in town. She took her cold with her; Addie kept her cold here and gave it to me. I kept the cold, the flu, or sinus infections for the next few months. Addie claimed that the air-conditioning was so cold at work that it often gave her a cold. I later found out that the man she was spending "secret time" with had a low immunity system and always kept a cold. Addie caught the colds from him and I caught the colds from her. Benita already knew about this and the other body fluids Addie and Crawley exchanged. I suspect that is why Benita suddenly stopped kissing her mother in the mouth, as she had done from earliest childhood. Often, Benita would turn her head when her mother tried to kiss her, and then she'd say, "I don't know where your mouth has been." I guess Benita was doing all that she could to "hip" me to what was going on. I paid attention without letting them know that I was paying attention.

Besides the habit of stating that she would sell her soul to Satan to keep her job, Addie developed the habit of "swearing to God" every time she opened her mouth. She was attempting to get me to believe what she said by invoking the usual "I swear to God" phrase.

This ploy; her gambling; and her fascinations with numerology, lottery candles, fortune cookies, good luck charms, and love potions led me to believe that Addie had not just made herself susceptible to satanic influences and demonic possession, she appeared to be a willing and active "devil worshipper." I am still saving one of the many "voodoo charm" catalogs she used to order from. Satan really led her around with a ring in her nose. Addie got to the point where she would bet her last dollar on anything and everything; then she'd blame me for not being rich, well-off, or free to work a regular job. Yes, the next man she slept with would have enough money for Addie and her daughter. The broken record played on.

After I found out about the telephone call to Addie from James Crawley, while he was at work at General Motors, Addie's method of operation reverted to its former pattern. She claimed to be at her relatives' most of the time that she was off work, and they continued to call to the house and leave messages on the answering machine asking where she was. This happened on Thanksgiving and on Christmas. The mother of one of Addie's friends from General Motors died before New Year's, and Addie claimed to be spending a great deal of time with her. Often when Addie was supposed to be comforting Betty and her sisters, Betty would call Addie's home and leave a message on the answering machine asking where Addie was. On the day of Betty's mother's funeral, many fellow General Motors coworkers were in attendance at the funeral. Everyone on the planet knew that Addie attended the funeral with James Crawley. Addie came home very late that evening. She claimed that she had a flat at the funeral home and had to ride with James Crawley. Supposedly, after the funeral, he changed the flat for her and followed her to a repair shop, where she had the tire serviced.

Several General Motors coworkers have long ago revealed that Addie never drove her car to the funeral; she came to the funeral with James. She left her car parked at his apartment. I took Addie's keys to her car from the kitchen table and went outside to open the trunk of her car. She followed me out there. I asked her what would I find when I opened the trunk and looked at the spare tire? Would the spare be dirty from usage after the flat on the original?

Would the original show any signs of repair as she had claimed? Could she even name the repair shop that serviced the tire?

Again Addie invoked the familiar phrase, "I swear to God," in an attempt to convince me. I opened the trunk and examined the spare tire. It had not been moved since Addie bought the car several years ago. The tire on the car that she claimed to have had serviced showed no signs of having been flat or of being repaired, and the service center she claimed to have gone to had gone out of business several weeks before. Lying Addie had struck again, and she knew that I knew it.

New Year's was spent in the usual way; I sat at home by myself while Addie made the midnight services at her church. Benita attended a party at Kent State University. At midnight Benita called to wish me a happy new year. Addie called to do the same, but she added that she was following some of her church members to another church, where they would continue celebrating until 4:00 am. I asked her about our intentions to celebrate the new year together after she attended her church services, and she replied, "This is the year 2000. Why would I want to spend it at home? We can celebrate together anytime."

Then I heard a man tell her to get off of the telephone so that they could go to the party. He said party and not to another church. I later found out that Addie had indeed attended a New Year's party with James Crawley; they also went to his church services after attending her church services. I got suspicious of Addie's actions when she got dressed for the midnight program at her church. I had always teased Addie about wearing the big blousy "old woman's" panties that she always wore. I tried to get her to wear the sexier cut panties and thongs. I even bought her several pair. She refused to ever wear any of them. On this particular night, she put on a pair of black, silk, see-through panties that only had a string going up the crack of her butt. As she stood in front of me and slipped into the seductive panties, I wondered if she actually thought that she was fooling me or if she just didn't care.

Addie and Benita got rid of their colds and I didn't. I was sick from Halloween of 1999 through Thanksgiving, Christmas, and

New Year's. I had been to the sinus doctor in Akron several times, but the medication didn't seem to be doing me any good. Valentine's Day, February 14, 2000, found me still sick and suffering from what I thought was sinus trouble. I wondered if the infection had developed into sinus cancer. I was spending a fortune with my doctor in Akron, but I wasn't getting any better. For Valentine's Day, I decided to send Addie some roses; not out of love, but out of mischief. I knew that Crawley would find out that someone had sent the roses to Addie and he would give her hell for it. Sure enough, she came home pissed off about the roses. She claimed that she didn't like her coworkers quizzing her about a secret admirer, who had sent the beautiful card and roses to her. I know for a fact that she was pissed off because James Crawley questioned her about the gift in front of a very large audience at the workplace. The roses caused them very much dissention. So much for him just being a friend. This man acted as if he had ownership rights to Addie. She had to kiss his ass for several days to assuage his anger. Like I said many times before, I was just there to finish my book, and now I was sidetracked by a debilitating sinus infection.

Addie received her insurance settlement sometime in April 2000. She had borrowed against the twenty-four thousand dollars she had coming, and she owed everybody. She repaid everyone she had borrowed from but me. She simply never got around to replacing my legal defense funds.

She must have run into the worst string of bad luck in the history of the world, or she was the worst liar on the planet. According to Addie, nearly all of her relatives in Virginia died off in one month's time. I never saw an obituary or a funeral program for the many funerals she supposedly attended in Virginia for the month of April 2000. Let Addie tell it, her cousins and some other distant relatives were dropping like flies. Coincidentally, none of the deceased was ever anybody that I had met before or anybody I had ever heard of. Every time Addie and Benita went to one of the funerals, I just happened to be critically ill. It really seemed to me that they waited until I got my sickest before they decided to go to Virginia.

Benita and Addie had just returned from a funeral in Virginia on April 22, 2000, and Addie was already giving me notice that she was about to go to another one on April 27.

Realizing how sick I was when they returned from the April 22 funeral, my daughter Benita told her mother that she would not be accompanying "the party" back to Virginia for the April 27 funeral. My daughter said that she would prefer to stay home to look after me. Addie returned from the funeral in a few days to find me totally congested and unable to breath. My legs and feet were swollen to three times their normal size and my temperature was off the charts.

Addie took me to Akron, just forty-five minutes away, and admitted me into the hospital under my brother's name, Robert Holmes. It didn't take much time for the doctors in emergency to diagnose that I had acute pneumonia in both lungs and that it had spread to the kidneys, causing total kidney failure. According to the doctors, I had only five days left to live.

I had been diagnosed as having most of, but not all of the symptoms of Goodpasture's syndrome, a virus that came from the fields of farms in England in the 1800s. Very few people had been diagnosed with the disease since the 1800s. A young teenager from the United States had just contracted the disease when he went to England on a trip with the Boy Scouts. The teenager died from the disease in about a week. The virus entered his nostrils, infected his lungs, and then spread to his kidneys, resulting in total kidney failure and death.

The appearance of my having contracted this rare and debilitating disease caused me to be the object of study of twenty-five doctors and specialists; they even conducted classes on me. The first question any of them asked me was had I been to England or Europe recently. The second question they asked me was had I been exposed to any wastes or chemical dumps.

Even though my doctors didn't expect me to live, they gave me some type of nuclear medicine that caused my urine and feces to glow a very bright fluorescent yellow. These doctors were quick to explain that this medicine would not treat the many problems I had, it would simply be used as a diagnostic tool. The gloom showed on my doctors' and nurses' faces. They were looking at a dead man.

Benita cried continuously. Addie looked a bit upset herself. The medications I had been given caused my shoulder-length hair to come out in spots, and Addie cut my hair off bald. She claimed to be afraid of contaminating me with her hugs and kisses, so she refrained from doing so. One day while she and Benita were visiting, Benita hugged and kissed me, then she asked her mother why she didn't do the same. Benita told her mother that she acted as if she didn't care about me. Addie responded that I knew that she loved me, she just didn't want me to catch anything from her. Posing as my brother Robert Holmes, my cover story was that Addie's husband had died and Addie and I got together as a couple and planned to marry. Supposedly, my former sister-in-law was now my fiancée. I think everyone at the hospital noticed that my fiancée was a little too standoffish toward me. Several of my doctors wanted to give some tests to my fiancée to see if she carried any of the symptoms that I had. They even offered to give the tests free of charge.

They were as astonished as I was that she refused all of the tests. Clarity set into my reasoning when I realized that one of the tests would have shown that she was sexually active with someone other than me. Even when my life was at stake, Addie was intent on keeping her adulterous secrets. Benita had gotten tired of the charade and blurted out words that reverberated in my mind for many days: "Nothing is more important than my dad's life."

I never felt that I was dying. I was weak, tired, and unable to breathe, but I didn't feel like I was dying. I was in a constant state of prayer. I called out loud to Father Yahweh every time I thought about him, and that was all of the time. I made sure to ask that my prayers be received in the name of Yahweh's son Yahshua Messiah. I knew that I would survive this illness because it had caught me while I was doing good. I had just finished observing the Feast of Unleavened Bread, when I was admitted into the Akron Emergency Unit. The Feast of Unleavened Bread is the celebration of putting away sin and evil from the world. Observers of this particular High Holy Day are given special blessings, and like I said many times before, I need all of the blessings I can get. I had another reason for believing that Father Yahweh would spare my life, other than because I called on him by his name and because I was observing the Feast of Unleavened Bread when the illness struck its hardest. I honestly believed that my Creator would spare my life because I had not finished my book. My book would expose Satan as the deceiver that he is, and it would help to direct mankind back to the true worship of our Creator, as taught by the Messiah and his disciples. I only had one chapter left to type when I checked into the Akron Hospital. I had to get better so that I could do what I had decided was my "life's work."

One, two, three, four, and five days ticktocked away on the clock in my bedroom. Not one time did I doubt that my Creator' would save my life. I had a purpose. I had work to do for Yahweh. I knew just what this sickness was all about. How can one explain my contracting a nineteenth-century virus from England while living in Youngstown, Ohio? It was apparent to me before I ever checked into the hospital that I was being attacked by Satan.

I knew that this was Satan's retaliation for my book exposing his deceptions of mankind. I knew that this was a test of my faith. Could I walk the walk, or just talk the talk? After several specialists told me that hydrocarbons, a class of chemicals like gasoline, solvents, paints, and antifreeze, were found in my lungs, the first question I asked was had I been poisoned.

Again the mysterious cup of cappuccino flashed through my mind. The toxicologists assured me that the hydrocarbons entered my system through my nostrils. If someone had poisoned me, they would have had to have done it with something like an inhalation mist or a nasal spray. As Addie paced the floor of my hospital room, wearing a worried-to-death look on her face, I wondered if she looked worried to death because she was concerned about my health or because she was worried about being found out. Was I just being paranoid? As "Lying Johnny" told me a long time ago, "Sometimes paranoia is a survival skill."

Benita's dormitory at Kent State University was only fifteen minutes away from my hospital room. She was there every day and several times a day. Addie used her job as an excuse not to come to the hospital; the truth of the matter was that she couldn't explain her sudden absences to James Crawley. I was scheduled to have a kidney biopsy on the fifth day of my hospital stay. The kidney biopsy involved cutting through the back muscles with a .22 caliber probe to take a sample of the infected kidney to see how diseased it was. No anesthesia could be used in the procedure. Benita withdrew from a final exam at Kent State to be there for me. Addie couldn't get away from James Crawley. Benita knew that, and she was mad as hell at her mother. I had no idea what was going on. I was fed that garbage from Addie about not being able to get away from her job. The kidney biopsy showed that my kidneys were not completely dead, as had been earlier diagnosed. Samples of my urine were taken around the clock to see if my kidneys would restart the filtering process. The kidney biopsy is usually given as a last option because of the damage it does to a kidney. The biopsy is equivalent to piercing the kidney with a .22 caliber, rod-shaped arrow. Instead of getting worse, my kidneys got better after the biopsy. At 5:00 a.m. a doctor came into my room to report that my kidneys were miraculously reversing themselves. They had restarted their filtering process. The doctor also reported that whatever virus had attacked my body was leaving it so fast that the specialists couldn't study it. As soon as the doctor left my room, I called Addie at our home to tell her the good news. She answered the telephone with a grouchy tone because she was mad about being awakened at 5:15 a.m. After telling her the good news, I was surprised to hear her say, "Call me later to tell me all about it. I'm too sleepy right now." I had thought that this good news was worth waking her for.

Dejected, I called someone else who might give a damn; I called my daughter Benita. Not only was she delighted that my kidneys were reversing themselves, she and several of her friends had been up all night long praying for Benita's "Uncle Bobby." Benita and her crew had a celebration at 5:30 a.m. because their prayers for "Uncle Bobby" had been answered.

Naturally, I thanked my Creator for doing what I thought he would do, and I remained in a constant state of prayer for many months afterward. My doctors told me that my kidneys were reversing themselves at so quick a rate that they were thinking about releasing me in a few more days. Today was the sixth day of my hospital stay. Addie showed up on the seventh day. Having overcome some mysterious nineteenth-century disease, I was elevated to celebrity status. Doctors and nurses from other wards on other floors came to see the "dead man." At the time, I had no idea that this new nickname would be given to me again at a later time for another reason. After being tagged with the new nickname, I don't really recall many people at the Akron Hospital calling me Robert Holmes, the name under which I was registered. The "dead man's" celebrity status caused me to be interviewed by many doctors and nurses who had nothing to do with my case. Several nurses sneaked into my room to keep me company at all hours of the day and night. I was given foot massages, body massages, and sponge baths to excess. Whether I was getting a massage, a bath, a shot, or an IV, somehow or another, the nurses always ended up handling my penis.

It got to the point that I didn't even pretend to be modest anymore. I acted as if it were perfectly normal for the nurses to handle my penis as they gave me a shot in the stomach or the butt. I could never understand how some of these nurses could pretend to have to hold my penis while they changed the IV in my lower thigh, down near my knee. I decided to cut into their fun by having my daughter Benita bring me a few pair of tight fitting briefs. Several nurses reacted just as I had anticipated: "Oh shoot! You're no fun." I was almost fifty years old and a nurse half my age was telling me about a man she was seeing who looked a lot like me. In the seven days I had been a patient at the Akron Hospital, she had gotten "friendly" enough with me to suggest that I move in with her. She was quick to point out that my "fiancée" Addie must not have really cared that much about me, since she rarely came to visit and since she didn't bother to come at all on the day of the kidney biopsy. There it was for all the world to see; Addie didn't give a damn about me. Not even when I had been dying.

It got to the point that I actually had to set boundaries, as far as the nurses were concerned. On one occasion, I actually had to make a comment when the nurse half my age decided to "out sit" Addie. I said, "You're my nurse and this is my fiancée," to the two women. After I designated their appropriate roles, the nurse got up and left.

She never spoke to me again. One nurse, who had the most beautiful green eyes on the planet, used to always tell me while I was in pain, "Just concentrate on these big beautiful green eyes and think about what we could be doing if you weren't stuck in this place." Green Eyes had no problem making that statement even when Addie was in my room. I was spoiled by the attention of young, beautiful, well-educated women, who actually had something to talk about. I didn't remember the last time Addie and I had anything meaningful to talk about. I assumed that she was all "talked" out, when she came home from Crawley's apartment each day, to bother talking to me. Believe me, I can always talk to anyone about anything. I have never been antisocial, and I have never been afraid to hear different points of view. Addie had been intentionally letting me starve from a lack of love or conversation. On many occasions, she even refused to speak. It was not uncommon for her to say, "I don't feel like speaking today." It wasn't until I was in the company of beautiful, friendly, intelligent, and articulate women that I realized what I had been missing for a number of years. I was really lonely at Addie's house since Benita went away to college, and that was just the way Addie wanted it. Seeing that so many other women were interested in me, Addie actually seemed to be slightly interested herself. She made several promises to me about what we would again grow to mean to each other after I was released from the hospital, finished my book, and cleared my name.

Speaking of different points of view. Nothing in the world can garner more debate, controversy, or anger than religion. If you want to get a really good argument going, that may even result in a preemptive strike, all you have to do is get a Moslem, a Jew, and a Christian involved. The twenty-five doctors and specialists who worked on my case ran the spectrum of races, nationalities, and religions. In the course of my seventh day in the Akron Hospital, the head of Internal Medicine, a Moslem, asked me if I believed that there was a God and a devil. After replying that I believed that there is a God and a devil, he went on to ask me what kind of work I did. I explained that I had been working on a book that revealed how Satan has deceived the whole world with his false religions. The Moslem doctor went on to explain to me that Satan often seeks physical retaliation in the form of sickness on those who are in his way. This Moslem adamantly exclaimed that there was no other way to explain my being attacked by a nineteenth century disease from England right here in Youngstown, Ohio, while I just happened to be working on a book that revealed Satan as the "Great Deceiver."

The head of the Nephrology department, the kidney doctor, was Jewish. He almost repeated the Moslem doctor from Internal Medicine word for word. By the time the Christian doctor from Infectious Diseases stopped by and gave me the third helping of "Satan and Unexplainable Diseases," I was convinced that I had not been paranoid or crazy to think that Satan might seek some revenge for my revelations concerning his trickery. I was glad that these three doctors from three varying religions saw what I suspected all of the time. Each of them warned me that such a thing might happen again, but more than likely, since I was aware of what was going on, Satan might come at me some other way. I had the three doctors tell Addie and Benita what they had told me. Benita seemed brave and sure of herself. Addie seemed doubtful of what the doctors had said and of what I believed. I knew then that Satan would come at me the second time through Addie, and I told her that. I told her not to let Satan come at me through her, since he had not been successful when he came at me directly. I told her that whatever she had done, I would forgive her for it because she was my wife and I loved her. I asked her to repent and sin no more, so that Yahweh would hear her prayers when she needed his help.

Her reply was, "Who are you to tell me how to worship my God? God is my judge and not you. I don't need your forgiveness; I only need God's. The scriptures say that he who is without sin can cast the first stone. You have sinned, so you can't judge me."

I told Addie that I had no intention of judging her, but I did remind her that the scriptures plainly stated that the adulterous woman was forgiven because she repented, she stopped her sin of adultery. Once again she swore to God that I had it all wrong; she wasn't seeing Crawley or anyone else. She actually called Benita to "cosign" her statement. Benita told me she had to go back to Kent

State to make up a final, then she shook her head and walked away without saying goodbye to her mother. Addie left behind her. I could hear Addie calling Benita as they went down the halls of the hospital. Benita was tired of lying for Addie.

CHAPTER 13

Until Death Do Us Part

I was a patient at the Akron Hospital for eight days, from May 1–8, 2000. In the early morning of May 8, a team of doctors came to my room to tell me that my lungs were so completely free of the pneumonia that it was as though I had never been sick; my kidneys were working so well that they decided to release me to outpatient status. I called my daughter Benita, who was just fifteen minutes away at Kent State University. I told her to come bust me out of that place. She was there in fifteen minutes, and she brought a friend, Jeff Vaughn. Jeff was also a student at Kent and a barber. He gave me a haircut and a shave before we checked out of the hospital. My daughter Benita is six feet tall, and I am four inches taller. Jeff looked like a younger version of me and could have been my clone or a son. One of the nurses remarked that my daughter and son looked just like me. We never bothered to tell her that Jeff was not my son but a classmate of Benita's. Seeing the three of us tower over the tiny four-foot-tall nurse was indeed a spectacle. She remarked that the doorknobs in our home must have been up pretty high. We laughed about her joke for a long time.

Benita had one of my nurses write her an excuse so that she could take a final exam she had missed when she stayed with me at the hospital on the day of the kidney biopsy. After that, Benita signed me out and we got out of that place as fast as possible. Benita, Jeff, and I stopped for turkey sandwiches at a submarine shop. I told Benita and Jeff how good it felt to be eating something other than hospital food. It was then that Benita asked me, "Isn't it great to be alive?" I replied that it was wonderful being alive.

Benita asked me what I intended to do next and I jokingly replied, "I'm going to Disneyland." It was at that time that Jeff told me that he was one of the many friends of Benita who had been up all night praying along with her for my survival. He was also one of the many who celebrated with Benita after hearing of my miraculous recovery. He continuously emphasized how much Benita must have loved her "Uncle Bobby," because she cried about my condition the whole time.

I had said goodbye and thank-you to all of the nurses and doctors at the Akron Hospital, but several had become lifelong friends: Drs. Yassir Farra, John Jacobs, Genny Zimora, Brian Cunningham, and Michael Sennfelt. I would see them often in the next few months as I trekked back to Akron for outpatient therapy. These particular doctors would eventually come to know Addie, Benita, and me on a first-name basis.

When I got home, my feet were still twice their normal size. My kidneys were not working efficiently enough to get the extra water from my ankles. That would take another month. Benita and Jeff stayed with me at our home for an hour, then they had to return to Kent State University to take makeup exams. Addie got home at about 4:00 p.m. My mother came up to visit at about the same time. Addie fixed me a bowl of oatmeal, because my feet were still badly swollen and the doctors didn't want me on my feet too much. That was the only time Addie fixed anything for me to eat the whole while I was recuperating. She only did it then because she was pretending for my mother. Addie stayed in the streets after work, but was sure to be home by 11:30 p.m. each night. Swollen feet or not, I cooked my own meals, washed my own clothes, and tried to do a bit of walking on the treadmill. I found that the more physically active I became, the more efficiently my kidneys performed. It took me three days before I worked my way up to walking one-quarter of a mile on the treadmill. On that third day, I also had my first outpatient appointments at Akron Hospital. I ended up walking over a mile inside of the hospital, by going to the various appointments there. Once I knew that I could walk a mile, I decided to walk a mile and a half on the treadmill. Slowly I increased my output until I was able to run six miles a day. I progressed to the point that I could lift four hundred pounds of weights for two hours every day. I also practiced my martial arts for one to two hours every day. In a few months, I was in the best shape I had ever been in in my entire life.

My first week at home was spent catching up on the local news I had missed. I had a large bundle of newspapers to read. U.S. Representative James A. Traficant Jr., the former sheriff, accused the local FBI of being in bed with the local mob bosses. Traficant accused the FBI of wanting to kill him because he was revealing the connections between the local mob and the local FBI. Traficant called for an investigation of whether federal agents, including Stanley Peterson, the former head of the local FBI, who retired in 1977 to become Youngstown's police chief, were tied to the mob. Traficant sent President Clinton a letter demanding a federal probe. Rumors were rampant that the mob had handpicked Peterson for his police chief's job. Traficant produced a witness who testified that she saw her husband give bribes to Peterson nearly forty years ago to allow illegal gambling in the area. Another article mentioned that in December 1996, his last month as Mahoning County prosecutor, James A. Philomena fixed a murder case for Dwayne Oliver, a man who shot a sixteen-year-old girl to death. A special prosecutor stated that Philomena reduced some cases and others just went away. Special Prosecutor Rob Glickman said that a fifteen-count state indictment was handed up against Philomena. Glickman said, "For each case, Philomena took thousands of dollars, but I haven't added all of the money up yet."

On my fifth day at home, I received another bit of information while I was sitting there catching up on the old newspapers. Addie's "Uncle Bernard" had remarried, after his first wife's recent death. His new wife was named Barbara. She was often called "Crazy" because of her humorous nature. Addie went so far as to state that she was a little "touched" in the head, because of a stroke she had. "Crazy Barbara" had called to Addie's house on my fifth day out of the hospital. Addie was not home and "Crazy Barbara" left a message on the answering machine, "Hi, Addie! We just loved having you and your fiancé over for dinner. We look forward to having both of you over again soon." Naturally, Addie and Benita claimed that "Crazy Barbara" was crazy, when they heard the telephone message. My mind wandered as I thought about the November 5 sea-cruise date that was rapidly approaching.

I ran back and forth to the Akron Hospital for the next few months, in an attempt to heal myself. When I was not running on the treadmill or lifting weights, I was finishing the last chapter of my book. Addie pressed me morning, noon, and night to finish the last chapter. I wasn't sure whether she wanted the book finished so that I could get out, or if she wanted the book finished so that we could get paid. She claimed that if I could get the book finished and sold fast enough, she wouldn't have to make a very drastic decision that would alter all of our lives forever. I knew that she had to be talking about marrying Crawley, but neither she nor Benita would admit it. I worked as fast as I could, but I didn't expect Addie to reverse the decision that she had apparently already made. Benita's birthday was on June 8, and I told her happy birthday. Her mother couldn't pass up the opportunity to add, "The daddy is the one who provides for you and not just the one who made you. Anyone can make a baby." By that outburst, I assumed that she was again referring to Crawley having money to provide for Addie and Benita, even though Addie swore to God that I got the wrong meaning of what she had just said. Addie's birthday was June 20. This was also the anniversary of our wedding.

Father's Day was a couple of days before. Neither Benita nor Addie ever said "Happy Father's Day" to me, even though they had a party for her "Uncle Bernard," and the telephone records show that they called James Crawley four times that day to tell him "Happy Father's Day."

On June 20, I took Addie and Benita to a restaurant out of town. This was to be our combination celebration for Benita's birthday, Addie's birthday, Father's Day, and our anniversary. Addie and Benita were surprised as I revealed a wallet full of one hundred dollar bills. Addie had nearly exhausted her twenty-four-thousand-dollar insurance settlement and she had nothing to show for it. Much of the money had gone to her relatives; some went to catch up on bills, but much of *it* went to pay for loans she had taken out in anticipation of the insurance check. I suspect that she owed quite a bit of money for gambling debts. I was never repaid my money for my defense fund, and Addie only paid three hundred of the thirty-five thousand I owed to the Akron Hospital for my stay there. She thought that the money I spent on medication came from my relatives. I led them to believe that this was some of that same money. Neither she nor Benita knew about the money from the diamonds, and they wouldn't know for another few months.

On the way back home from the restaurant, Benita wanted to stop at a car lot to look at some of the new cars. She immediately fell in love with a black minivan. We went inside of Courtesy Chrysler, where Randy was glad to negotiate with us. Addie could get the van for Benita by putting down seven hundred dollars and making payments of two hundred a month, after trading the car in that the real "Uncle Bobby" had given Benita for her graduation present. I was surprised to find that Addie had to speak of borrowing the seven hundred to put down on the minivan. Addie didn't have a penny left in the bank. Her entire insurance settlement was gone; her five-thousand-dollar income tax refund was gone; her 2,500 dollar profit sharing check was gone; and the money she had gotten from me when I sold my coins was long gone. I counted out the seven hundred to Randy, as I asked Addie if she could afford to pay the two hundred a month for the minivan. She claimed to have perfect credit, but I remembered that all of her credit cards had been revoked because they were overdrawn. It was my guess that filling out the credit application for the minivan was nothing but an exercise in futility. I pulled Benita off to the side and cautioned her against getting her hopes up over the minivan. I really didn't believe that her mother had the necessary credit.

After three days, Randy from Courtesy Chrysler called our house to tell us that Addie's credit application had been denied because she had a history of paying her bills too late. She also had too many outstanding loans for which she had cosigned for relatives. It seems that

Addie had been named as the secondary responsible party for too many of her relatives' loans to initiate anymore loans on her own. She needed a cosigner. Benita became severally depressed over the realization that her mother had spent all of the money she had come into in just the last three months. Benita asked her mother over and over, "How do you earn sixty five thousand dollars a year then get a twenty-four-thousand-dollar settlement, and a five-thousand-dollar income tax refund, and not have any money or credit? Now that you have cosigned for everyone else, who's going to cosign for you?"

The only thing Addie could come back with was, "Well, if I had a husband who worked a job, we'd have the necessary credit to buy the minivan."

Again, Addie was quick to add that the next man she slept with would have enough money and credit for her and her daughter. Benita was quick to point out that her mother couldn't have come up with the seven-hundred-dollar down payment even if she did have the necessary credit. Benita asked Addie the same thing I wanted to know: "What have you done with all of your money?" A search for Addie's missing money revealed what we all knew from the beginning: Addie had spent a fortune on the lottery, sports betting, and illegal gambling.

One day in that month, Benita and Addie ran into the house and excitedly explained that Addie's sister Pat was down the road a few miles, and she was on her way to our house from Virginia. They had just talked to her on their cell phones. She would be arriving at our home in one hour, and she was bringing other relatives from Virginia with her. I had to get out of the house and find somewhere safe to stay while they were here. My mother already had out-of-town guests at her home, so Benita suggested that I go to a motel near her campus at Kent State University, until "Aunt Pat" and her crew went back to Virginia. I had only been out of the Akron Hospital for a little over a month. The only place I had been was to the hospital for outpatient therapy. Benita took me to the motel a few blocks away from her Kent State campus, then she returned home to Addie and the out-of-town company. It wasn't until 6:00 p.m., when it was time to take my kidney medication, that I realized that I had forgotten to bring the medication. Several calls to Addie's and Benita's cell phones were fruitless. I didn't want to call them on their residential telephone because Aunt Pat might answer the telephone and recognize my voice, even if I disguised it. I thought about the time that I called to the house and Addie's brother Calvin and her sister Pat answered the telephone at the same time. I mimicked the voice of another one of Addie's brothers, Alan, so well that Pat and Calvin told me that they would call me back in a few minutes. When they returned the call to Alan, he told them that they must be on drugs; he hadn't called them. Pat and Calvin were convinced that Alan must have been drunk and didn't remember calling them.

By midnight, my kidney pain was killing me. The cell phone messages I had left Benita and Addie were not being responded to. Did I dare to call directly to Addie's house and take the chance of my disguised voice being recognized? Instead, I opted for leaving a message on Benita's dormitory telephone. I knew that she would check her messages on it even when she didn't check her cell phone messages. I was in pain, the air-conditioning in the room didn't work, and I felt like I was going to pass out. I left the door open and went to sleep to deal with the pain. I was awakened by someone putting cold water on my sides. It was Benita. She told me that she had been putting cold compresses on my kidneys for an hour to reduce the swelling. She had also given me a dose of my medication that she brought with her. Benita had gotten my message from her dormitory telephone's answering machine and hurried to my motel with the medication. The clock on the motel dresser showed that it was two o'clock. I told Benita that I couldn't believe that I had been asleep for two hours. That is when she corrected me and told me that it was 2:00 p.m. I had been asleep or unconscious for fourteen hours. Benita and I went to the motel's restaurant for lunch. After she was sure that I was all right, she went back to her mother's house to see Aunt Pat, who had already left for home. When asked why she had deserted Aunt Pat and the other relatives, Benita replied, "I had something more important to do." That was the only explanation Benita ever gave Addie about the matter.

Benita returned to the motel to get me and we went to a late dinner; then we returned home when it was dark. I spent the next few days finishing the first writing of the last chapter of my book. Later, I did some proofreading and rewriting of that last chapter; the bibliography wouldn't be finished until early September. Morning, noon, and night I worked on my health and my book. Fourteen hours at the word processor became the norm. Realizing that Addie and Benita were both still bummed out over the minivan fiasco, I rode to Cleveland one day in July with Benita to get them a few surprises: concert tickets for Whitney Houston, followed by a LeVert concert the next week. Benita and Addie had just returned from a July 4th celebration at Put-in-Bay, a boating resort. The holiday seemed to do both of them some good. Addie brought me a tee shirt from the resort as a souvenir. Months later, I would find out that Addie and Benita went to Put-in-Bay with James Crawley and that he "unknowingly" bought the tee shirt for me. While Addie and Benita were in attendance at the Whitney Houston concert, someone rang our home telephone once many times. It was obviously a signal. I suspected that James Crawley didn't know where Addie was and he was getting upset that she was not returning his calls. Eventually, he did as I anticipated. He let the telephone ring long enough for Addie's caller ID to record the number from which he was calling. I had seen that telephone number before and Benita had told me that the telephone number belonged to her best friend's aunt. Supposedly, Benita's friend Renee called Benita and Addie from her aunt's telephone, morning, noon, and night to discuss her unhappiness over her parent's divorce. Because Renee was such a "delicate and fragile" child, Addie and Benita made "special allowances" by letting her call them anytime of the day or the night.

These "special allowances" extended to Renee calling Addie or Benita when they were at work, in church, out of town, or asleep at 2:00 a.m. I wasn't buying it. I called the telephone number that was illuminated on Addie's caller ID. The male voice on the answering machine said, "Hello, you have reached the residence of James Crawley. Please leave a message at the sound of the beep." I never told Addie and Benita that I found out the truth about Renee's aunt's telephone number. I was there to finish my book and then I planned on turning myself in to the FBI in Cleveland. I had Addie hurry to finish cutting down the suits my brother Darnell gave me. I knew that I'd need them for court in the next few months.

Benita and Addie returned from the Whitney Houston concert with some wonderful souvenirs. Naturally, both of them called all of their friends and relatives to tell them every little detail about the show. Neither of them ever told me a thing about the concert. Benita actually had to ask her mother to thank me for paying for the concert and the dinner. In another week, this same scenario was repeated when they went to the LeVert concert. As before, Crawley played games on the telephone. The telephone number he was calling from was the same one he called from when Addie and Benita went to the Whitney Houston concert. I had enough of the lies; it was way past time to get the hell out of there. Addie and Benita got in late that night from the LeVert concert, and they didn't bother calling "Renee" at her aunt's house.

Early the next morning, we were all awakened by what sounded like someone kicking the front door of our house. Benita looked out of her window to see James Crawley and his car in our driveway. Addie was hysterical. "What in the hell does he want?" she whispered. "I told him I didn't want to go out with him."

Benita asked her mother if she wanted Benita to tell him that she wasn't home, but it was too late. James was peeping into the window of the garage. He could see Addie's and Benita's cars there. Addie and Benita decided that they would just remain quiet until he left. James pulled out his cell phone and called our residential phone number, then he called Addie's cell phone number and followed that by calling Benita's cell phone number. I laughed at Addie's and Benita's charades. They actually thought they could convince me that James was just another pest whom Addie couldn't get rid of. Addie and Benita chose to call James Crawley a dangerous stalker that day for my benefit. I got James's cell phone number from Addie's caller ID before she erased it. This number looked familiar; Addie had told me that it was one of her relatives' cell phone number.

Crawley left our driveway that day, but he returned three days later. It was the middle of the week, and Benita was getting dressed to go to a friend's party at 9:00 p.m. Her roommate at Kent State University was on her way to our house to pick Benita up to go to the party. When we all heard the kicking sound at the side door of our house, we wondered if one of the neighborhood dogs had gotten loose and was chasing Gemise. When Benita looked out of the side door window, she whispered to her mother and me that it was James Crawley kicking at the side door. As before, Addie and Benita waited quietly until he left. He returned five minutes later and started kicking on the side door again. This time Benita was putting some of her dirty dishes in the kitchen sink and the sound of the dishes hitting in the sink was enough noise to make James Crawley holler through the door, "I hear the pots rattling. I know you're in there. You may as well open the door."

Benita opened the door immediately, while Addie ran upstairs to her bedroom and stretched out on the bed. "Oh my god! Oh my god!" was the only thing Addie could say. Benita stopped James at the door and told him that her mother was at Eileen's house, the cousin whom Addie always claimed she was visiting when she was actually visiting James. Now Benita was feeding that same lie to James. James told Benita that he saw Addie's and Benita's cars in the garage, so how did Addie get to Eileen's house? Benita replied that Eileen picked Addie up in her car. James took a step out into the driveway of our home and dialed Eileen's telephone number. Eileen told James that she had not seen or spoken to Addie or Benita all day. James snarled that message to Benita and stomped off to his car, slammed his door, and burned his tires, as he sped off down the street. Then Addie's residential and cellular telephones started ringing alternately. It was James calling from his cell phone. This was his way of letting Addie know that he knew she was in the house. Once again, Addie and Benita chose to put on the charade that James was some kind of dangerous stalker, who just wouldn't take "No" for an answer. I pretended to fall for their lies and I acted as if I were going to call the police out to our home to run James Crawley off. Addie and Benita both made a mad dash toward me to prevent me from calling the police. "I'll handle this at work tomorrow," Addie yelled. I told her that she wouldn't have to wait that long because James had just pulled back into our driveway.

Our residential telephone and Addie's cell phone started ringing alternately once again.

James sat there in the driveway for a few more minutes, then he started blowing his car's horn, in long drawn out blasts that caused some of our neighbors to come out on their porches. Benita refused to answer the door again and Addie was terrified that Crawley had the nerve to come to our home after she had told him not to. I was really enjoying the charade and went so far as to pull the curtains back from one of the windows so that he would know that someone was in the house. Crawley finally pulled off again, spinning his tires as he went. Our neighbors went back into their homes and Benita's roommate from Kent State University pulled into our driveway. She had finally arrived to pick Benita up for the party they were supposed to be attending that evening. Benita ran out to Gemise's car and jumped in while the car was still moving. Benita rushed Gemise in backing her car out of our driveway, then they sped away in a haste.

A few minutes later, Benita called her mother, cell phone to cell phone, to tell her that James Crawley had staked out our house and had actually followed Benita and Gemise when they left. Crawley had circled the block four times, as he followed the two college roommates to see who was in the car. When he saw who was in the car, he blew his car's horn and sped away. Again, Addie put on the pretense that James was some kind of a dangerous stalker. I told her, "James seems to be showing that he has ownership rights. How long is it before the two of you are supposed to get married? Don't forget that the honeymoon cruise is scheduled for November 5; you're running out of time."

Her reply to this was, "You're the one who's running out of time. If you turn yourself in to the FBI, you're going to mess up everything for me. It would be better for everyone, if you just stayed dead."

Then Addie sneaked outside, stealthily slipped into her car, and sped away. I wondered what tale would she and Benita tell Crawley; and would he be stupid enough to believe it.

Nothing was said between the two of us for the next two days. Then Addie said that she knew that I would never forgive her for what she had done. I told her that she was my wife and that I would always forgive her anything. I asked her again if she and James had gotten married. Addie swore on several Bibles that she had not married James Crawley in Virginia. She went on to explain that she was near bankruptcy and that she would have to make some tough decisions in order to survive. I told her then that she didn't have to worry about any money because I had stashed some away for a rainy day, and right now it was pouring. She questioned me about how I was able to sell the diamonds and coins without her or Benita knowing it. I didn't answer that question, but I was quick to answer that she spent money like we had a money tree. I added that her gambling habit and her recreational spending were leaving us broke. She admitted that she had problems with overspending and gambling. She asked me how much money I had stashed, but I would not tell her. I counted out one thousand dollars in one-hundred-dollar bills and asked her if that would hold her for a while. I told her that the money I had stashed was for my legal defense fund and that I didn't intend to spend it on nonsense. That date was September 29; she deposited the money in her credit union on October 2. From the day that I gave Addie the one thousand dollars, September 29, to October 5, we made love several times a night, every night. The only reason we stopped on October 6 was because of my observance of the weekend Sabbath. As soon as that Sabbath weekend was over, we went back at it like two rabbits in heat. Addie was so aggressive in our lovemaking that I actually had to tell her to slow down; I wasn't going anywhere anytime soon. I had no way of knowing that she had already made other plans.

On Thursday, October 5, I called Addie at her job, as I have done thousands of times.

Again, her coworkers answered her phone and informed me that Addie had been receiving threatening telephone calls and her coworkers were now screening her calls. Once again, I identified myself as her brother-in-law Robert Holmes and the coworkers called her to the telephone. Once again, she told me of someone making threats to her on her work phone and I suspected that it was James Crawley. A wild thought crossed my mind for just an instant: "What if no one was threatening Addie and she made the whole thing up as part of some setup designed to paint me as some villain who was living in her home against her will?" That would be the perfect allegation if she or James chose to murder me in my sleep or to turn me in to the police. Maybe the two of them were married. Benita would never tell me the truth. If James was willing to let me sleep with his new bride every night since they were married, then he had to be in on the plot to murder me or to turn me in to the police. Benita had to know about this.

The next day, Friday, October 6, Benita came home from Kent State to take me to the Akron Hospital for some laboratory tests and some new prescriptions. I asked her point blank if Addie and James were married, and if all of them planned to murder me or turn me in to the police. Like her mother, Benita swore to God that her mother and James were not married and no one planned on doing anything to me. My private detective had already told me of the many lies that Addie and Benita had told me. I couldn't trust anything either one of them said. The next day, Saturday, October 7, I mailed a copy of my manuscript to my brother in Los Angeles. I included a letter, in which I told him of my suspicions. I also informed the other members of my family of those suspicions and I told all of them about the information and evidence I had compiled that exonerated me from the bogus charges of twenty years ago, as well as documents, tapes, and photographs that would expose Addie and Benita as liars if they claimed that I was living with them against their will.

The next day, Sunday, October 8, at sunset, was the beginning of the Day of Atonement, the High Holy Day on which one attempts to be at one with the Creator by fasting and prayer. As I fasted and prayed from the sunset of October 8 to the sunset of October 9, I prayed an additional prayer to the ones I usually prayed on this day: "Father Yahweh, I ask that what I suspect does not come to pass, but if it does, I ask for your protection. I ask this in the name of your holy son, Yahshua Messiah. Amen." Whatever would come to pass, I knew that I would survive it in good fashion. After all, I still had to get my book published and explained.

That was Yahweh's will, therefore it was my will as well.

The next day, Tuesday, October 10, Kay Jewelers called our home and left a message on the answering machine while Addie was at work. They were sorry that they couldn't get the wedding ring resized in time for the wedding, but it was ready for pickup now. Naturally, Addie denied knowing anything about this message, in spite of the fact that the jeweler congratulated Addie and James in the message that was left on the answering machine. Addie claimed that James must have put the jeweler up to this as some part of a sick joke. My reasoning told me that the message was for me and not for Addie. James wanted me to attack Addie so that she could shoot me and claim selfdefense. I called my relatives and told all of them what had happened; I made a point of informing them as Addie stood next to me and listened. I called the jeweler and pretended to be James Crawley. The jeweler told me that they were sorry that the ring was not ready in time for the wedding, but it was ready now. I thanked them and hung up the telephone. Addie heard the entire conversation, yet she still swore to God in heaven that she was not married to James. She continued to claim that this must be a sick joke on his part. My answer to this was that if it were a sick joke, he'd have to know that I was there in the house with Addie. The message was for me and not for Addie.

The next day, October 11, was even more ridiculous. This time Affordable Insurance called the house and left a message on the answering machine while Addie was at work. The message stated that Addie and Benita's car insurance rates were drastically reduced when combined with James Crawley's because of the family discount. The insurance agent also congratulated Addie and James on their recent marriage. I waited until Addie got home from work, then I called the insurance agent while Addie listened. Again, I pretended to be James Crawley and the insurance agent was glad to explain the specifics of the savings on insurance because of the family discount rates. Again, Addie claimed that James was sick in the head to pull this type of stunt. Again, I responded that the message was for my ears, not Addie's.

James knew I was there in the house because Addie had told him. He either wanted me to flee from the home or he wanted me to attack Addie so that she could shoot me in self-defense. I did neither. I kept my relatives informed and I kept my eyes open. Addie claimed to have to go to the pharmacy to pick up a prescription. I knew that she needed an excuse to get out of the house so that she could inform James that their plan to get me to attack Addie was not working. That is when James took it upon himself to call the home and leave a message for me to hear. Before Addie returned to our home from the pharmacy, James called to our home and left a message on the answering machine. He stated that he was tired of waiting and that he was moving in the next day. Again Addie claimed that James must be out of his mind. To prove to me that she was being honest with me and that she only loved me, she asked me to follow her upstairs to our bedroom to make love. She was going to show me how much she loved only me. I wasn't buying her lies for a minute, but I was sure that this would be the last time that I would ever be with Addie. I planned on turning myself in the next day.

Addie stripped naked and stood in front of me rubbing her breasts, butt, and groin. Like the consummate prostitute she had become, she turned the topic from sex to money, while she stood there as naked as a jaybird. Even though I had just given her one thousand dollars a few days before, she claimed to be broke. She claimed that she didn't even have gas money. I told her that I had money stashed in the house, but I only had one hundred on me. I gave her the hundred and her role as the seductress continued. She undressed me very slowly as she kissed and licked me from head to toe. She bit me on my ears, neck, nipples, and my penis. I remember thinking that she hadn't worked this hard in bed since the time she proposed to me in 1976.

We went at it like rabbits during the mating season; all through the night and into the late morning. She was supposed to be getting ready for work that morning, but she complained of the usual back pain she got from our rigorous lovemaking. As usual, I massaged her back, prepared the usual "healing herb" tea and the accompanying hot chocolate. This patented ritual lasted nearly two hours, and I was more fatigued from rubbing life back into her than I was from the lovemaking; or so I thought. After taking a few swallows of my own hot chocolate, I couldn't keep my eyes open. As I passed out, I remember hearing Addie in the closet downstairs.

The closet downstairs was mostly filled with my clothes; and something else that I couldn't think of in my groggy state of mind. I wondered if she planned on stealing another one of my dress shirts to wear to work. I couldn't recall what else was stashed in that downstairs closet. I dozed off for a second, as I heard her walking back up the stairs. All of a sudden, her slow, deliberate walk turned into a hectic-paced run. I heard a thunderous sound and I recognized the unmistakable smell of gunpowder. Now reality slapped me in the face; I had been drugged. I suddenly remembered the other thing hidden in the downstairs closet. It was a gun! A burning, paralyzing pain hit me in the stomach. I groaned, let out a gasp for breath, and went silent; playing possum. As the "would-be" assassin crept forward to admire her handiwork, I suddenly lifted up and reached for the outstretched gun in her hand, but she was ready for me, and she shot me again. I got the gun and hand on the second try, as many more bullets exploded in the bedroom. I didn't know at the time how many rounds hit me, but I was hit many times before I got the gun away from her. Of the original nine rounds in the gun, only two remained. I was hit five times in the stomach and chest area. Of the two rounds left, one hadn't been fired, but the one she attempted to fire into my head, had misfired. Praise Father Yahweh in the name of his son Yahshua Messiah.

From the time that I was finally able to wrestle the gun from her, and then check it for unspent rounds, she had dropped to her knees, half begging and half praying. I pressed the gun hard against her head and asked her: "Murderous bitch, do you love this fake ass preacher enough to kill your only child's father?" She replied that she had done this for my daughter Benita. I was enraged: "Do you mean to tell me that my daughter wanted me dead?"

She went on to explain that Crawley had access to eighty thousand dollars, and that he would spend it all on Benita and her if I were out of the way. He didn't have the nerve to take me out himself, so it was left up to her. According to her, Benita thought that Addie was going to turn me over to the FBI, since Addie and Crawley had secretly been wedded on September 22. They had agreed to remain apart until the murderous deed was done. The more she talked, the more I thought about putting that last bullet in her brain. She uttered the only name that would make me spare her life when she said, "Benita refused to give me away when I got married to Crawley. My sister Pat had to do it."

As she remained on her knees, with the pistol still at her temple, I finally realized that I was spurting blood like a spigot. I had so many holes in me that I wondered why I hadn't passed out from the lack of blood. A joke passed through my mind; I felt like a piece of Swiss cheese. I was starting to weaken and I knew that I needed to get to the hospital immediately. There was no time to get dressed, or to ride forty-five minutes to the Akron Hospital. I told Addie that she was taking me less than two blocks to our local Northside Hospital. I no longer cared about being recognized, I really had planned on turning myself in as I had told her so many times. She voiced some concern about having to pay back Social Security and the insurance companies she collected from, when she had me declared dead. I didn't give a damn about any of that, and I ordered her down the steps before me, on our way to the car and then to the hospital. She didn't see me toss the gun on the bed, as she started down the steps. My stomach really started hurting as I caught a glance of the quarter dollar-sized holes the bullets made in our bedroom walls. I put the fingers of one hand in the bullet holes and prayed that I didn't bleed out before I got to the hospital; a survival skill I learned from an episode of *Magnum, P.I.* I used the other hand to steady myself with the handrail on the wall going down the steps. Halfway down the thirteen steps, I must have passed out. I only remember waking up after what had to be a couple of hours. I still had my fingers in the bullet holes, and I hadn't lost any more blood, at least not on the outside. Addie was nowhere to be seen. I managed to get to my knees and fold my hands long enough to get off one badly needed prayer. "Hezekiah's Prayer," 2 Kings 3. This prayer was taught to me by my grandmother when I was twelve years old. I've used this prayer several times before and I believe that usage is one of the reasons that I'm still here today. In Hezekiah's Prayer, King Hezekiah pleads his case to the Creator when Hezekiah is stricken ill and near sure death. Hezekiah cites the covenant between the Creator and him, in which the Creator promises him a long life if he obeys the Creator. This was a conditional agreement, in which Hezekiah had to do his part first.

I was in and out of consciousness, and I could hear the telephone ring, but my temporary paralysis did not allow me to go to the telephone or to open any door or window to call for help. In truth, all that I could do was to try to regulate my breathing and my heart rate, and to try not to go into shock. Unknown to me at the time, Addie had gone to my mother's home with a concocted story about having a bad reaction to some medication that caused her to hallucinate and shoot me to death. She assured my mother and my brother that I was dead because she emptied the gun on me. My mother's exact words were, "Ben is not the type to die so easily, besides that, if my son were dead I'd know it." She sent my brother Jerry and Addie back to the scene of the shooting, in the home I secretly shared with my wife and daughter, only to have Addie refuse to give my brother Jerry the key to the house. He had to kick the very, heavy security door in. When Jerry got inside the house, he found me in the same spot I had originally fallen, at the foot of the steps. The sound of the door being kicked in awoke me once again. My exact first words to him were, "What took you so long?"

My brother Jerry went outside to Addie's car to inform her that I was just barely alive and he told her to call 911, if she didn't want to catch a murder rap. He came back inside to attend me. The records from the dispatch officer at "911" show that Addie called them three times and hung up the cell phone. After the third hang-up, the dispatcher called her back. By this time, Jerry had gone back to her car to see what the holdup was. It was then that he realized that she was stalling for time and waiting for me to die. He took her cell phone and gave the dispatcher the necessary information. He also took Addie's car keys so that she could not flee from the scene. I wondered what the minister who married us would have to say when she heard about this tum of events. I don't think this is what she had in mind when she said, "Until death do you part." The police arrived with the ambulance and I recall hearing the paramedics say that my blood pressure was 75/40, and dropping fast. I've seen death before, and this wasn't it. For me, death was not an option; I had things to do. I passed out again.

CHAPTER 14

Twenty Years After

A day and a half later, I awoke in the emergency ward of St. Elizabeth's Hospital, Youngstown, Ohio, just ten blocks from the shooting. I still don't know why I wasn't taken to Northside Hospital, which was just two blocks away. Several female nurses were standing around my bed, and one of them made the startling remark, "Well, do you want us to call you Robert or Benjamin, Mr. Holmes?" Obviously, they knew my real identity as well as my alternate identity. One of the nurses went on to explain that a driver's license with the name of Robert Holmes was found in the pocket of the pajamas I was wearing. She also went on to explain that Addie had told the police that I was using that identity but that I was actually Benjamin Robert Holmes Jr., fugitive-at-large for twenty years. This revelation to the authorities placed me in no jeopardy because as the local police and the FBI went on to explain my case of twenty years had been dropped for a number of reasons, in June of that year, just four months ago. Most people thought that I just outlasted the statute of limitations, others later found out that most of the authorities involved in my persecution were in jail or on their way to jail. Yes, it took a while, but the criminals in uniform had been found out, just as I asserted twenty years before.

Most of the employees at St Elizabeth's Hospital, on the north side of Youngstown, were former classmates of mine, who grew up with me in that very neighborhood. I was inundated with former friends, girlfriends, and relatives. My brother Jerry and two detectives finally put an end to the three-ring circus, and got down to business.

Addie originally claimed that she had a bad reaction to some medication and that resulted in her hallucinating and then attempting to murder me. Now, the new story was that neither she nor my daughter Benita had seen or heard from me for twenty years. She claimed that she thought I was dead until I popped up on her doorstep four days ago, demanding half of everything she owned because we were still married in spite of the fact that she had just recently remarried. Supposedly, I also threatened to kill her, the new husband, and my own daughter. According to the new story, she was raped by me and then had to shoot me in self-defense after I passed out. One more twist to her convoluted story: my brother Jerry had kidnapped her for me for four days. The detectives were quick to point out that they had checked with her job and that she had reported to work each of the four days in question. Further investigation and interviews with the neighbors where she, Benita, and I lived, revealed that I had been living there for three years steadily, and up to ten years on and off. The detectives also found fifty pairs of my shoes, twenty suits, a hundred sweaters, and five manuscripts of books I had written. Thirty boxes of research for those manuscripts were also discovered. The discovery that truly decimated her latest statement was a cache of photographs of her, Benita, and me, together on various occasions and holidays, for the last twenty years, and all of them were dated in her handwriting.

The various authorities had all of this information and evidence to not only prove Addie to be a perjurer and would-be murderer, but they also had received information over the years from some anonymous source that directly resulted in the arrest, conviction, and incarceration of various officers, judges, prosecutors, defense attorneys, and politicians in and around the immediate vicinity. Coincidentally, most of those prosecuted and or killed had been a direct threat to me and mine for the last twenty years. The detectives told me that it probably wasn't safe for me to stay in town after my release from the hospital. They inferred that it wasn't worth sticking around to face my assailant in court. Addie was in jail, awaiting bond. Her new husband knew about me for at least three years, and even after marrying Addie, agreed to live separately from her until they got rid of me. My daughter Benita and my brother Jerry knew about the affair for three years, the engagement for one year, and the marriage for one month. Both of them knew that I would either be turned in to the authorities or killed, yet neither saw a need or had the nerve to intervene.

Depending on who's counting, I had been shot three to five times. I counted four holes and one drainage hole that was actually a fifth bullet hole. I sustained a bullet in each kidney, my liver was completely cut in half, several feet of intestine were damaged and removed, and one bullet passed through the stomach and lodged in the spine. None of the bullets were removed because of the danger, and the wounds were simply cauterized to stop the bleeding. Truthfully speaking, the exploratory incisions to check the damage from the bullets hurt more than the actual wounds themselves. I was only given ice chips for ten days and then released from the hospital. My daughter Benita and my Uncle Sanders took me to my mother's home. We made a stop at the scene of my shooting to gather my belongings; that took two days, six pickup truck loads, and six able-bodied men. It was at that time that I was given a copy of *Jet Magazine*, in which a women's group was promising to raise money to help defend Addie.

They were not privileged to the information the authorities had proving her guilt in this case and my innocence in the past case of twenty years ago. It was time to pull the ace from under my sleeve. Just for the record, Addie and Benita share a very bad habit; they talk in their sleep, and they speak clearly when they do so.

Benita's recurring nightmare included her continuously saying; "Don't hurt my daddy." Addie's recurring nightmare included calling me "James" and continuously saying, "You'll never forgive me for what I've done." I had no choice; when in doubt, bug the damn telephone. I learned to bug telephones when I worked as an investigator for the law firm of Haines, Haines, and Breckinridge, of Youngstown, Ohio. I amassed a bushel basket of audio tapes featuring Addie, Benita, the new man, and me in various combinations of interaction. After letting my brothers hear what was afoot on the tapes, I decided to let Addie and Benita know that I was there to finish writing my book and then I was turning myself in to the

172

Cleveland FBI, so that possibly there would be no suspicion that she had any knowledge of my whereabouts for the last twenty years. She agreed that things would work out for all concerned, if I meant what I said. I even told her that I had a bug on the telephone. As I suspected, she looked until she found the bug and destroyed it. She had no idea that I had a second bug on the telephone. It was from that second bug that I got the really juicy information that would later be evidence against her. The second bug provided the ace up my sleeve.

As soon as Addie found out that the neighbors had told the investigators just how long I had actually been around, she decided to try for a third version of the events. In the third rendition, I was living at her residence against her will for years and had backup to keep her in line. She and Benita were nothing more than prisoners. That's when I dropped the ace on the investigators. The tapes from the second bug featured the new man telling Benita that he knew that I was living in the house. The ace also featured Addie stating that I had remodeled the home twice since I had been living there. She went on to say that the new man was just a way out of some financial problems she had incurred from unrestrained spending and gambling debts. The ace featured the new man saying that Addie was his wife now and he was determined to get me out of the house, immediately, one way or the other. I was sure to get Addie and Benita on tape saying that I never threatened them and that they begged me to stay as a way of stalling the new man.

The tapes and the photographs made Addie's guilty plea a foregone conclusion. The only thing we haggled over was the paying of the seventy thousand dollars in medical bills. I had to sue her for that. In exchange for some of my family's property held in her name, I agreed to drop the suit and pay the medical bills myself. The only thing left was for her to be sentenced and to do her time. In order to get my family's property back from her, I had to agree to the stipulation that she do forty-five days in the county jail and then complete two years on probation. In this way she could keep her job and pay back the insurance money and the Social Security money she claimed when she had me declared dead. Another twist of events included the prosecutors in the case against her, offering her a deal in which they would give her the lightest sentence possible if she turned state's evidence against me concerning charges from twenty years ago; charges that had already been dropped. As the prosecutors stated it, "Who in the hell does he think he is that he walks out of serious charges by outlasting the statute of limitations and then expects to profit by writing a book about it and suing those who originally charged him?"

Once the facts of the case concerning *The State of Ohio vs. Addie Holmes Crawley* were made available, the women's groups withdrew any offers of helping Addie with her defense fund. All of a sudden, the media were interested in what I had to say. Addie's attorney was seriously entertaining the idea of her turning state's evidence against me until the time to tell what she knew arrived. At that time she actually asked in front of witnesses, "What do you want me to say? Just tell me what you want me to say and I'll say it." So much for testifying or 'testilying' against me.

The *New York Times Magazine* did a five-page story on me, on December 5, 2000; in it they revealed transcripts of the tapes I had on my crooked persecutors from twenty years ago. Present prosecutors and policemen, who had nothing to do with the case of twenty years ago, considered the *New York Times* article a black eye for all of the area, past and present. Authorities in the area actually stated that they considered the article to be spit in their faces. The crooked policemen who plagued me twenty years ago had been convicted of racketeering, violation of civil rights, drug trafficking, aggravated felonious assault, and misuse of their official positions by protecting drug dealers aligned with them. The prosecutor of twenty years ago was connected to a "hot car" scheme, in which he personally was convicted of altering odometers and titles to automobiles. My, how the mighty have fallen! The article also revealed transcripts of the tapes I had on Addie, Benita, and the new man.

Delphi Packard, a division of General Motors, like St. Elizabeth's Hospital, is a large employer of my former classmates, running buddies, and relatives. When the article came out in the *New York Times*, the news came to me that she was again denying that she had me hidden in her house, while she was engaged to and later married to another man.

She even went so far as to brag that if she had shot me in the head, she wouldn't be having so much trouble out of me. I was not angered, but I did feel it necessary to put her in her place by letting the truth kick her in the ass. After all, she had it coming. I spent a small fortune sending three thousand photographs to her coworkers at Delphi Packard; audio tapes added to her embarrassment. I did not stop there; I also sent photographs and tapes to all of her relatives, in town and out of town. I made sure not to forget copies for her pastor, church members, and the Mother of the Church. Copies were also sent to the new man's family and church, especially since he had been misrepresenting himself as a preacher while plotting my murder.

I was contacted by investigators from Delphi Packard's insurance company, as well as investigators from Social Security. They asked me the same question that her coworkers at Delphi Packard asked: "Are these pictures and audio tapes real?"

My response was the same to everyone: "These pictures and audiotapes have been authenticated by the Mahoning County Crime Lab, and that's good enough for me."

Addie called me to beg me not to send anymore photos or tapes; she was at risk of losing her job. I had broken the steel maiden.

Mention was made in the *New York Times* article that I had survived financially while on the run by selling blueprints of silencers and by selling prefabricated parts to assemble those silencers. This proved to be better advertising than any of the ads I paid for in the backs of *Guns and Ammo* types of magazines. When I was shot and then taken to the hospital by the paramedics, the investigators found another gun, other than the one Addie shot me with.

Accompanying that gun were a silencer, an extra clip, and a box of bullets. One of the stories Addie told the investigators was that the gun and silencer were mine and that I had threatened her with it, making it all the more necessary to kill me in self-defense. The only problem with that rendition was the fact that the gun was her gun, legally purchased and registered to her, twenty years ago. She thought that the conversion to computers and discs, recently, would obscure any old paper trail of the original purchaser and owner of the firearm.

It didn't. The saleswoman of that time even remembered the original sale, because the first gun was prone to jamming, and a second one was issued. Both serial numbers were recorded together. This information became common knowledge for those "in the loop." In Youngstown, the judges, the prosecutors, the defense attorneys, the policemen, the insurance agents, the bondsmen, the private detectives, the bounty hunters, and the taxi drivers all eat lunch together and exchange information—even confidential information. Imagine my surprise, before the *New York Times* article that discussed silencers, when everybody in Youngstown came to me about silencers. These inquiries multiplied tenfold when the *New York Times* article was published.

To further illustrate my point about the "Good-Old-Boy Network" and their inability to keep confidential information confidential; consider this: I hired two attorneys. The first attorney was to handle Civil Rights' lawsuits from the past and to fend off any revised and reissued charges stemming from the charges of twenty years ago. The second attorney was to sue Addie over the shooting injuries and the medical bills, thereby forcing her to relinquish property of my family's that she refused to relinquish after I returned from the grave. The second attorney was also given the task of retrieving valuable telephone records by subpoena before Ohio Bell, AT&T, and Sprint destroyed them. I took a writer from *The New York Times Magazine* everywhere I went, and she witnessed the payments and the orders to the attorneys. I saw the first attorney at 11:00 a.m., and the second at noon. Later in that day, I was having a late lunch with the writer when I remembered some other details that I thought were important to give to both of the attorneys. When I called the attorneys' offices, I was told four times by each of the attorneys' secretaries that they were tied up for the rest of the day, and that they would get back to me the following day. Meanwhile, both of them were blowing up the writer's cell phone, while we were having our late lunch, at about 4:00 p.m. Both of them left numerous messages. Frustrated because they weren't taking my calls, the writer and I decided to answer the attorneys' calls just to see what was really going on. The attorneys were too busy to talk to me but not too busy to ask to be in the writer's article and possibly in my book. Furthermore, there was a discussion about what I paid the first attorney compared to what I paid the second. Apparently, this was the topic of their luncheon gossip. When told that I was with the writer and wanted to speak to them, again both of them stated that they had to go. The next day at the courthouse and at the lawyers' offices, policemen, secretaries, and other lawyers revealed that they too were present for the luncheon gossip and heard it all.

My point here is this: Not only were people coming to me about silencers after the *New York Times* article, but they were coming to me before the article, simply because those who collected evidence from the scene of the shooting divulged sensitive and confidential information concerning an ongoing investigation, apparently just to have something to talk about over lunch. No consideration is given to whether they are hurting the good guy or helping the bad guy. Some defendant, plaintiff, prosecutor, or judge should consider filing Obstruction of Justice charges against some of these gossip hounds. Loose lips do sink ships.

The *New York Times* article hit the newsstands on December 5, 2000. By Christmas of that year I was once again "The Silencer Man." Now, more than any other time in my life, people were contacting me about silencers. But it didn't stop there. They also wanted fully automatic weapons' conversion kits, remote control bombs, poisons, and formulas for synthesizing the more popular drugs. Thousands of requests came in for alternate identification papers and hiding places in foreign countries that didn't have extradition treaties with the United States of America. Many of these requests came in the form of letters; from foreign countries, like Mexico, Canada, Venezuela, Brazil, Argentina, Saudi Arabia, Germany, France, and Italy; these scared me. The foreign names scared me. The names of some of the organizations scared me. I was contacted by every Alphabet Soup agency in the United States that was concerned with crime, espionage, and Homeland Security. There were attempts at recruiting me and my notoriety to draw in and snare "enemies of the State." I had been here before; I didn't like it twenty years ago and I didn't like it now. Thank you, but no thank you. The full-court press from government agencies, who wanted me to work for them, plus being caught between warring factions of a gangland "turf war," are just two of the reasons why I had to "take a powder" twenty years ago. It further complicated my situation that one of the more prominent gangs of that time owned the police, the prosecutors, and the judges.

Many requests for "tools of the trade" came from the locals. One request came from one of my old racing buddies, Ernie. Ernie had become a "beyond-his-means" gambler who supplemented his United States Steel Mill pension by doing freelance hits—murder for hire. Ernie was also president of one of the larger black biker gangs of the area. Most of them were under indictment for using their "seemingly," harmless, cross-country, biker treks to smuggle drugs. On the day in question, Ernie was showing me the twenty-two motorcycles in his garage, when he switched his attention to an early model Volvo. Supposedly, I could have the Volvo if I wanted it. It was in his way. All the vehicle needed was one clamp on the gas line.

He'd do it himself, but his knees were too messed up. All I had to do to get the Volvo was to crawl up under it, while the hydraulic jack was in place, and put the clamp on the gas line. I told Ernie that my health was worse than his and that I couldn't go under the car. It was then that he broke down and confided to me that he was hired to drop the hydraulic jack and let the Volvo crush me to death, for five thousand dollars. He went on to tell me who hired him. It was Addie's new husband's brother, one of my old racing buddies. I never went to Ernie's place again, but I did hear that he met an untimely death three years later. It is rumored that someone gave him poisoned cocaine that eventually killed him.

Ernie also told me that most of our old acquaintances were dead, locked up, or on their way to jail. The ones going to jail considered me their "get out of jail free" card. Most of the authorities in law enforcement openly pursued the "Big Fish That Got Away." Publicly, I exposed the corruption of the past and of the present; and behind closed doors, some of those same corrupt officials had painted a bulls-eye on my back. I was much more than a subject to be watched; I was *the* target. I was guilty by association and anyone doing anything illegal must have been working for me, out of fear of me and my three gangs. At least that's what the rumor was. Old friends in trouble with the law kept discussing things with me that they shouldn't have. "My god! Was everyone wired or what?"

It was a safe bet that most of the old and the new friends were "wired." Unknown to me at the time, Jimmy, his wife Angela, Booker, and his partner Marv were all subjects of a DEA investigation. Booker was after Jimmy's wife Angela, a gorgeous little thing, who also worked at Delphi Packard. Booker had amassed a small fortune, doing whatever he was doing. He got to the point that he could afford to hire "muscle" to do his dirty work, and he did. There were rumors that he hired someone to rob one of my brothers, while he pretended to love my other brother Jerry and me. Booker had the bad habit of pressing too hard when pumping me or anyone else for information that was only useful to the police. Jimmy told me after he was raided and incarcerated that Booker had set him up, but that I was the inevitable target. His wife Angela concurred. I actually found a "wire" on Booker once. He claimed to have the electronic surveillance equipment to listen in on his own adulterous wife Val and her young stud. Nonetheless, I felt like I was playing Russian roulette being around him and I've never considered myself suicidal.

Not being able to catch the big fish, Booker and Marv eventually had to do their time, a little after Addie got out. Addie had to report to court for sentencing, a measly forty-five days that actually turned out to be thirty days, because she had a nervous breakdown and had to be hospitalized. That was in late 2001. Through continuances and medical emergencies, her lawyer had strategically delayed her "vacation" in the county jail for over a year. That thirty days was like thirty years to her and she aged badly from it. She emerged from jail with raccoon-like circles around her eyes that are still there to this day. Beauty had turned into the beast. It was really a wonder that she went to jail at all, considering the rumored plea bargain deal she was offered from the prosecutor's office to turn state's evidence on me, concerning criminal charges of the past. Before Addie went to jail, the prosecutor's office actually sent me a registered letter refusing to accept any evidence from me concerning Addie's assault on me. I had to contact the Youngstown Bar Association and the Ohio

Disciplinary Council in an attempt to get the Youngstown authorities to do their job. Actually, I accused the prosecutor's office of case-fixing and obstruction of justice. Concerning the Bar Association, I was referred to a representative of the Bar who just happened to share the same highly, uncommon last name as the assistant prosecutor I was complaining about. That questionable representative referred me to the Ohio Disciplinary Council, which in turn told me that they could not force the prosecutors to do their jobs and that I might be better off contacting the Bar Association.

Caught up in a "Catch-22" situation I decided to write the prosecutor's office a twenty-five-page registered letter, outlining the evidence I had in the case of *The State Of Ohio vs. Addie Holmes Crawley*. Knowing that they knew that I had the ear of many newspapers and television talk shows, I included in the registered letter to the prosecutor's office a note that I was sending a copy of the "letter of evidence" to all major newspapers and television stations so that the media could see how justice was practiced in Youngstown.

The prosecutor's "phone tag" tactics, continuances, and pseudo-investigations served their purpose: delaying sending Addie to jail until they found out if she had anything useful against me. Not being able to squeeze any water from the stone, the state relented and Addie went to jail. I concentrated on healing up, as well as I could, and stayed as "invisible" as I could—which turned out to be not quite invisible enough.

I recall how difficult it was getting former friends and family members to turn over assets that they had been holding for some time, as in the case concerning Addie and the house in Seattle, where the "D.C. Snipers" rented a duplex from my family as they trekked across the United States killing Americans at will. I got my own driver's license, for the first time in twenty years, and didn't have to worry about the legality of using someone else's driver's license. I had intentionally forgotten my Social Security number and had to relearn it. Before I could be "legal" again, I had to find someone "credible" and in authority, who could positively identify me, because officials claimed that accurate photographs and reliable fingerprints of me were no longer available. George Ross of the Youngstown Police

Department grew up ten houses away from the home my four brothers and I grew up in at 774 Fairmont Avenue, Youngstown, Ohio. We went to school together, played basketball together, and our parents are very, good, longtime friends. His father, Rev. Ross, was even a mentor to my baby brother, Rev. Darnell Holmes, and was influential in Darnell's pursuit of a doctorate in ministry. In order for me to be legal and declared "alive" again, Officer George Ross, of the Fingerprint Department of the Youngstown Police Department, had to write out an affidavit swearing that he recognized me as Benjamin Robert Holmes Jr., and then fingerprint me and file those prints with the affidavit. A birth certificate, a Social Security card, and a driver's license followed. I was "legit." All I needed next was a set of wheels, and I knew just who to look up from my distant past. Lying Johnny, my old mentor, was rumored to have a car lot full of pristine automobiles. I recall leaving him thirty thousand dollars' worth of cars and racing parts, when I decided to pull a Houdini. I just knew that he'd look out for a brother.

Lying Johnny, my old mentor, had so grown in notoriety and invisibility that many were referring to him as the "Living Legend" or "The Ghostman." He really did have a secret car lot of pristine, collector's cars; high-performance, "muscle" cars; and low-mileage, classic, luxury cars. I fell in love with the ice-blue, metallic, 1990, Lincoln Continental, Designer's Series. In early 2002, this 1990 automobile looked like it had just been driven off the showroom floor. I lived on the north side of town, and I had no way of knowing that there were three other cars identical to this one, from the other three sides of town; driven by tall, Black men, who looked a lot like me. They had "thirty day tags" on their cars, as I did. As John explained it, I'd either blend in with them or get blamed for something they did. According to John, "keeping everyone confused" was a good thing.

Lying Johnny had served as an intelligence officer for Special Forces when he was in Vietnam. He hadn't missed one step since he retired from all of that to civilian life. He had his finger on the pulse of everyone and everything in the area. What he didn't know, he could find out very quickly. After all of this time, he still had a well-oiled, information-gathering machine. John went on to tell me about the twelve thousand dollars that Booker and Jimmy had collected from delinquent accounts by claiming that the money was actually mine and that I was contemplating sending my own personal "collection agency" to collect that money. I had been put at risk and had not gained a cent of the twelve thousand dollars. I probably would never have found this out, except for John. Jimmy was already in jail and Booker was soon to join him. I was alive and free. I'd get over their deception. John pointed out that it was smart of me to sever any ties to them, because they were trying to get the authorities to believe that they worked for me.

They and others went so far as to claim to be lieutenants in one or the other of the "rumored" three gangs I headed. Two years had passed since I had "returned from the grave," and many of my closest former associates had chosen to remain invisible to me or to handle me with a ten-foot pole. I was "too hot." Quite a few benefitted from the myths about my secret army. Many sold bogus "product" to unsuspecting dupes and claimed that they sold it for me. "If you got a problem with the product, take it up with Ben Holmes" became the great intimidating remark for a while, until I sought out the perpetrators and saw to it that they returned the money they had swindled in my name. I had to "insist" that Booker return money that he had suckered from drug buyers, by claiming that he worked for me. In his personal show of disdain for me, after he returned the money in question, Booker paraded past my mother's home, consecutively, in several of his more expensive vehicles, to show me that I hadn't hurt him financially at all. "The parade" included a customized Jaguar; a Lexus; a 1962, convertible, Chevy Impala; a 1966, convertible, Buick Wildcat; a Ford Explorer; a Ford pickup truck; a Harley Sportster; and a Harley Full-Dressed Hog. Shortly after that, the DEA took all of them and twelve houses when Booker was busted for supplying cocaine and heroin to clients spanning from New York to California. Various newspapers claimed that he had been doing this for five to ten years, which was the same amount of time he was sentenced to serve.

Youngstown used to produce steel for the car plants, the military and civilian aircraft, the military and civilian seacraft, roads, and buildings. Steel in this area started dying around 1975–1979, and has been hemorrhaging ever since. Cheap foreign steel was the culprit.

Almost overnight, the domino effect went from one industry to another here, and many weren't even steel related. General Motors made severe cutbacks and Delphi Packard went from a healthy work-force of six thousand to just six hundred overnight. Chances are that if you aren't a mailman, working for the utilities companies, working for Youngstown State University, or working for the hospitals, then you're probably not working. One of the hospitals is threatening to close right now. Statistics show that more people in this town are on food stamps than ever before.

Teachers and policemen are among the lowest paid in the nation. Youngstown State University awards more chemistry degrees than all the rest of the state universities in Ohio combined. Correlations have been drawn between the low pay of the local police officers and the tendency for some of them to steal or go on the take. Chemistry students and professors here are believed to be one of the sources of chemicals and glassware to make synthetic drugs that far surpass the poor quality of street drugs in this area. Some argue that if it weren't for the "underground economy" here, there wouldn't be much of an economy at all.

The drug game, the whore game, the hot car game, the paper game, the gambling game, and the killing game all took severe hits when Lenny Strollo and his faction of the local mob decided to turn state's evidence against their own "invisible empire" of organized crime, to avoid doing a little time. Those following Strollo modeled themselves after him when it came time to play "Let's Make a Deal." Sheriffs, deputies, judges, prosecutors, defense attorneys, politicians, and mob figures have all been jailed by the dozens for RICO viola-tions, obstruction of justice, racketeering, theft in office, paying and receiving bribes, case-fixing, and conspiracies concerning gambling, drugs, and prostitution. Cell phones, house phones, GPS systems, confidential informants, and good old "wires" played a role in nab-bing the subjects.

John reminded me to stay off the computers and the cell phones, "and don't ever forget that the prosecutor, Phil Gains, was on the front page of the *Youngstown Vindicator* essentially declaring open season on Ben Holmes." He further admonished me not to fall into a false sense of security because none of the old charges had been re-filed. The authorities were more interested in finding some "new" charges to file. In this town, I was a target forever.

It seemed like every time I got in the Lincoln, I was followed. Essentially, I led a "parade" all over town. I met the owners of the other three Lincolns like mine, and one day we paraded past the police department and several other places that the task force was known to frequent. Then each of the four of us parked his car in the drive of one of the other owners of the Lincolns and rode with someone else. Lying Johnny was quick to send word to me that the police scanners weren't talking about anything but me and my new alliance with the owners of the other three Lincolns. For the next three days, I was stopped eleven times; nothing was found. The owners of the other three Lincolns reported that they had been stopped at least that many times also. For me, it was always the same conversation when the police stopped me. They wanted to know what everyone in town was up to; most of these people I had never even met or heard of. The authorities must have really been desperate to ask me about people I didn't even know. As John was fond of saying, "They were on a fishing expedition."

John had "associates" everywhere, and very little escaped his attention. He surrounded himself with characters known only to me as the Wizard, the Warlord, and the Mad Scientist. I never knew their real names or their functions, except that the Wizard had done some federal time for hacking into FBI files.

CHAPTER 15

In Jail without the Bail

John's information retrievers caught wind of a conversation amongst "officers of the law," in which it was mentioned that I was wanted so badly that many would look the other way if someone decided to do something to me. Policemen had a running joke that if Addie had been a better shot, she would have been doing a lot of people a big favor. The gist of all of this was that sooner or later one of these trigger-happy cops was going to go nuts on me, or at least find something on me, whether I had anything on me or not. Two very good friends, who I grew up with and went to college with, were robbed and shot. One was shot in the leg and sustained a very survivable wound. However, he panicked, ran too far too fast, and bled to death in no time flat. My other old schoolmate had the presence of mind to remember my shooting incident, and put a finger in his stomach wound that was made by a .357 magnum.

He is alive and well today. I'm glad that some good came of my ordeal.

I knew that I was drawing too much attention to John by being around him as often as I was. I don't know if that is why someone killed his wife, chopped her up in little pieces, and then buried her in a shallow grave with some dead dog parts. John and I parted company permanently for our own good. His parting words echo in my mind. "You need to get invisible again for a while." That's what I thought I was doing, but time and circumstances would prove that I wasn't quite invisible enough. I had not yet mastered the art of invisibility, as John and many of our old running buddies had.

The Lincoln I got from Lying Johnny was plush and had been very well taken care of. He was quick to point out that the car was the subject of a recall notice; meaning that it had a mechanical problem of such significance that the manufacturers were willing to make the necessary repairs, if you waited your turn. Another option was to have it repaired yourself and then submit the receipts to them for reimbursement. The nature of the mechanical flaw was a giant nut and bolt that connected the front frame of the car to the rear frame of the car. Once this nut and bolt were tightened, they were then welded in place to prevent loosening. Poor welds allowed the nut and bolt to loosen and the front and back halves of the frame were moving; they were attempting to separate. In that attempt to separate, gas lines, hoses, brake lines, and brake cables were being stretched and damaged. On my Lincoln, the brake cable was being stretched to the point of making the driver's rear brake engage while the car was rolling, thus causing the brakes to continuously wear out prematurely.

I had the recall notice and simply had to wait my turn. While waiting several months for my turn to get my Lincoln repaired, I had to have three sets of brake pads and one rotor replaced on the rear, driver's side just to be able to drive the car. No one dared to attempt to repair the broken weld on the nut and bolt that held the two portions of the frame together.

That was precision work that the manufacturer and the dealer would have to do. I kept the car running well enough to make local visits to my many doctors; all of whom were no more than ten blocks away. I had to take several blood tests several times a month. I'd be so weak from those tests that I'd often stop one block from my doctors to rest at a lifelong friend's home. His name is Reggie, and as of this date, our families have been close for forty years.

Often, while sitting in my car in front of Reggie's home, or when leaving his home, the police would pull me over for a routine license and insurance inspection. The event would end with the officers asking me about Reggie's son Sean, who also lived at that address.

Sean played college football against one of the task force officers in question. Sean was one of the quarterbacks who led Ohio State to back-to-back championships over the task force officer's team, when they were still in school. As Sean explained it to me, there was also a woman involved, whom they were both seeing. According to Sean, the three of them had actually partied together, at various college "sets." Sean said that no good came of the relationship and harsh words were eventually exchanged. Years later, that same task force officer was instrumental in sending Sean to jail for drug possession, but Sean still had the girl. That seemed to be one of the task force officer's main concerns when he "talked" to me: "Who else is in the house; any girls? What do they look like; do you know their names?" It really pissed him off that I never knew, saw, or heard anything. According to that officer, I had it coming for not "cooperating" with him. The threat was made that I might even be charged with hampering an investigation or obstruction of justice. All because I wouldn't be his snitch. Truthfully speaking, he was more concerned about the girl than he was about crime.

On May 25, 2002, I was up early and on my way to the west side to get another set of brakes put on the rear driver's side of the Lincoln; still waiting for my turn on the recall list.

One of my old racing buddies had a shop on the west side where he restored old classic cars and motorcycles. I waited all day for him to finish the automobile he had in the single-car garage so that he could get to mine next. His gorgeous, high-maintenance girlfriend slowed his progress considerably, with constant attempts at his seduction; he had just gotten paid and he was loaded. According to Lulu, "Dennis can finish that car and Ben's any old time." In her own words, she was hungry, horny, broke, and in need of a few drinks. After way too many breaks, and way too many trips to the closest tavern, we all realized that Dennis wouldn't be getting to my car that day. I was about to head back home to the north side, when he asked me to take Lulu to her home on the north side. At least he'd be able to finish the car on the rack in the single-car garage, and maybe get to mine the next day.

Lulu and I loaded up the Lincoln with the car parts I had brought and a change of clothing she had brought to Dennis's garage. I hadn't driven a mile when I heard the rear brake pads screeching horribly against the rotor. It had been this bad before, and I had still been able to make it home another four miles many times before. After all, Dennis would get to my car tomorrow. It was dark and late. I suddenly realized that tonight was jazz night at the Elk's Lounge. I had to pass it on the way home. I drew all kinds of attention from the crowd outside of the Elk's Lounge, as the brakes made a very embarrassing screech every time my gorgeous, ice-blue Lincoln moved. That's when one of the members of the crowd standing outside approached my car to tell me that my car was sparking fire near my gas tank every time the car moved. My mother's house was only four blocks away. I could make it to her house and then use her car to take Lulu home. That was the plan that got shot down three blocks from my mother's house. The same "plain clothes" task force officer who had stopped me so many times before, in his quest to get information on Reggie and his son Sean, turned on his siren and lights to stop me because the sparks from the brakes were dangerously close to the gas tank. He was right about that and I had no problem with his decision. I was taking a chance trying to get the car home and I knew it. I had spotted the officer and his partner, when their task car was two cars behind me, in front of the Elk's Lounge. I told Lulu not to get out of the car and definitely not to make any sudden moves until the officers said so. I knew these two and they knew me. They had reputations on the street, on the force, and at Internal Affairs for being trigger-happy violators of civil rights, who also had no problem macing or roughing up their targets.

The two officers exited their vehicle and approached both sides of mine from the rear.

Both of them had their hands on their firearms. I was told to exit my car and I was in the process of doing so when I was told to leave my cane in the car. I had been walking on two canes, using leg braces, and wearing two back braces. The very medicine that my doctors were giving me to heal my liver and kidneys had the side effect of leaching calcium from the bones and leaving them brittle. I left both canes in the car and was about to meet the two officers at the rear of my vehicle, when they ordered me to turn off my car. My Lincoln has computer-regulated shocks that deflate when the automobile is turned off. This caused the rear end of the car to descend about eight inches toward the ground. This alarmed the trigger-happy officers who thought the sudden movement of the car meant that someone was in it moving around. They asked me if I had a passenger in the car. "Yes, I did." But the policemen couldn't tell because my windows were one-way mirrored glass. I could see perfectly well from the inside out, but no one could see from the outside in. Lulu was ordered out of my car and both of us joined the officers at the trunk of my vehicle, where they ran our names to see if we had any outstanding warrants. I was strictly legit, but Lulu wasn't. Not only did she have a bench warrant issued by the court for failure to appear at her trial for driving without a license, but she also told the officers that she had two crack pipes hidden in body cavities of her anatomy. She was quick to point out that I had no knowledge of her carrying the paraphernalia on her person. That didn't matter. Two crack pipes to them meant that each one of us would be charged with possession of one of the pipes, and we were.

From what I was able to deduce from the conversation between the two officers and Lulu, they knew her very well, as in the biblical sense. They didn't really care about her bench warrant but were more concerned that I was having sex with her, or even worse, pimping her out for pay. "Riding around in this 'Ghetto Cruiser,' picking up white chicks to play with or to sell, is this a hobby for you or a job?" Stevie Wonder could see that these officers knew Lulu from some spots on the west side and that they had "spent some time together," on a regular basis. I felt like Reggie's son Sean. These trigger-happy thugs with badges were more concerned that I was sleeping with a white woman for free, and they had to pay to get her.

They didn't really give a damn whether or not a crime had been committed. Lulu was verbally assaulted by them because they assumed that she and I were intimate, and that thought pissed them off. If she would just claim that I was forcing her to have sex with me and others, they promised to get the bench warrant dropped. When she refused to lie on me, they took the threats and the physical contact up a few notches. After putting Lulu on the back seat of the task force cruiser, they returned to me at the rear of my car and handcuffed me. I don't know what they said to Lulu in the cruiser, but she was crying her eyes out.

The first thing out of the mouth of the driver of the cruiser was, "You hitting that?" To which I answered that I was doing her boyfriend, my mechanic, a favor by taking her home when my car started giving me trouble. The driver of the cruiser slapped me upside my head so hard that my baseball cap flew six feet away from me. I said, "Don't you see all of these people gathered around us? Some might construe your actions as police brutality."

The driver replied, "If we blew your brains out, right here and right now, somebody would probably give us a medal."

Reggie's son Sean was among the ten people who had gathered around the two cars to see what was going on. When asked what he was doing there at that particular time, Sean responded, "I was bored to death and there's nothing good on cable. Besides that, we're gathered here to make sure that nothing strange happens to Uncle Ben."

That really inflamed the driver of the cruiser and he forearmed me in my right jaw with his left forearm; then he forearmed me in my left shoulder with his right forearm. I heard my left collarbone break on impact and I ended up on the trunk of my own car, with the antenna poking me in one of my damaged kidneys. Many in the crowd used their cell phones to call the police department to report what was going on. Sean called my mother to let her know what was happening. Frightened by the outraged crowd, the two task officers called to the station and to other cars in the area for backup. "We've got Ben Holmes here on Belmont and Madison; his friends are giving us a little trouble, and we need backup."

After the other three police cars arrived, carrying two officers each, they dispersed the crowd and one of the cars took Lulu away. The blow to my kidneys made me need to urinate in a hurry. The driver of the first task car told me to piss on myself. His partner led me over to the side of the road, where the Women's Crisis Shelter is located, searched me from head to toe twice, re-cuffed my hands in front of me, and allowed me to walk fifteen feet away from him to an outside patio of that crisis center, which was surrounded by very dense foliage, ten feet tall. I couldn't see the officer and he couldn't see me. We kept calling out to each other so that he could be assured that I hadn't wandered off. Blood was in my urine and it burned like hell when I was finally able to release the urine I had been holding for nearly an hour.

Just before the backup cruisers arrived, when the first task officer forearmed me in the jaw and the collarbone, he boasted to Sean, "Remember how I used to hit them like that when we used to play football?" The officer went so far as to mention the name of the school he played for. After the backup crews ran the crowd off, while I was taking my badly-needed leak, thanks to the second officer, the first officer claimed to have found a pistol that I was supposed to have dropped, in a section of that block some twenty yards away, where I had not been at any time. Keep in mind that I had been on the opposite side of the street, with the second officer, taking that badly-needed leak. I called the entire charade bogus and insisted that they take me to the hospital. Many of the members of the crowd that had gathered around the task force car and mine were actually just getting off or going to the night shift at St. Elizabeth's Hospital. Many of these hospital workers were my old classmates, with whom I had reacquainted myself. The police were well aware of the number of friends I had at that hospital and decided to take me ten blocks to Northside Hospital, instead of a block and a half to St. Elizabeth's Hospital. The officers also needed to stall for time, while they worked out the particulars of their bogus story. Much time was spent fine-tuning their lies in the hospital parking lot, so that they might pass scrutiny. They had already attracted the attention of Internal Affairs some time ago. I got to see a doctor at Northside Hospital. He was told by the officers that all I needed was a few Tylenol for my back pain, and that is what he gave me.

From the hospital I was taken to the Mahoning County Jail for processing and lockup. It was like a family reunion at the jail. Most of the policemen were my former high school and college classmates. Several of the women working there were former girlfriends of mine or of my four brothers. My brother-in-law works there. When he heard that I was to be a guest of the county, he came down to see me and brought the head of Internal Affairs with him.

Everyone there was well aware of the reputations and the actions of these two task force officers. I had a host of blood relatives and in-laws there who held some decent rank, after twenty to thirty years on the force. Two of my former karate students talked to me about them making bids for sheriff and chief of police in the next few years. They even talked about rumors of a Black man running for mayor. In the next three years, all of that came to pass. Instead of being tarred and feathered, as the two task officers pushed for, I was actually treated as a celebrity by my former friends and classmates, who wanted autographs. Like the workers at Delphi Packard and St. Elizabeth's Hospital, they make up most of the workforce here.

Two representatives from Internal Affairs came to see me before I was completely finished being booked. Not only had Internal Affairs been made aware of the beating I took, but there was an even more important question they wanted to ask me. "How in the hell did I manage to get the gun back from the Police Evidence Vault, that was taken from the scene of my shooting while I was being taken to the hospital by the paramedics?"

The two representatives from Internal Affairs had to rephrase that question several times before I understood what they were asking me. Then clarity hit me like a ton of bricks. When Addie first shot me, she told the officers on the scene that I had pulled a gun and silencer on her; and that she had to shoot me in self-defense. Later it was found that she was lying and that the second gun was in fact another weapon of hers. That second weapon of hers had become an essential part of the case and had been logged into the Police Evidence Vault until trial time. Now, after the two task force officers had beaten me to a bloody pulp, they had the audacity to charge me with carrying a gun and silencer that had already been logged into evidence in another case. Then the silencer disappeared and reappeared, several times. Internal Affairs informed me that they knew just what was happening, and they smelled a couple of rats—maybe even six of them. Before I got to my cell, many officers in the county facility told me to play it cool, because the truth was already known and that Internal Affairs was on the case. I had confidence in them for a while, until they started to spin their tires in the mud and I ended up having to save myself.

Originally, my bond was set at twenty-five thousand dollars for the concealed weapon. Once it was found out that I had "disappeared" for twenty years, the judge said that there would be no bond because I was a flight risk; furthermore, the ATF had a hold on me because of the silencer. I was destined to sit there until trial time, unless Internal Affairs came to my rescue. I'd give Internal Affairs a reasonable amount of time, but if I had to go to plan B, I already had a very competent team of lawyers who won every case they ever had against Mahoning County.

One thing for damn sure, my team of lawyers was not from the local "Good Old Boys."

My choice of "legal" hired muscle was the Akron, Ohio law firm of Armbruster and Kelley, simply because they weren't of the local "Good Old Boy Network." While living in Cleveland and Akron, I heard nothing but praise concerning this law firm in regards to not selling out to the powers that be in Youngstown. If anything, "Arm Twister and Kelley," as they were affectionately called by the Mahoning Valley authorities, had a reputation for going after corruption here in Youngstown; also called Bomb City, Murder Central, Killers Are Us, Dodge City, the Wild Wild West, and Gangster's Paradise. They seemed to have a vendetta going with authorities in Youngstown, and I absolutely loved that about them. My enemy's enemy is my friend. I'd give Internal Affairs a little more time, then I'd call in the cavalry.

Thirty days in jail without the bail dampened any hopes that justice would prevail without a good stiff kick in the butt. Internal Affairs was playing the same old broken record: "Have a little patience, these things take time." I had five bullets in me. Both of my kidneys were full of lead. My liver was on a slow mend from being shot in half. The steroids I was taking to fight the Goodpasture disease were leaving me with the brittle bone disease. My blood pressure was nearly untreatable. I had just received heart surgery a few months before incarceration, and I had a bullet in my spine that was threatening to paralyze me. I had recently spent two thousand dollars on orthopedic leg braces so that I might be able to walk without help. I wasn't permitted to use the leg braces, the back braces, or the canes in jail. Even though I spent much of my time in Medical, I was refused many of my medications, because they were "unnecessary" or too expensive. Someone playing God here had decided that I was to die a slow, tortuous death, while patiently awaiting the results of Internal Affairs' investigation.

I had been the epitome of patience for twenty years, and I didn't have any patience left. I drew encouragement from reports from my private investigator: If the gun in question were ever in my possession, why weren't my fingerprints on the gun, the clip, or the bullets? As a matter of fact, no one's prints were found on those items. A report from the towing company, used by the police to tow my vehicle, mentioned that the rear, driver's-side wheel had locked up because of the friction from the brake pads dragging against the rotor. That same towing company mentioned that a brown cane and a black cane were among the items found in my car. The dark, tinted windows on my Lincoln were found to be impossible to see through, from the outside in. The police tore my car apart and found nothing. No drugs were found in my urine or blood tests at the County Jail Medical Ward. The crack pipe charge was dismissed after Lulu claimed it in writing. The silencer charge was dismissed after it disappeared again. There was another development; I was receiving death threats at home.

The task force officers' statements read like a comic book. They were great entertainment, but full of fiction. The officers claimed that they saw Lulu through my black windows and pursued my vehicle to apprehend her. They further asserted that they never noticed or mentioned any sparks coming from the rear wheel of my car. These same two officers claimed that they never saw any leg braces or canes, and that they suspect that the wide, back belt was used to hide the pistol in question. They claim to have searched me twice without finding a weapon, but also claim not to have searched under the wide back belt. My private detective gave me plenty to work with. This information was made available to Internal Affairs, but I wasn't waiting any longer. It was time to launch plan B.

My mother and my brother Jerry had my Lincoln towed home from the police impound a few days after the cops had it towed. I gave specific orders not to move the vehicle after the tow truck brought it home, not to start it up, and not to make any of the repairs that it needed.

If my turn came up on the recall list, let it pass; at this point it was better to let the car sit, preserved as evidence until trial time. There were policemen living all around my mother's home, where she had it towed. A longtime officer lived next door to my mother and another lived directly across the street from her. George Ross, the officer in charge of fingerprints at the Youngstown City Jail, had a father who lived ten doors from my mother. In short, these officers' presence insured that no claim could be made that the windows had been recently tinted, or that the rear wheel of my car had been mechanically altered to match my claim that the police stopped me because of the mechanical safety hazards that necessitated the recall notice. It was one thing to have evidence proving my innocence, and it was another thing to be able to preserve it. I was in jail and could not get to any of the evidence I needed to have "safeguarded." I needed someone in authority to take possession of my evidence before it was tampered with or disappeared altogether. I thought I had the right authority in mind.

According to the task force officers' statements, even though I was cuffed, I had to be restrained by them after they cuffed and charged "the white woman." Supposedly, that is how I sustained my many injuries at their hands. Again, as far as they could remember, I had no obvious physical ailments and fought them to a standstill, even though I was cuffed. They went on to say that they had some fear of me because I am known to be a very dangerous karate instructor. Mention is made of the fact that they were about to use pepper spray on me, when I relented and claimed to have to use a restroom because of my kidneys. While I was urinating behind some bushes, the first officer thinks that he saw me toss something that turned out to be the firearm in question. The second officer, who actually accompanied me close to the bushes in question, did not make that same claim. Even though the second officer was much closer to me than the first, the second officer said that it was very foggy and dark that night. "Visibility was at an absolute minimum."

Photographs were taken of that spot, under those same conditions, in the nighttime.

Expert photographers couldn't get a visual development that anyone could recognize. It wasn't much better in the daylight because of the thickness and the height of the foliage. It was obvious that the first officer was lying about what he saw, and the second officer was guilty of some perjury, but he was not about to commit to that particular perjury. At some point, these officers were warned about the penalties for filing false charges and for perjury. They were also warned about violating civil rights, which doesn't have a statute of limitation. They stuck to their basic stories, with minor "amendments" and "fine-tuning." I was still a flight risk and Internal Affairs was moving too slowly. My lawyers were convinced that I wouldn't see a bail hearing until I had been in jail for close to the amount of time I would have to serve if I had pled guilty, no contest, or had been found guilty by a court of law on the gun charge.

The estimated amount of time that I'd have to sit in jail until the bail hearing was six months to one year. I had only been there four months. My evidence had not been safeguarded, my bail had not been set, Internal Affairs was stuck, and there was no Scottie to beam me up in the transporter. It was time to reach out and touch someone through my writing campaign.

Despite the evidence that my private detective uncovered, and despite a total of five letters that I sent to Judge Durkin, who was the judge in this case, no intervention was made and no special investigation was conducted, other than that of Internal Affairs. They ducked out of the whole process when talks of budget cuts and layoffs became prevalent. Judge Durkin responded that he could not and would not "safeguard" any evidence for me until trial time. The Mahoning County Bar Association was referred to me when I contacted the Inmate Assistance Program at the Akron, Ohio School of Law. Next I contacted the U.S. Attorney at the U.S. Department of Justice and the Federal Public Defender Program; neither of them was even willing to safeguard my evidence for a while. The Northeast Ohio Legal

Services and several prominent local and out-of-town lawyers followed suit and also refused to save my evidence. I contacted Barry
Schect, of the Defender Program, also known from the O.J. Simpson
trial. He was too tied up to even consider getting involved for at
least another year. Finally, I filed a complaint with the United States
District Court, in Cleveland, Ohio. It was there, on March 13, 2003,
that they let my letter explain that my civil rights had been violated,
that I was a victim of police brutality, that exculpatory evidence was
being hidden, that perjury had been committed, and that I could
prove that evidence had been planted. I listed all of the responsible
authorities who take oaths verifying that they will defend individuals'
rights to fair trials, yet they all reneged on that oath when it came
time to get off their butts and do a little work. I stated my evidence
for my defense, where it could be located, and asked that the U.S.
Court seize that evidence and safeguard it until trial time. I also asked
for a reasonable bond and adequate medical attention. I had been in
jail for ten months, and looking at more.

To amuse myself until I got a response from the complaint I
filed with the U.S. District Court, I started helping others with their
legal problems. It wasn't long before police officers at the county jail
were referring "newbies" to me for legal advice. I had the dubious dis-
tinction of being called "The Jailhouse Lawyer." A very strange thing
happened; representatives of a faction of the police department came
to me, in jail, for help when they felt discriminated against by the
management. One officer in particular had a bad habit of calling the
"guests" of the county "slaves." Most of us were there awaiting bond,
and had not been convicted of anything. Nonetheless, this particular corporal literally enslaved the guests with subservient chores and
with his constant name-calling. None of the guards was as hated as
this particular corporal. He was a bastard to say the least, but there
was a deeper cause for his bitterness. It was revealed that he had peti-
tioned the county for years to make testing available for the sergeant's
position; all to no avail. So the story went, he and others had been
corporals for ten to fifteen years, with no chance of advancement
because the authorities wouldn't make the sergeant's tests available.
These were forty-five- to fifty-five-year-old men, with families, and

they couldn't even earn a decent wage to support those families. One of the better known reasons why these officers weren't making progress in their lawsuits was the fact that they had employed several local lawyers who were a part of the "Good Old Boy Network." These lawyers worked with the prosecutors, the judges, and the police. They were all friends and partners.

I had contacts with lawyers in Akron, who launched a surprise visit on the county jail, after having a representative from the Akron Law School Legal Aide verify my claims that the officers were abusing the guests, that the toilets were not functional, that the food was subpar, that adequate health care was not available, that medication was going to everyone but the patients, and that lawyers did not come to the jail to counsel the guests. There was a standing policy that you only got to see your lawyer when you posted bond and went to his office. For some reason the gangs in jail always had the medicines that the patients were supposed to have. The guests were locked down twenty-three to twenty-four hours a day, unless they became the "slaves" of the jail and did whatever they were ordered to do. All of this was in violation of the civil rights of prisoners who had not yet been convicted of anything. Knowing that my mail was being read and trashed, I had to smuggle my mail out with those who were being released. Furthermore, I had lawyers in Akron send me responses through other guests in my particular "pod." That incoming mail was disguised by putting it in envelopes addressed by individuals' girlfriends and wives. Perfume and lipstick decorated the incoming envelopes to further convince the prying eyes that this was nothing more than lover's mail. Impressed with my ability to get powerful Akron lawyers to come to the Mahoning County Jail to see me, and then to issue legal threats against the management, the corporals courted me in an attempt to use my contacts against the managers of the jail, who refused them the sergeant's test. An alliance was proposed, at three o'clock in the morning, while everyone else was asleep, by the very corporal who called the prisoners his slaves. If I wrote to the Akron lawyers and asked them to represent these disenfranchised corporals, the corporals and other guards would make things much better for the guests at "Hotel Mahoning." These guards promised to get the heat and air-conditioning fixed; they promised to get the toilets fixed; they promised to stop forcing us to wash our clothes in the washing machine that AIDS patients used; they promised us movies; and they promised us real health care. What we should have taken for granted, we had to bargain for. I showed the letter that I had written to the Akron lawyers to the corporal and he made sure that it was mailed, after showing it to several of his partners. Things got much better in my pod, but stayed uninhabitable in the rest of the jail. As soon as the Akron lawyers agreed to look into the corporals' complaints, things went back to the usual—just as I suspected they would.

Once the corporals' complaint was filed by the Akron lawyers, there was no more recreation time, there were no more movies, the showers went on the blitz, the toilets wouldn't flush, and medical care was nearly inexistent. There was a guest of the county living in my pod, who had full-blown AIDS, and he bled from the penis. Again, we were forced to wash our clothes in the washing machine with his. We were forced to use the same unsterilized clippers and razors. The guards used gloves and hand sanitizer, but the slaves were subjected to all types of infections by handling things the guards wouldn't. As I had discussed with the Akron lawyers before they agreed to represent the police, the detainees at Mahoning County were nothing but whores for the jail; once they got finished pimping us, they'd move on to other prey. I had anticipated that action and had never stopped filing my complaints through the Akron lawyers, to the U.S. Attorney. A dangerous outbreak of staphylococcus broke out in the entire jail, and treatment was refused because the medicine cost too much. I still have the response from the jail's doctor, in which he denies that there is such a problem, and if there is such a problem, get it taken care of when we get out of jail.

Things really got crazy for the next three months, and I must admit that I intentionally added to the chaos. The county jail guards were particularly proud of the fact that they had some heavyweight drug dealers in custody. They were located in my pod, T pod, so designated for "terrorist" pod. All of the dangerous killers and big drug dealers were with me in T pod. Many of them grew up with me and my four brothers, on the north side of Youngstown, and went to Rayen High School with us. I reviewed all of their cases. The ones my age called me "Cousin" and the ones younger than me called me "Uncle." Some of the prisoners and the guards actually believed that half of the prisoners and many of the guards were friends of mine, blood relatives, or in-laws. This suspicion became more prevalent when two heroin dealers got busted with four million dollars' worth of top-grade heroin. They were ten years younger than me and they went to school with my younger brothers. They lived behind my mother's home and their backyard adjoined my mother's. They had been stripped of everything and didn't have any money for commissary. They called my mother and asked her to tell me to give them something to eat until they got on their feet. I talked to my mother daily on the telephone, got the message, and complied. When the guards witnessed me handing twenty-five dollars' worth of commissary to each of the two men, they started calling them and many others "The Holmes Family."

Even more frightening was the fact that many in jail and outside the jail were beginning to call themselves part of "The Holmes Family." Released prisoners wrote back to me in jail and confirmed that there were several "crews" claiming Holmes affiliation or protection. All types of things were being done, in my family's name, and we knew nothing about them.

Several big-time drug dealers came to me for advice. One was a Dominican, who was facing seven years and forfeiture of all of his many assets, after a long plea bargaining arrangement. I made real enemies of the Mahoning County authorities when I told him that he should have had an interpreter present when he and his local "Good Old Boy" lawyer negotiated his plea deal. I was warned by guards at the county jail not to help the "big fish" get away.

Angered by the "little corporal" once again calling me and others slaves, I did my best to get the Dominican a reduction in time or a trial. He didn't know that he could change his plea to not guilty and demand a jury trial. Rather than go through that, the state reduced his time in half. I did exactly the same thing so many times that I became the nemesis to the DEA and the task force. The threats continued at home and in jail. A relative, who is a guard at the county jail, warned me of a possible physical retaliation against me, by one of the prisoners working for the police. That attempted retaliation came at the hands of J. Brown.

J. Brown was a half-wit, who was as strong as an ox. Born a few ticks from normal intelligence, his body compensated with phenomenal strength. He had been a contender in the Golden Gloves program, when he was younger, and was in the process of turning professional when he caught several criminal cases for theft, assault, stolen cars, and possession of drugs. He had already demolished several prisoners who made fun of the scar tissue over his left eyebrow, that looked as if he had shaven it. Some made the mistake of calling him "sissy" because of that eyebrow and paid the price. They got knocked out. I got along fine with everyone, including him. The prisoners had been locked down for twenty-four hours, for four days straight. Imagine how relieved everyone was when it was announced that we would be allowed to go to gym, and then take showers. No one was allowed to stay in their cells; it was mandatory that everyone went to the gym. I smelled trouble, but I had no idea that it was coming from J. Brown, whose case I had just finished reviewing. Many of the guests at Hotel Mahoning occupied themselves playing basketball or volleyball. Having everything medically wrong with me that you could imagine, I leaned against the wall and watched. Only J. Brown approached me, which was suspicious in itself. On the few occasions that we did have gym, many who did not participate did as I did and lined up on the "spectators' wall." This time no one joined me but J. Brown.

He didn't speak, except to say, "I got to fuck you up, Uncle Ben." Then he started swinging and I started blocking. He threw fifteen unanswered blows at me before I retaliated. The fact that I caught all of his blows on my arms and hands sent him ballistic. There was no doubt that he was a power puncher, because my arms and hands were killing me. After catching fifteen punches with my arms and hands, he was completely surprised to get dropped by a single chin-shot that he never saw coming. I was amazed that he got back on his feet immediately, only to have me plant my size 17 shoes in his chest with a sidekick that dropped him once again. As before, he got back up immediately. It then dawned on me that he was too dumb to feel pain, and that I was hitting him but hurting myself. I wondered if I had broken any of my brittle bones on his hard head. Abandoning his boxing skills, he attempted to run under me in a tackling effort. Bent over with his head in my stomach, I leaned on his back and bear hugged the air out of him. I then kneed him in the stomach and stood him up. Out of air, he was the perfect target for my left and right, edge-of-the-hand, kidney blows.

Devastated by the kidney blows, he could do nothing when I grabbed him by the back of the neck and the back part of the belt of his pants. With all of my might, I rammed his head into the con-crete-reinforced cinder blocks that the gym walls were made of.

Afraid that I had killed my "punching bag," I quickly walked away from him as if I had no idea what had happened to him. It didn't matter that I had reviewed everyone's cases in T pod and other pods; those bastards gave me up like the true Judases that they were. Before I knew it, there was talk of charges against me for attempted murder, or at least for aggravated assault. Fortunately for J. Brown, he only sustained a severe headache and a blow to his ego. Out of a pod of sixty prisoners, twelve claimed that I started the fight and only three said that J. Brown started the fight. The guard was conveniently absent at the time, taking a cigarette break. That's when I told the investigating authorities to review the two surveillance cameras positioned at each end of the gym. Fifteen minutes later the guards returned and carried J. Brown away. I heard that he spent the night in "the hole" and was shipped to the penitentiary the next day. A relative of mine on the force told me that he had to be shipped away before he started talking about who put him up to his attack on me. Keep in mind that J. Brown was a half-wit, and it wouldn't have been long before he started running his mouth uncontrollably about everything he knew.

I had something new to complain about to the Akron lawyers, who in turn filed complaints with the Justice Department. Because of the shortage of food and medicine, the whole pod had degen-erated into gangs or factions aligned with whom they had to, in order to survive. Robbery, assault, theft, gambling, and smuggling were the basis of the jailhouse economy, and activity in that economy wasn't reserved for the prisoners, but actually "enabled" by the guards themselves. These guards brought cigarettes, lighters, fast food, cell phones, and confidential information to anyone who could meet their price. If you had money on the outside, you simply put your order in to the guard of your choice, then you arranged for your partner, relative, wife, or girlfriend to pay that guard, at some mutually agreed upon location. Once payment was made, the guard would deliver your order along with that day's mail. I got some static from one of J. Brown's friends in T pod, after my run in with J. Brown. Apparently, he was Brown's partner on the outside. Several "handymen," or "muscle" men offered to hurt J. Brown's friend very badly for as little as a few candy bars and a pack of coffee. Most of these prisoners didn't trust the court-appointed lawyers, who invariably went the routes of plea bargains, no contest, and deals involving giving up someone else. They also couldn't afford a real lawyer; the authorities had stripped them, so they were stuck with me, and they had no intention of letting anyone or anything hurt "Uncle Ben."

Whether I wanted it or not, everywhere I went I was "bodyguarded" by the prisoners whose cases I was working or had already worked. The Dominican sent me a letter from the penitentiary, with a picture of his gorgeous sister enclosed. She was interested in meeting me when I got out of jail, in the Dominican Republic, and she would pay for the airplane ticket.

Her family and friends called her pretty, but they should have called her gorgeous. It seemed to me that it would be a while before I'd get to see her, because Mahoning County had other plans for me. I used my usefulness to the many gangs in T pod as a bargaining ploy to cut back on the hostilities; I was dubbed the "peacemaker" and the "ambassador."

Truthfully speaking, I felt more like a babysitter in a daycare center. Most of these rowdies were my daughter's age and some of them actually knew her. The older gentlemen had the bad habit of acting like the younger men, out of fear of being criticized and attacked for being old. After beating the devil out of J. Brown, I had only two other challengers the whole thirteen months I spent at Hotel Mahoning. These two challengers disliked each other immensely. They were the ultimate "muscle" of the pod. Each hired out on the inside as they did on the outside. I had no need to hire protection and told them so. Then each one independently attempted to extort commissary from me. That's when I hired each one to attack the other. The result was that they both were relocated to other pods and I didn't have to break my brittle hands on another hard head.

The "D.C. Sniper," John Williams Muhammad, and his apprentice hit man, John Malvo, were all over the news every day. Suddenly it was being revealed that my brother Robert Holmes had been in the military with Muhammad and was renting an apartment to the two assassins at the time that he turned them in for the half-a-million dollar reward. A totally unnecessary tidbit of information was included; former fugitive from justice for twenty years, Benjamin Robert Holmes had in the past used his brother's identity while on the run. As of yet, it was unknown if I knew these assassins or ever employed their services, but a connection was suspected. It didn't help that Muhammad claimed to have discussed some business with me on the telephone, and that my brother Robert was the one to put us together. According to the many authorities who interviewed me about this incident, while I was in the county jail, Muhammad claimed that I was to make silencers for his rifles.

The authorities plagued me about my former Muhammad associates of twenty years ago; was this "John Williams Muhammad" one of my old associates who had resurfaced after all this time? The authorities intimated that Muhammad and Malvo were just the tip of an iceberg, consisting of many cells in the United States, paid to carry out the will of Muslim extremist terrorists. According to the authorities some of the shootings took place in locations impossible for the captured duo to have traveled that far that fast. Furthermore, the shootings didn't stop immediately after the duo was apprehended. There were others out there taking orders from the same "managers." A deal was proposed that I set up an advertisement in some local *Gun and Ammo*-type magazines, or set up a website on the Internet to lure these terrorists with the promise of blueprints and parts for homemade silencers. Two hundred thousand dollars a year was offered as my beginning salary. My family had already been worried to death about my mother and other elderly relatives, when my brother Robert went public and granted television interviews about his relationship with the D.C. Snipers. There is no doubt in my family's minds that there were more snipers than just the two that were apprehended, because we received threats from them; most of those threats were directed to Robert's mother—my mother.

According to those same authorities, my cooperation with their sting operation would convince them that my family had never been in business with these assassins, and that we were as anxious as anyone else to bring the rest of them to justice. I stood firm with my response: "Who's going to guard my mother and father, twenty-four hours a day, for the rest of their lives? Don't forget about my daughter, my aunts, my uncles, and my cousins also."

No deal; I wasn't going for it. I didn't really give a damn whether the authorities believed I knew more than I was telling or not. Mahoning County couldn't keep me in jail much longer. I'd be out in a few more months, and I didn't have to put my family in danger to get out. You can imagine how all of this added to the notoriety of "The Holmes Family." The very thought that I could have anyone killed, from coast to coast, while I sat in jail, was enough to make most of the prisoners reluctant to aggravate me. Some of the prisoners I had "words" with were intentionally "spooked" by some of my closer associates in jail. Those associates of mine spread the rumor that I could "call in a hit" on anyone I wanted gone, and I could do it from the jail's T-pod telephone. Naturally, if I couldn't get my original target, because they were in jail or on the run, according to the rumors, any family member would be killed instead. The jokes abounded every time I used the telephone. Was I dialing in a hit? Was I going to reach out and "touch" somebody? Not every prisoner, nor every guard, took the rumor lightly that I could "dial a hit." Clearly, more believed the rumor to be true than those who didn't.

There were also the issues of the home in Seattle and the half-a-million dollar reward. What was Robert Holmes's property and what was Ben Robert Holmes's property? According to the authorities, that line had been blurred, and "Holmes Family" assets were just that. By the way, the Holmes Family was no longer a traditional family but a network of gangs called the Holmes Family. I had blood relatives, in-laws, and much younger cousins "doing their things"; I didn't know them. They got lumped into the "family." Anyone with whom my brothers and I ever associated, who now had any kind of a hustle going, were also lumped into the "family." Last but not least, anyone claiming to be in the "family" was lumped in.

News from the Akron lawyers representing those who wanted the sergeant's test allowed my friends and relatives on the force to come out of the closet and openly converse with me in the daytime, instead of through notes and midnight visits. I had done something to help them, and then too, there were those worrisome rumors about my dial-a-hit. Obviously, no one wanted me as an enemy, and most went out of their way to endear themselves to me. One officer assigned to T pod told his fellow officers and the prisoners that I gave him a ride in one of my three racing cars when he was a little boy of seven. Many more officers came forward with revelations about how they knew me. Before the week was through, it was revealed through a number of reliable sources on the force that I went to high school and college with many of the officers and their wives. It was revealed that some of these officers were present at the scene of my shooting, helped collect evidence, and interviewed neighbors who stated that I had been living in the home Addie shot me in for up to ten years. Some of these officers helped collect the very gun and silencer that Addie claimed I drew on her, causing her to shoot me in self-defense, supposedly. Some of these officers were bold enough to state that I had been searched many times on the night the wheel on my Lincoln caused the police to stop me. These officers assert that I had no weapon on me and that the two officers in question got the weapon that was already in the police evidence vault and claimed that some-how I had regained access to it and had it on my person the night they stopped me. They went so far as to state that Internal Affairs and the U.S. Attorney had launched inquiries into all of this. Their advice to me was to keep the faith. I had plenty of faith, but unfortunately my health was fading fast, and I was still in jail without the bail.

CHAPTER 16

Connected: Who I Met in Jail

The D.C. Sniper fiasco only added to my notoriety. Soon prisoners in my pod were asking me to talk on the telephones to their children, parents, and wives. The first thing they all wanted to know was if the snipers worked for my family, and next was what were we going to do with the half-a-million dollar reward? Many of the people I talked to on the telephones I knew from twenty years ago, some I just met since my shooting, and some I had never heard of.

There was the expected plea that I take care of their loved ones while we were in jail, but you'd be surprised how many women wanted to "get with me," and I was even more surprised at the number of "underground businessmen," who implored me to look them up so that we could make "The Yo," Youngstown, like it used to be. Everybody, everywhere, wanted to be hooked up to the half-a-million and whatever else the Holmes Family had access to—including assassins and silencers. Some were so bold as to propose alliances and ventures on the jail telephone. In retrospect, were they that dumb, that desperate, or wired?

Someone representing every gang in the area was present in T pod, and each of those representatives made sure that I communicated in some form or fashion that I'd look them up on the outside. I remember on one occasion a young brother talked on the telephone to his mother, then he came back to me with the most astonished look on his face. He then proceeded to tell me his mother's name and he told me that she ordered him to show "Uncle Ben" the proper respect; "After all, he was almost your daddy." I admitted to the young brother that I had indeed dated his mother for a long period of time, but no, he wasn't my son. She never even hinted at that, but she was concerned that he show the proper respect to someone who might be able to do him and her some good, somewhere down the road. The prisoners came and went on T pod, and many came back often. Often prisoners whose cases I had reviewed would write to me and let me know what was going on in other parts of the county jail, at the penitentiary, or on the outside. Many wrote to say that they were waiting for me to get out of jail so that we could embark on some of the "business" ventures we discussed in jail. It was not unusual for a prisoner to be shipped to the penitentiary, serve six months, and be back on the streets, while I was still in jail without the bail, but you wouldn't believe who I met in jail.

Before he even got to our pod, everyone was telling me about the "Jamaican." I hadn't been active on the streets of Youngstown for twenty years. Since I was outted by the shooting, the only places I went on a regular basis were to doctors, hospitals, and pharmacies. Jail opened my eyes to activities that were invisible to me and the casual observer. There really was an active and thriving underground economy and an invisible empire in Youngstsown, right under our noses. The Jamaican was discussed in the newspapers, on the television, and by the guards on T pod. The Jamaican had smuggled, into the United States, two hundred pounds of a very, high quality of marijuana. No one knows how he does it, but apparently he's been doing the same thing for years and has accumulated some real wealth. The Jamaican was in his apartment, near Youngstown State University, where he was known to set up shop, when one of his neighbors called in a complaint about the noise he was making while he was playing his reggae music. He didn't heed the many warnings the black, female neighbor gave him and went so far as to call the young, black sister a bitch. Well, that pissed her off more than the music ever could. She bugged the hell out of the police until they finally arrived. They found the Jamaican puffing on a huge joint of weed called a spliff, which consists of a couple of ounces of weed rolled in one complete sheet of newspaper. A search of the apartment led to the discovery of a hidden compartment in his closet that yielded the two-hundred-pound bale of marijuana. The Jamaican was also loaded with cash and tried to bribe the authorities.

Officers on the scene visited T pod on several occasions after that incident and just couldn't help telling the story to anyone who'd listen, and I listened. The Jamaican tried to smoke the spliff' by himself. That act temporarily left him deaf and blind. He was lit up. When he finally came down enough to realize what was going on, he made the mistake of offering the officers a bribe of two hundred dollars. The officers said that the Jamaican had ten thousand dollars on him and had the nerve to try to buy them with two hundred dollars. One of the officers made the crack on T pod, in front of the Jamaican, "I can be bought, but I don't come cheaply." There is no doubt that the officer who made that comment did have an affordable price tag, because it wasn't long after he made that comment that a group of drug dealers and users claimed that they made arrangements for him and several other officers to get paid with assets outside of the jail. The payoff was for a guaranteed way to get drugs into the county jail. The officers would bring cigarettes, lighters, and legal documents to the prisoners for a stiff price. They would not bring drugs, but they would provide a route for them to be smuggled. The visitor's window had a surveillance camera fixed onto it. For those who paid the proper price to the right people, the cameras were turned off or diverted long enough for the visitor to dig the grout from the bottom of the window and send whatever would fit under that window. Then toothpaste would be used to fill in the space dug out by the visitor. Pills of every type, heroin, cocaine, ecstasy, and marijuana all found their way to T pod in this manner.

After consuming the drug of their choice, the participating prisoners now had to deal with their "munchies." Six to ten people would combine whatever they had to contribute to what was called a "break." Sausage, noodles, cheese, peppers, beans, and just about anything else that was okayed by the participants was mixed together in huge bags; then it was split into equal portions. The break meal was never the same because some new ingredient was added each time. The Jamaican was the king of the break, because he had enough money to bribe the guards to bring him the ingredients he wanted from the outside, or the guards would allow his friends on the outside to leave a bag for him. I've heard the Jamaican say that he paid so much bribe money to the guards at Mahoning County Jail that he could have bought a new Cadillac. Often I'd be called upon to split the break up evenly because the Jamaican had funny ideas about what an even split was.

The guards there seemed to have funny ideas about fair and even splits also. They were paid a king's ransom just to let cigarettes and various foods into T pod, but they went a little too far when they decided to take whatever they wanted of the gold chains, the Rolex watches, the designer clothes, and the wallets of money supposedly "safeguarded" in the property lockup, preserved for the prisoners until their releases. It was common to see your own jewelry and clothing being worn by the guards. When I filed a complaint with the sheriff and the warden, a notice was posted, in which the guards asserted the right of impound.

I saw some of my own property being paraded by the guards, and some of that property was evidence I needed for my defense. This was the same evidence that I had written about to the Justice Department, in an attempt to get them to safeguard that evidence until trial time. The Justice Department literally dared anyone to touch my evidence, yet there it was in front of me, being worn by one of the deputies, just like they paraded any of the other prisoners' property.

In a Class Action Complaint, to the Justice Department, through the Akron lawyers, I had the signature of most of the prisoners in the Mahoning County Jail as cosigners to my complaints about the theft of our property, the theft of evidence, solicitation of bribes, perjury, extortion, case-fixing, smuggling contraband, and violation of our civil rights. The filthy living conditions, poor medical care, overcrowding, and lack of security were thrown in for good measure. I was no longer a single voice screaming in the wind. I now had backup. There was strength in numbers. The lawyers who refused to visit their clients in jail came running after they received responses from the Justice Department. All of a sudden, the warden, the sheriff, and the commissioners came to inspect the jail. Now the medical staff came through two to three times a day—to every pod.

When a lawyer visited a client on T pod, both the lawyer and the client requested my presence to discuss the Class Action Complaint.

The Jamaican had a lawyer come all the way from Jamaica to see him; he didn't trust the "Good Old Boy" local lawyers. The Jamaican ended up taking a deal that involved setting his brother-in-law up with a telephone conversation. So much for anyone looking him up after we all got released from jail. He was eventually shipped out to the penitentiary, and there were no hugs, handshakes, or goodbyes for the snitch.

A police officer was scheduled to get married, but went to an early grave instead, when he stopped what he suspected to be a stolen car being driven through downtown Youngstown, Ohio. The driver of the suspected stolen vehicle executed the officer without mercy or hesitation. There was a nationwide manhunt for the perpetrator, and eventually he was located out of state and returned here for trial. He had accomplices in his getaway. One of those accomplices, Kuzan, was twenty-three years old at the time, just as my daughter was. As a matter of fact, Kuzan was the first cousin to another Kuzan who was a schoolmate of my daughter from kindergarten to their graduation from high school. I knew this kid's whole family.

Kuzan, the "accomplice," was placed on T pod with the rest of the terrorists. He knew my daughter and told me so. He started hanging out at my lunch table, as many people did, including the guards. Threats of usurping power from the warden and the sheriff, by the Justice Department, made the actions of the jail managers a little more humane. Those who needed it got regular medical attention. Twice a day the nurse would bring my medicine and check my vitals. On one particular occasion, the nurse requested that I follow her back to the medical ward to see the doctor. Letting my imagination get the better of me, I suspected the worst. The super-extreme fluctuating temperatures in T pod left me with a cold all the time. I had an extremely low immune system, as a side effect of the Goodpasture's disease of the kidneys. Medically I had plenty to worry about, especially since the jail's medical ward refused to give me the same medicines I was prescribed on the outside. I never got to the medical ward and I never got to see the doctor. Instead the nurse led me to the same gymnasium in which I had the altercation with J. Brown. She told me to sit tight for a minute and then she left.

Totally confused and just a bit alarmed, I waited until a sixty-something-year old, whitehaired, white woman of three hundred pounds entered. She wore eyeglasses and a very jovial smile. She looked for the world like Santa Claus's wife, except for the black and gray Mahoning County Deputy's uniform. Getting right to business, she asked me what Kuzan was to me and why did I allow him to sit at my lunch table. "Is he one of yours?" she asked. I gave her the story about Kuzan's cousin being a schoolmate to my daughter. The jovial smile vanished and the demon in her showed on her face. 'That bastard helped a cop-killer escape and he's going to pay. Keep away from him and keep him away from your table. We'll deal with him in our own way and time; don't interfere!" I nodded yes in agreement, then she said, "Have a nice day," and went back out of the gym door. I waited until the nurse came for me and escorted me back to my bunk.

Kuzan took one hell of an ass whipping, as evidenced by his facial injuries, when they brought him back from the private session in the gym. According to the many rumors on T pod, one of Kuzan's fellow accomplices was also a guest at Hotel Mahoning. Supposedly, this second accomplice didn't make out so well; he was found dead the next morning, with a sheet suspended from the ceiling and tied around his neck. When I inquired of the authorities at Mahoning County Jail about any truth in the rumors, they refused to deny or confirm anything. Kuzan shipped out to the penitentiary shortly after that. While he was still in my pod, he ate alone in his room, and we had no conversations at all.

Constantly looking for something to occupy the time while in jail, the other guests and I spent most of the time we were allowed out of our pens gossiping. Sometimes the gossip proved to be frighteningly truthful. The Mad Bomber was all that I had been told that he was.

Majoring in math and science, the Mad Bomber excelled in both. According to him, his IQ was off the charts. He graduated early from high school, college, and graduate school. His hobbies were robotics and remote controls. I was tutoring a class of prisoners, who were interested in getting their GEDs while they were incarcerated; may as well do something with all of that time on your hands. This genius sat in on my classes just to see if I had any idea of what I was talking about. A few questions arose concerning geometry, trigonometry, and calculus. I gave the explanations that I had been given when I was an engineering major.

The Mad Bomber stood up and took over the class, "There's an easier way to do it than that," he growled. At first I was pissed off that he interrupted me; then I was pissed off that he knew a whole lot more than I did; then I was in awe of the way that he made it all so easy to learn.

After the class, I bought him a cup of coffee and we exchanged ideas about many things, and our conversation wasn't limited to math, science, or engineering. Possessing a true photographic memory, the Bomber only had to download schematics from the Internet, then access those plans and photos from his mind when he needed them. I was not in the area when the Bomber originally had his run in with the law. What I had been told about him wasn't half of what he told me himself. By his own admission, he was stopped by some policemen because they thought he was driving erratically after leaving one of the local clubs. Apparently, he called the officers something that they objected to and a fight ensued. The Bomber was on the losing end and also went to jail. After posting bond, the Bomber designed a high-yielding bomb from the many plans he had downloaded from the Internet, and added a few new twists of his own, just to make the bomb not defusable by the local bomb squad.

It's not clear whether the Mad Bomber planted many bombs or just one, but it is clear that several bomb squads, in the immediate vicinities, admitted that they were way over their heads in defusing this scientific product of criminal genius. Apparently, the Bomber was arrogant enough to use his own name when he sent a list of demands to the police department and to the mayor. Knowing who he was, and by his product what he was capable of, the authorities promised in writing that they would look into his list of demands and grievances.

Furthermore, it was secretly mentioned that no charges would be forthcoming, if he defused the bomb and kept his mouth shut, so that the authorities would not be embarrassed by his extortion tactics. It seems that the Bomber had an accomplice and partner in demolitions, who also happened to be on T pod on charges unrelated to demolitions. This character was affectionately called "Hawkeye Hymie." I know that Hymie is a slur name for Germans.

Hawkeye admitted that his name was Hymes and that he was German. The Hawkeye part came about because he was so deadly accurate with a crossbow, especially when he loaded his arrows with a homemade C-4 explosive. Long before the Bomber and Hawkeye came to me looking for employment on the outside, I suspected that someone in authority had put them up to propositioning me in some type of illegal activity. Later I would find that they represented invisible, underground factions of the various gangs in the Youngstown City and the Mahoning Valley areas. If I didn't recruit them, then they were to recruit me.

According to the Bomber and several guards, the Bomber was never charged for the bomb or the extortion demands. The entire event was written up as though the Bomber were an innocent bystander, who was willing to do his part as a civic-minded citizen, to defuse a very explosive situation. Supposedly, there were some, ignorant of the real facts, who proposed some type of recognition for this civic-minded hero, but the shy hero chose to remain anonymous. The Bomber and Hawkeye had a gifted cartoonist as a friend, who was in the habit of cartooning many of the duo's exploits, even when the duo asked Vinnie, the cartoonist, not to. Many of the guests at Hotel Mahoning made the mistake of conspiring in the front of Vinnie, only to see their best laid plans revealed in cartoon form for all the jail to see.

Fortunately, Vinnie had sense enough to assign false names to his cartoon caricatures, but the prisoners knew who they were, and by Vinnie's accurate descriptions, the guards knew too.

Vinnie was in jail for pimping underage girls, corrupting minor females with drugs, and burglarizing churches. Most of these idiosyncrasies were overlooked by the jail's population. It is ironic that what he was nearly beaten to death about in the Mahoning County Jail, by the prisoners and the guards, was not illegal. Vinnie made the mistake of cursing his elderly mother out on the pod telephone, in front of witnesses. Those witnesses spread the word to the rest of the pod, including the guards. I had witnessed child molesters, rapists, and wife beaters get beat down to the ground in jail, because there were some things the inmates just didn't go for. I have never witnessed such ferocity in administering an ass whipping as I did in the case of the inmates versus Vinnie the cartoonist. I still think that the prisoners were more upset over Vinnie snitching on them in the form of cartoons than they were offended by the way he talked to his mother on the jail's telephone. I think the pretended outrage over Vinnie's mistreatment of his mother was worthy of an Oscar. Some of the prisoners rationalized to me that Vinnie had beaten and stolen from his mother, on a regular basis, in the recent past.

Vinnie caricaturized me as the boss of three gangs, recruiting "talent" from inside the county jail so that I could put together the ultimate crime family. He did not fail to make use of the fact that my family had some exposure to John Williams Muhammad, the D.C. Sniper. Vinnie gave suspicious minds something to cling on to when he portrayed me as the manager of several cells of assassins, including the team of Malvo and Muhammad. As in the cases of Billy the Kid and Wild Bill Hickok, "When the legend is more interesting than the man, print the legend." Every bank job, every hit, every turf war, and every gambling joint that Vinnie claimed I was responsible for was thrown back in my face many times in the form of the inmates' and the guards' interrogations: "Well, if it isn't true, why would Vinnie tell a lie?"

Officer Dowd had just written me up as the perfect model prisoner, because I tutored those studying for their GED tests, and I started a non-denominational Bible study and church services there at the jail that was not limited to T pod. There were many gifted cartoonists on T pod. Once Vinnie perfected the prototype, he put the other lackeys to work duplicating the fictionalized account of an organization that didn't exist. Officer Dowd wasn't the only officer to come to me with a copy of the comic books. Someone was having them copied on the outside and sent back into the jail. The more I denied the accuracy of the comic books, the more the fiction seemed to take on a life of its own. Anyone observed conversing with me was guilty by association; they must be an integral part of the Holmes Family. Imagine how shaky it got in the county jail and on the outside when the story broke that my family was intent on taking over all of the gangs in the area. They'd either work for me or "take a one-way ride." Was Vinnie trying to get me killed before I got out of jail or what?

I actually had to "babysit" Vinnie. By that, I mean that I literally had to monitor what he said and drew. I kept him very close and gave him a place at my dinner table, next to me. It seems that Vinnie had no source of commissary except for what he was paid for his comic books. I must admit that the story lines were interesting and the artwork was exceptional. The cons must have actually thought that they had an inside glimpse of what I had going on by reading Vinnie's inside scoops. To prevent hostilities and deaths in T pod, and in the jail in general, I actually fed Vinnie what I wanted him to write about. My version of the comic book series depicted a kinder, gentler, more inclusive type of a network of mobs; in short, "The Brotherhood." This concept swept the jail overnight; everyone wanted a position in "The Brotherhood." Unheard of connections and riches lay in store for anyone connected to "The Brotherhood." There was a constant jockeying to get a position at my table, or just into T pod.

The comic series became analogous to Adolf Hitler's *Mein Kampf*, in the sense that everyone assumed that the comic series revealed what I had already accomplished, and what I intended to accomplish, once I was released from jail. The only good thing about this new slant that I caused in Vinnie's writing was the fact that networking, franchising, and brotherhood were emphasized instead of dog-eat-dog domination and turf wars. "The Brotherhood," whether fictional or fact, made more sense to everyone concerned than did a continuation of the warlord tactics of the past. Even some of the guards thought that a new and inclusive type of a mob would be better for Youngstown in general. Vinnie the cartoonist, the drug addict, the want-to-be, had conceived and sold an organization that only existed in his mind and in his comic series, so that he could get a few candy bars and a few cups of coffee.

I kept Vinnie loaded up with food. He became my shadow or I became his. The pen was much mightier than the sword. Vinnie's comic series actually smoothed over the hatred that gangs in this area held for decades. I was surprised that Vinnie, an Italian Catholic, actually reached out to other Italian Catholics, Mexicans, Puerto Ricans, Dominicans, and Columbians, in the name of Catholicism and brotherhood. According to Vinnie, the followers of Catholicism were already brothers in the faith, and that was their common ground. According to Vinnie, "We'll all have to stick together to survive Armageddon. There will be no future underground economy, unless we create it now. Without an underground economy, none of us will survive Armageddon, our future." Vinnie the drug addict had become a prophet.

Privately, I called him the "False Prophet," and he loved it. Publicly, the others and I called him "The Prophet." I saw no need in disrespecting Vinnie, especially since he now wrote his comics in a way that not only didn't hurt me, but in a sense, actually helped me.

Newly released prisoners wrote me in jail to let me know that they had visited dermatologists to verify their skin infections. They did in fact have serious strains of the Staphylococcus aureus superbug, and it was killing people. The infection was pervasive in hospitals, schools, the military, and jails. The former prisoners at Mahoning County Jail rained new and old newspaper articles down on me about the staph invasion. I got more mail because of the staph topic than all of the other guests on T pod together. Again, I went to Medical and begged the staff to do their jobs. I still have a hand-written response from the doctor and the head nurse, at Mahoning County Jail's Medical Ward, stating that the other prisoners and I had become hypochondriacs from reading the newspaper articles.

The corporals who wanted a chance to become sergeants had one thing correct when they called us slaves. Except for the commissary, we ate like slaves; we ate the leftover garbage from master's plate. The coffee was actually an inexpensive tree bark called chicory; no sugar was available from the jail. The oatmeal was served without butter or sugar.

We got meat, chicken, once a month. Imagine the inmates fighting over that. There was no salt for the boiled eggs. Stockpiling sugar, salt, or pepper for later usage was forbidden. The janitor told me that there was nothing wrong with the heater or air-conditioning thermostat. Tired of lying to the prisoners, the janitor finally admitted that the managers of the jail intentionally turned the heat or the air-conditioning sky high, just to torture the guests at Hotel Mahoning.

The janitor was willing to go on the record, if anyone cared; "These sadistic bastards turn the heat up in the summertime and they turn the air up in the winter time, just to make these poor prisoners suffer. I think the guards get some kind of a kick from it." The janitor also swore that the toilets weren't working because he was ordered to turn them off from the main pump. We were told by the guards, when we questioned these actions, that if we wanted things to get better in the jail, we'd better write our loved ones at home and beg them to pass the levy.

There it was for all to see; we were intentionally being tortured to make us influence our families to pass the levy, which would give these sadists raises and better benefits. I commissioned Vinnie to put his staff to work telling that tale in the comic series. I made sure that the lawyers in Akron were notified, the U.S. District Court received complaints, the warden was told that it was known that he was a part of the conspiracy, and the Health Department was contacted about the filth and the staph infections that the sheriff refused to address.

The guards also stated that there were more than enough of them to manage the jail. They had been intentionally overcrowding us in cells like sardines, for twenty-four hours at a time, just to make us riot. Vinnie and his staff were right on the mark, in his comic series, when he noted that these ingrates were the same corporals who enlisted the aid of the prisoners and the Akron lawyers, in their bid to get the sergeant's test reissued. But guess what? The corporals were mad as hell because they were issued the tests, but the dumb bastards flunked the tests.

Some of these ignorant thugs in uniform had been on the force for fifteen years, yet they couldn't pass the sergeant's test. Instead of blowing their own brains out, they took it out on us.

I took a special delight in helping Vinnie and his staff any way that I could. I intentionally ridiculed the corporals in the comic series; I pushed their buttons like they planned on pushing ours. They came at me full force, just as I planned it. The place really was filthy. The janitor had already stated many times that the managers tried to cut costs by having him install cheap fiberglass air filters on the furnace and on the air-conditioning. This resulted in a horrible fiberglass lint settling on everything and everybody; needless to say we were breathing death. What was thought to be allergies or colds turned out to be bronchial poisoning; the fiberglass residue clogged the sinuses, the bronchial tubes, and the lungs. Upon blowing one's nose, nothing was found in the excretion but blue and black fiber-glass dust. The stuff was also found in the eyes and the ears. It was necessary to have the eyes, the ears, and the sinuses rinsed every few days, just to be able to function. The air-conditioning was turned sky high again. It was freezing. Because I was taking a super huge dose of blood thinner, I was allowed to have several blankets, since my thin blood would not hold body heat. When the torture began, my extra blankets were confiscated. The guards knew that I was instrumental in Vinnie's portrayal of them as "Keystone Cops and Assholes." The air was turned up so high that you could see your breath. The blue fiberglass residue was so thick that you could cut it with a knife. It looked like blue fog in T pod.

My Goodpasture disease affected my heart, lungs, kidneys, and my blood's thickness. I had suffered from nearly terminal pneumonia a year before. I was next in line to have my ears, nose, throat, and eyes rinsed of the deadly blue dust. The gentleman in front of me, Chuck, started screaming like hell and grabbing his eyes. The nurse had put the hydrogen peroxide meant for his ears, into his eyes. She took him to Medical, where they rinsed his eyes to no avail. He was taken to the hospital for "professional care." Later he was released from jail early so that he could receive proper care for his eyes, and also in hopes that he would keep his end of the deal, by not suing the jail's medical ward. So there it was. If the medical ward were guilty of medical negligence or incompetence, you might get released early, for medical reasons, if you agreed not to sue the offending party. Chuck was long gone. The staph infection had already lowered my resistance, and the Goodpasture disease had left me with a poor immune system to begin with. On the night in question, the guards had again taken my blankets and turned the air-conditioning as high as it would go. I coughed until I passed out. The cold had thickened my blood to the point that my heart was overstrained trying to pump it. My blood vessels to the main organs of my body constricted from the cold, and my heart went into an irregular rhythm. My blood pressure went up to 225/160; I was unconscious and having a stroke and a heart attack at the same time.

I awoke several times and hit the emergency switch located next to my bed. I got no response for at least two hours. I passed out again and lost track of time. Finally, a guard came to my cell and told me to hold on; a nurse was coming for me with a wheelchair. I passed out again. When I awoke again a whole day had passed and I was in the jail's medical ward. That is when I was brought up to date on my condition. That is when I was told about the extremely high blood pressure, the irregular heartbeat, and the thickened blood. I did not remember that this same little nurse had been in my cell most of the night taking my vitals, until they got so erratic that she went for the wheelchair. I had indeed had a stroke and a heart attack. As soon as I was stable, the judge would set a minimal bond so that I could be released from jail to see my own specialist on the outside, just as Chuck was allowed to do when the nurse put the ear cleaner in his eyes. It was no coincidence that I had been in jail for thirteen months. I had refused to plead guilty to the trumped-up charge. Nonetheless, I essentially served my time for the gun charge and then some; the gun charge carried a sentence of six months to a year and a half. Because I was deemed a flight risk, no bond was set for me for nearly a year; then the bond was set at two hundred and fifty thousand; now the bond was set at a mere twenty-five hundred. That's two hundred and fifty dollars through a bondsman. My former private detective was now a bondsman and I gave him a call.

A few days passed before the judge did her job and set the low bond. My outside doctors actually wrote letters to the jail's medical ward, to the warden, and to the sheriff asking them if they were trying to kill me in jail. Even after the bond money was paid, it still took another two days before I was actually allowed to walk out of the jail.

I have a hundred blood relatives living in the immediate vicinity. They all have excellent jobs or very prosperous hustles going for them. Every one of them has benefitted from the lie that the Holmes Family was more than a family; it is an organization. Yet, my baby brother had to fly from Los Angeles, on June 11, 2003, and leave his birthday party to pay the two hundred and fifty dollars to the bondsman, because nobody else thought enough of me to pay it. There was no "Holmes Family." I was on my own. The cons in jail showed more sincerity when talking about the "Brotherhood" than my own family had shown the whole while I had been in jail.

Thank God for my brother Darnell and the few others who cared about me. My new motto is, "I love who loves me, and the rest can go to hell." They were all just a bunch of freeloaders.

When it was time to leave T pod, every one of the prisoners in that pod, and some of the guards also, lined up to hug me or shake my hand, as I walked out of T pod, on my way to Processing and Property. Five gangs were well represented on T pod, and they all said the same thing to me as I departed: "The Brotherhood is real, man; we'll hook up when we get out." My mother sat outside in the parking lot of the jail for two hours, waiting for me. It was not unusual for the guards to steal gold chains, watches, and designer clothes from the prisoners' property room, but why on earth had they "misplaced" my back braces and my leg braces?

Those items weren't misplaced; they had been stolen and done away with. Those items were a few of the pieces of property that I needed as evidence of my medical condition at the time that the cops beat the hell out of a fifty-two-year-old cripple, because I was chauffeuring an attractive white woman in my very, clean Lincoln. After having eluded the police for twenty years, when I did pop back up and they couldn't press any charges, most of the authorities felt like I had beaten the system. They said that they felt as if I had spit in their faces. The truly sad part about all of this is the fact that the policemen uttering this disgruntlement weren't even around twenty years ago. They had nothing to do with me or anything that happened in those days. As far as I was concerned, they were just looking for excuses to be assholes.

After two hours of pretending that they didn't know what happened to my back and leg braces, the attending officer gave me a receipt for the missing property and told me to file for reimbursement of those items. I was allowed to leave jail with the orange flip-flop rubber sandals that were mandatorily confiscated by the guards, when the prisoner was released.

Up to this point in time, no prisoner had ever been allowed to take the jail's orange sandals out of the jail and onto the street. I was the exception, because my orthopedic shoes were also missing. The shoes, the back braces, the leg braces, and the two canes were mentioned to the Justice Department as evidence that I wanted them to "safeguard," until my trial. I had contacted state and federal authorities, while I was in jail, and told them that if they did not take possession of certain pieces of evidence, that evidence would be stolen or destroyed, because it was powerful evidence that the arresting officers perjured themselves, planted evidence, violated my civil rights, falsely charged me, and nearly beat me to death for nothing. As I had predicted, some of my evidence was gone, but the attending officer signed on the dotted line. She wrote a statement confirming that certain items were checked into my property locker when I was originally booked, a year ago. She was concerned that I be reimbursed for the loss; I was more concerned that they give me some type of document admitting that evidence for my defense had been in the custody of the police, and now that evidence was gone.

Once I hit the streets, I wore the orange flip-flops everywhere I went. I was proving a point and bragging too. The police had kept me in jail for thirteen months on a trumped-up charge. They further violated my civil rights by stealing evidence I had for my defense, and they had no choice but to issue me a document stating that that evidence for my defense was "misplaced," while in their custody. The orange shoes said that and more. Anyone who had ever been a guest of Hotel Mahoning knew that the orange shoes were never seen on the street, and if you did see those shoes on the street, there was a very good story behind them. I had stayed in T pod longer than any who had been there. Most of the prisoners had done six months in the penitentiary and had been released on parole, while I was still locked down on T pod. I had been receiving letters from the representatives of the various gangs, while I was in jail and since I had been released. We couldn't talk to anyone on the telephone, out of fear of being recorded, but I read the hundreds of letters that were left in my jail locker until I was released. New mail came every day to my mother's house. The old mail and the new mail all had the same requests, from the local gangs and from interested parties all over the world: "We need hookups on silencers, fully automatic weapons, fake IDs, foreign bank accounts, remote control bombs, synthetic drug formulas, automobile titles, motorcycle titles, and VIN numbers for cars and bikes." The letters would end with, "Let's make the Brotherhood real."

Somebody was actually buying that crap that the Holmes Family had access to a whole lot, and that we weren't sharing with others. Many of the local letters had a common message: "The Brotherhood is a mutual thing, not one-sided, with a few having everything and many having nothing. Help us to help you. Remember the brothers you met in jail."

CHAPTER 17

The Brotherhood

Wherever Vinnie and the rest of T pod happened to be, they always kept in touch with me. When Vinnie got finished doing his time, in various places, he dropped by my mother's house to see me. Vinnie had been making ends meet on the outside by acting as the liaison, or deal maker, between the five or more gangs. In a "supply and demand" town like Youngstown, often making a very healthy profit was just a matter of putting the supply with the demand.

Gangs that weren't in the habit of "networking" for a mutual benefit would often pay a handsome finder's fee to anyone providing a demand for a particular supply. Vinnie wasn't the only one benefitting from the new and kinder interaction of the gangs. It wasn't unusual for these various deal makers to gain acceptance by claiming to represent me or my family, especially if it were known that these so-called representatives actually knew or were related to the Holmes family. Some of my relatives and some of my associates were making good money in my name, and I couldn't even get a ride from them to my doctors' appointments.

I had a thousand doctors' appointments. In addition to seeing doctors for my heart, kidneys, blood pressure, and brittle bones, I now had to see a specialist for the staphylococcus infection that had left black, bald spots on my head. This infection was not just on the scalp but throughout my body. Super doses of antibiotics and antifungals were taken in an effort to combat the superbug. The side effect was diminished kidney function, out-of-control blood pressure, and an irregular heartbeat. Walking on concrete and steel, in T pod for thirteen months, without my back braces, my leg braces, or my canes left my ankles, legs, and knees bowed, painful, and weak. My Lincoln sat in my mother's driveway the thirteen months that I spent in Mahoning County Jail. The Lincoln is still sitting in that same spot, and it may sit there forever. The Lincoln is proof in itself that the police did not look through my dark-tinted windows to see the young white woman, who had a warrant out for her arrest. The locked-up, rear driver's wheel is proof that the police stopped my car because the wheel was sparking fire near the gas tank. I still save the original recall order that describes this type of mechanical malfunction in detail. I had to wage an uphill battle to get the county officials to pay me for the orthopedic shoes and leg braces, because payment would be an admission that they had "misplaced" valuable evidence for my defense. Finally, they apologized and paid me.

There is a perfectly preserved 1970 GTO in my mother's garage, which my brother Carnell left when he died in 1992. The candy-apple red beauty would be a pleasure to drive to my many doctors' appointments, except that the car is a stick shift and I can't push the clutch down with my damaged left knee, ankle, and foot. The GTO is still sitting. My mother owns a 1979 four-door Cadillac. The car is banana yellow with a white landau top. The vehicle has very little mileage on it and is an authentic, original collector's item, which she will be getting historical plates for. This vehicle is taken out of the garage in the spring and summer only, when it is dry and sunny outside. If I didn't pay someone to take me to the doctors, then I would have to take a cab. This went on so long that all of the cab drivers knew me by my first name, and they knew which doctor I was going to, on which date, without me having to even open my mouth. Then the "Brotherhood" sent me a few guardian angels.

I was walking on crutches, until the warden paid me for my leg braces and the orthopedic shoes. When I didn't have the money to pay for a ride to the doctors or to the hospitals, I'd walk, even in the winter time, in the snow. Some of the very same friends and relatives, who were making a fortune claiming to represent the "Holmes Family," passed me as I was walking to the doctors, in the snow, on crutches, and many times the bastards had the nerve to blow the horn, wave, and speed on their merry way. Then my angels came.

Tish was a forty-year-old, gorgeous Italian woman, who looked like a twin to her twenty-three-year-old daughter. Tish had kept her weight down so well that she could wear her daughter's jeans, and she looked better in them. Tish claimed that the Indian in her accounted more for her jet-black hair than the Italian genes did. Tish drove a blood-red SUV that was always freshly washed and waxed. Tish first presented herself to me at one of my doctors' offices and told me that she was sent to pick me up when the doctor was finished with me.

Not wishing to look such a beautiful gift horse in the mouth, I asked few questions and assumed that my mother had paid someone to pick me up after my mother had dropped me off. In her car, Tish asked me if I was in a hurry to get home. I responded that I was not and we ended up at one of the local bars, known to be frequented by the remnant of the old Italian mob and their offspring. Some of the older faces I remembered from twenty years ago; they were there just to break the ice and introduce me to the new regime, many of whom I had already met in jail. One of the older Italian gentlemen said, "None of us has what we used to have. We gonna make this brotherhood thing work or what? We didn't come to the party empty-handed; we got a little something to offer. No strings attached. You be the judge. We'll show you what we can do, and if you decide to work with us, so be it. You can do a whole lot worse than having us for friends, Brother."

I had a few shots and a few beers. Some of us discussed my old racing shop, just one block away from this bar. I had raced cars with and against some of the gentlemen my age, who were present at this sit-down. Now it was obvious why the younger Italians came at me about "hooking up" when we met in jail. They were sent by the old heads. I went to high school and college with some of their parents.

Tish gave me her home telephone number, the bar telephone number, the number at her pizza shop, and two cell phone numbers. When she dropped me off at my mother's house, she was very careful in helping me up the stairs and into the house. She insisted on meeting my mother and the three of us enjoyed cups of coffee, as we watched the news and talked.

After Tish was gone, I stretched out in my bed and reran the day's events. Was Tish my driver and bodyguard or was she just my new prison guard? Time would tell. After all, I had been told that I could exchange her for a different model. My first few months out of jail were filled with appointments to five doctors, and trips to the hospital for blood tests for four of those doctors.

When Tish wasn't available, Tasha took me to my many medical appointments. Tasha was a twenty-three-year-old golden-skinned beauty, who was slightly related to me through marriage. She was the daughter of one of Addie's first cousins. Those cousins were well-represented on the local police force. I used to race cars with Tasha's uncles, who later became police officers, and I frequented a bar that her family owned. I knew Tasha's many relatives before I met Addie, and remained friends with my in-laws, Addie's cousins, even after Addie shot me. When I told Tasha that she looked like my daughter, she responded that she knew Benita.

Indeed she did. They were cousins; they had met at many family functions, and they knew many of the same people. The time came when Tasha told me about an older man she used to date. To which I made the reply, "I don't mess around with any young girls my daughter's age. It would be too much like incest. I would be more inclined to adopt you than to have sex with you." I quoted this line to her often; she and Tish were too determined to get me in the sack. Someone was pulling their strings. I suspected that they were part of a bribe to me. I wasn't buying any of this, except the transportation, which I soon began paying them for quite handsomely. Knowing that the time would come when they would want something in return, I made sure that I had not compromised myself, and that I didn't owe anyone anything.

Many other drivers were made available to me, male and female, of every possible nationality and color. I got the message. The Brotherhood was everywhere. It was every race, every economic background, and every educational background. The Brotherhood existed before me and it would exist after me. I had gotten past the crutches and the canes. The new leg braces that the warden paid for were working just fine. For a minute, I was even able to do without my "drivers." My brother, Robert, who received his reward money for turning in the D.C. Snipers, sent me a car; a Dodge Intrepid. The car was driven from Seattle to Youngstown, without burning a drop of oil. It made it to my mother's driveway and died.

Engine knocking, front end trouble, gas line leaks, water hose leaks, and a bad computer made me park the car more than I drove it. All of my doctors' appointments were only two blocks away. I could keep my "money pit" running well enough to go that far, for a while. I still wouldn't dare touch or move the Lincoln, until I found out whether I might need it as evidence.

I remember one of the rare occasions when Tish, Tasha, and I were together at one of my doctors' offices. When I walked out of the office and into the parking lot, for the three of us to get into Tish's SUV, people I used to know and had not seen or heard from in twenty years, yelled at me, whistled, and approached me in that parking lot. Some of them hugged me and some simply shook my hand, but all of them handed me their telephone numbers and begged me to call them. The first thing that came to my mind was that they wanted to beg me for some of my brother's reward money. Then I thought that maybe they were concerned that I might be able to hook them up with something or somebody. Then it dawned on me—it was all of the above. Someone told them that I'd be at that particular doctor's office, at that particular time. They had waited for me to finish my appointment, then they presented their sales pitches. I remember stating to Tish and Tasha that, "This is enough to make a person a little paranoid."

To which Tish responded, "Just because you're a little paranoid, doesn't mean that there isn't someone out to get you."

I laughed a fake laugh and seriously thought about what had just happened and what Tish had just said. Then I remembered one of Lying Johnny's old favorite quotes, "Ain't nothing wrong with being paranoid; sometimes it can be a survival skill."

The routine was the same all of the time. I'd call one of my many drivers and they'd take me where I had to go. At the conclusion of whatever business I had to attend to, the driver for that day would suggest stopping somewhere for a drink. In that way I got introduced or reintroduced to most of the underground businessmen, in Youngstown. They got to give their sales pitches and I got a chance to say, "Let me think about it, and I'll get back to you."

I was very careful not to become indebted to anyone of them. I didn't plan on being their slave.

I also didn't intend to break the law, or put myself in a position where I might be judged guilty by association. In Youngstown, you were guilty when the authorities said so. Here, there is no emphasis on law and order, or truth, justice, and the American way. Here, in Youngstown, there is only the "Good Old Boy Network."

The many letters from my Akron lawyers remind me of the way justice is meted out in "The Yo." From the time I first stepped into the Mahoning County Jail, I started a continuous correspondence with the lawyers in Akron, with the intention of filing class action lawsuits, over the violations of the prisoners' civil rights and the deplorable living conditions. Now that I was on the outside again, I received mail from many of the agencies I had contacted while I was incarcerated. My Akron lawyers had filed lawsuits with the Justice Department, over the HIV, tuberculosis, hepatitis, and the staphylococcus infections present at the county jail. The filthiness, the freezing cold, or the burning hot environments of the jail were investigated and found to be intentional, just as the maintenance man had sworn. The misuse and slave-like abuse of the prisoners was also investigated and found to be factual. The overcrowding of the prison and the day-to-day lockdowns were found to be unconstitutional. Charges that the guards were smuggling contraband and extorting from the prisoners was investigated and found to be factual. A gang mentality has been found to be instigated by the authorities here.

The guards have been heard trying to incite riots and fights among the populace here. The guards have been heard threatening the prisoners to get their families to vote for the levy, or else. It is also a fact that an environmental group and an infectious disease group have toured this Mahoning County facility, and they have ordered the cleaning and sanitizing of the air-conditioning vents, the heater vents, the cafeteria, the kitchen, and the washing machines. All of these areas were determined to be "dangerously contaminated," to the point of fomenting serious infections that might lead to illness and death. That mysterious blue and black fiberglass dust that was found in the vents of the air-conditioning and the heaters was determined to be clogging the prisoners' lungs to the point of no return.

It was found by the Justice Department that corruption and incompetence in Mahoning County made it impossible for the managers to continue, and that a panel would be empowered to operate the facility until further notice. The Brotherhood had shut down the jail.

CHAPTER 18

A Little Help from My Friends

Vinnie's mythical Brotherhood seemed to be turning into a reality. I couldn't get anywhere, in my solo attempts to bring the proper outside authorities in to visit the corrupt Mahoning County machine. Even the Akron lawyers insisted on having some cosigners, some co-complainants; in other words, some backup on these serious complaints against the county. There is strength in numbers, and I gave them plenty of numbers, almost the entire prisoner population of the county jail. But it still took time before the Akron lawyers felt that they had enough evidence to go to the Justice Department. Many from the county jail were subpoenaed, and many testified voluntarily. My letters were the main basis for the lawsuits, and those complaints would not have gone anywhere without the many signatures of the prisoners and the guards. I complained to various agencies from May 25, 2002 to June 11, 2003. I had suffered a stroke, a heart attack, and had been released from jail, after a stay of thirteen months, and the Justice Department was just finally bringing the managers of the Mahoning County Jail up on charges. Policing the police is a very slow process, and it couldn't have been done without a little help from my friends.

I was contacted by the media about the role I played in organizing our complaints against those who called themselves our masters. I had nothing to say but, "Justice was served." The so-called incompetent faction of the police force was laid off. Supposedly, the corporals, who couldn't pass the sergeant's test, were the scapegoats for the entire department, and they were indeed mad as hell. They were dangerously mad.

I decided that it was time to master the art of invisibility. I did not feel safe at all, with the large number of marked and plain clothes cars passing my mother's house, twenty-four hours of the day. I had attacked the system and disappeared. Many of the officers lost their jobs, while many others were transferred to lesser-paying positions. Some of them actually said what they all had to be thinking: "While we were torturing him here in jail, he was killing us." Every month that I spent in the county jail, I filed a complaint, which later became a lawsuit. I can't say who won in this whole process, but I can definitely say who lost. Every case that was ever made by the Mahoning County Sheriff's Department was reviewed or claimed to be. All of the neighboring police departments openly criticized Youngstown and Mahoning County for planting evidence, destroying evidence, filing false charges, and for abusing detainees. The comment was made that there are no civil rights for prisoners in this area.

I had pissed off the cops and everyone went into hiding, out of fear of revenge from the goons in uniform. Personally, I was trying to get the impotent media in the area to do their jobs, by further investigating and exposing these charlatans, who claim to protect and serve. The spotlight was on the entire community. We were all under the watchful eye of the scandalhungry media, and they found plenty to chew on. My second girlfriend in my lifetime, and one of my former coworkers in the garage at the Ohio Edison Electric Company, were both working as writers at the *Youngstown Vindicator*. I also had a female friend whose former boyfriend used to race cars with me. She was an investigative reporter for the *Vindicator*, and I had already given her many interviews and scoops about many things. I went to high school with one of the press setters and one of the engineers at the *Vindicator*.

In addition to all of these connections at the *Vindicator*, I also had a friend who worked there, whom I babysat and taught to drive a car when we were much younger. He went to school with my baby brother, and in many ways was regarded as a younger brother. I also had friends who worked for the Cleveland *Plain Dealer*, the

Pittsburgh Gazette, the *Akron Beacon Journal*, the *New York Times*, and the *Los Angeles Times*. I had more access to the news media than one man should. It was just a matter of time before the media contacted me or I contacted them. We had a very intimate relationship. I learned very early after my resurrection that the media can be your friend. Again taking a cue from Vinnie, I realized that the pen is mightier than the sword. Speaking of Vinnie, he was convicted of beating his elderly mother, nearly to death, with a metal foldup chair. At the same time that Vinnie was on his way to the penitentiary for that crime, his baby brother was being lauded in the newspapers for earning his Eagle Scouts award.

Because of the many lawsuits, the watchful eye of the Justice Department, and the feeding frenzy of the local press, many criminal cases in which evidence had been lost, stolen, or destroyed were dropped. Many prisoners were let out of jail with time served. Many of those prisoners didn't have the nerve or the money to pursue those who planted evidence or falsely accused them in the first place. Many of those wronged were just glad to get out of jail. They didn't give a damn about a lawsuit or revenge; they were just glad to be free. Two of Tasha's cousins were robbed and killed. All kinds of rumors abounded. Neither she nor I know yet what or who was behind it. I am comfortable in knowing that she is safe in her own special hiding place. I still hear from her, through her family, my in-laws. Tish gave me a painting that I had been admiring for quite a time. Then she disappeared too. Upon having the painting inspected and appraised, I was shocked at how much it was actually worth. So far I have not been in such poor financial shape as to have to sell it.

Once again my "money pit" automobile was giving me trouble and I had to call on one of my former drivers, whom I had re-met through Tish and Tasha. I had originally met "B-Boy" when we were in jail together, in the county; thirteen months for me and eleven months for him. He was on T pod the second longest time, and I was there the longest. I was glad to see the brother again, but I was alarmed at the fact that he was on his way back to jail for three years on a drug sales rap. He took me to many of my doctors' appointments, until the time came for him to turn himself in to start doing his time. One day, just before his departing time came, we were talking about his case, after he had just picked me up from my doctor's office. Somehow or the other we ended up at one of the local bars to get a few shots and some beer. An old classmate approached me in the bar and asked me to buy him a drink. I responded that I was broke and only drinking because of B-Boy's generosity. The old classmate, Ron, pulled a knife and said that he wasn't afraid of the sword that I carried in the walking cane I had with me. This cane was used for walking and that was all. Somehow this fool got the notion that I carried a sword in the cane and came after me with the butcher's knife.

A friend of B-Boy's, K-Dog, was present in the bar at the time, and he had been listening to our conversations. As Ron walked pass B-Boy toward me, K-Dog grabbed Ron from the rear, by his wrists, and held them. B-Boy slammed Ron in his left jaw with a right-handed roundhouse blow. Ron dropped like a sack of potatoes. As Ron attempted to get up, B-Boy broke a Budweiser beer bottle over Ron's head. Again Ron dropped to the floor. This time he was all the way unconscious, but he looked dead. That's when B-Boy and K-Dog were told by the manager of the bar, "Take that piece of trash outside and do what you want to him." My two wannabe bodyguards worked out all day, every day. They earned their livings as bodyguards, collections agents, bouncers, and general all-around muscle. They were more than anxious to step up to the next pay grade as killers, and it really looked like Ron was going to be their evidence that they were more than ready for that next pay grade.

B and K carried Ron outside by an arm and a leg, each, and threw him into the street. I followed them to the door to see that much, and then I returned to finish my beer and talk to the manager, with whom I went to high school. As a matter of fact, he married one of my first cousins. So here we go again. The manager had the crowd in an uproar when he told them who I was and what I had caused to happen to the county jail. I couldn't drink all of the beers and shots that the patrons of the bar bought me. Every five minutes or so, I'd go to one of the windows to see that B and K were still giving Ron the ass whipping of the century. Knowing that B and K would kill Ron, if I didn't intervene, I took four of the six beers that were bought for me, outside to the killers-in-training, and gave them two beers, each. The manager of the bar didn't give a damn about Ron getting his ass kicked in front of the bar, but he was a little worried about the police seeing opened bottles of beer being consumed in public, in front of his bar. He told the three of us to come back inside with the beverages, and we did. That's when Ron made his getaway. I figured that a forty-five minute ass whipping by these two would give him something to think about for a long time.

While I was at the bar, the conversation turned to Tasha's two cousins being robbed and killed. For some reason or the other, everybody in the bar took for granted that I was going to put a hit on the people who did Tasha's relatives. Many in the bar asked me in front of everyone there how much would I be paying for the job. Others offered to do the job if I gave them a silencer to keep; still others offered to do the job as an initiation into the Brotherhood.

These would-be-assassins only did in public what many had done in privacy; they wanted to be paid for what they thought they were good at: killing. Most of the people in the bar were old enough to have been to Vietnam. Some of them came home to steel mill jobs, General Motors' jobs, and Packard Electric jobs, but many never found meaningful jobs or couldn't hold a job because of drug habits, post-traumatic stress disorder, Agent Orange, or battle injuries. Many of these men were snipers then, and were still pretty good now. They wanted jobs in the fields that Uncle Sam trained them. Many of them were now among the homeless.

The complete night at the bar was filled with stories of stealth and killing, in Vietnam and stateside. None of this night at this bar was coincidental. I was brought here for a reason. I was brought here to recruit from the available talent. Even Ron's severe ass whipping was planned. If it hadn't been him who got out of line and caused himself to be made an example of, it would have been some other poor, drunk, unsuspecting soul. I learned from the patrons of the bar that Vinnie had been moved to an institution for the criminally insane. Months later, I was interviewed by the FBI, who wanted to know about my three gangs that Vinnie managed for me as my general. It was at that time that I was again propositioned to work for several law enforcement agencies. Again I aroused the authorities' suspicions by declining their offers.

According to those authorities, "You must have been made a better proposition by someone else, if you're refusing us." Yes, I had been made some very lucrative offers, but I had no intentions of taking those offers either. Poor health and ailing parents did not leave me in a position to take any job, especially the more dangerous ones. The incident at the bar was the last time that I laid eyes on B-Boy or K-Dog. I do know for a fact that they are locked up. They did the best they could for Uncle Ben, when they could do it. Which just happened to be an occasional ride and a little muscle, when it was needed. At least they prevented me from having to break my brittle hands on somebody's head again. I continued to get a little help from my friends. In most cases I didn't ask for the help; in some cases I didn't know of the help until much later. The important fact is that this aid was directed by managers who wanted me protected, but indebted to them. In most instances I had some idea who sent me a care package or a bodyguard. In a few other instances, I had no clue who my benefactor was.

I looked up my friend "P," the private detective. He had gone from that line of work to bondsman to restaurateur. His restaurant was the perfect place for buying, selling, or trading information. The strange mixture of law enforcement and hustlers there only worked because the owner demanded that his rules be adhered to, regardless of who you were. P confided to me that much of what he had accomplished was only because his business associates knew of his closeness to me. It was assumed that he was in contact with me always, even though I was relatively invisible to everyone else. Knowledge of my medical problems was common, and served as the most likely excuse of my absences, so often. That fact allowed family, friends, and associates to reap benefits in my name, without my knowledge or permission.

These people were working this "Brotherhood" thing to death, and they were making serious money from it. No wonder I received an occasional care package at my mother's house from some anonymous benefactor. They all owed me. I really didn't mind if they prospered from being connected to the "Brotherhood." No one was able to commit me to any serious obligations. No one could speak for me. I alone reserved that power. To me the Brotherhood was still a figment of Vinnie's imagination, that some were slick enough to use to their advantage, when seeking hookups in waters and territories, heretofore, taboo to them.

The time would come when I would find out that the "Brotherhood" was more factual than I thought. There were "outsiders," who thought that this area was fragmented, weak, and ready for taking. Legal gambling had been voted down here several times, but there still existed a very prosperous "underground" gambling network here. A very large number of weapons find their way from this area to New York and Chicago. For an area this small, we have an unusually brisk and profitable drug trade going here. There was a time when the different factions of the Italian mob, in this area, had killed off or informed on each other, to the point of near extinction. It was at that time that the remnant of those Italian factions sold franchises to black drug dealers who were rich compared to the cash-poor Italian remnants. Keeping that in mind, outsiders see the "None Italians" generating large incomes, but they do not see a strong united front to repel invaders. They were wrong. Just because the invaders or the outsiders didn't see the weapons, the soldiers, and the warlords didn't mean that they didn't exist. It simply meant that those forces had learned the benefit of being invisible. As soon as it was learned that an invasion was probable, every major gun supplier in the area was burglarized.

The sensational news accounts about the gun burglaries were enough in themselves to cause the would-be invaders to rethink that whole "invasion thing." The theft of so many weapons, at one time, sent a message: "There is nothing in this area for outsiders but death." The next step for the outsiders was to attempt to feel out how much "heart" we had in this area. In other words, if we had guns, would we use them? Unknown to me at the time, a dinner was to occur at P's place, just for the purpose of networking; associates coming together with some mutual business interaction in mind.

The dinner was later revealed to me to be a type of a peace treaty between some of the outsiders and some of the locals, who sided with P. P had told me to wear my best suit and he'd pick me up promptly at 9:00 p.m. Supposedly, he simply needed to be seen with me to get some assholes off his back. P's police friends had the security in hand. Armed and in uniform the officers searched everyone who came into the restaurant. I was introduced to some ladies and some gentlemen; then I was ushered to a table in the back, where I sat alone, while P talked in whispers to his guests. In less than ten minutes, he walked back to my table and asked me what I wanted to eat. I told him. He went back to the guest table, shook the strangers' hands, and the guests waved at me as they left.

The message was so clear that Stevie Wonder could have seen it: Ben Holmes stands with his friend P, and we have the hustlers and the police on our side. I knew for a fact that P had a lot of dirt on a lot of policemen and politicians, from his days as a serious private investigator. I also know that he used hookers, almost exclusively, in gathering his information. Add to this mix the fact that P was a pimp before he took up investigating, and you really can't even imagine just how much dirt he has on whom. No wonder he climbed so far, so fast.

I had no problem playing P's game, for a little while anyway. So long as it didn't cost me too much. I had no problem letting him be king, and that made me the king maker. What I really needed and continued to seek was invisibility, but it was necessary to surface, from time to time. Just to make the world stand up and take notice of the fact that Ben Holmes stood with his brother P, P insisted that I drive his red Lincoln for a while since he had plenty of transportation. I stashed the red Lincoln in a garage that only I knew of and got in another vehicle that I borrowed from time to time. That vehicle had totally blacked-out windows. Talk about being invisible! On one of the few occasions that I actually brought P's car out into the open, I stopped at one of the local spots where cars are hand-washed. One of the car detailers was a good friend to Lying Johnny, my old friend from whom I bought the ice-blue Lincoln, which was still sitting in my mother's backyard. This car detailer, Earl, thought that I had bought another Lincoln, while the one that I bought from John was going to waste in my mother's backyard. Earl made some comment to the effect that I must have conned another sucker out of their car, like I conned Lying Johnny out of his. Stunned by this verbal assault, from an associate whom I had hauled in my vehicles, free of charge, too many times to count, I watched in further amazement, as Charmaine, another car detailer working alongside Earl, dropped her bucket to the ground and delivered a crushing roundhouse blow to Earl's heart, which caused him to collapse as if he had been shot. Charmaine may have weighed one hundred pounds, soaking wet. After chastising Earl for harassing Uncle Ben, she turned back to her work. Even though she wasn't the detailer to work on the car I was driving, I tipped her ten dollars anyway. I was pleased with the show; after all, there wasn't anything on cable.

I know for a fact that Earl and Charmaine recognized P's red Lincoln that I was driving. Earl just couldn't resist the urge to act a fool, and Charmaine couldn't resist the urge to put him in check. Besides acting a fool, Earl was also checking me out to see what I was made of.

He, like many others, wanted to know if and how I had changed in twenty years. Earl wanted to know what he could get away with when I didn't have anyone to fight my battles. At the age of fifty-six, he still had a thirteen-year-old's bully attitude. He and everyone in the area had heard about the time I had to run a young brother's head into the walls of the jail, but everyone had also heard that I suffered a stroke and a heart attack in jail. It had also become common knowledge that certain entities had provided me some minor protection, and that several good ass whippings had been given to those who threatened me.

I guess the whole town was concerned about what I would do next. There were rumors that the DEA, the FBI, and ATF had attempted to recruit me. Then there was the hot story about my brother collecting the reward for the D.C. Snipers, and what my role was in all of that. But what really concerned the local authorities and the local underground economy was whether or not I would openly step into the leadership role that was waiting for me in the

Brotherhood. When and if my health permitted, would I come out of the shadows and be more visible in the Brotherhood? Many who wanted to "barter" with me refused to deal with anyone else claiming to represent me. These relatives, friends, and associates knew that nothing could be believed until you heard it from my mouth, personally. As my health improved and I became more visible, more of my old friends came out of hiding as well. An old racing buddy and classmate was now running for Congress, and it looked as if he might win. Another classmate was the son of a very successful Congressman. Still another classmate was now a judge. I had many relatives, in-laws, and friends in the Mahoning County Sheriff's Department and the Youngstown Police Department. In addition to that, I went to high school or college with the families who owned most of the businesses in this area. When you get into the connections I made in the areas of basketball, football, boxing, and martial arts you get into uncountable numbers. Among these acquaintances were many who represented the media, publishers, and movie producers. Everyone wanted to know my secrets, and book deals and movies were talked about. But when it came time to actually make it happen, those interested claimed that they had been threatened by some of the authorities in the area, to the point that they gave up on the project.

I still have a pristine copy of the *Youngstown Vindicator*, November 3, 2000, in which Mahoning County Prosecutor Paul Gains is featured on the front page stating that he finds it offensive that I have avoided prosecution for all of these years and now return and expect to profit from it. When it was brought to his attention that the FBI and other authorities were satisfied that I was a victim and that there never was anything to charge me with in the past, present, or future, the only thing Prosecutor Gains could say was, "Oh."

I recall the astonished look on Prosecutor Gains's face when there was a discussion about turning audio tapes over to the FBI, which I had made twenty years ago, of some crooked policemen. I guess my bringing in the Justice Department, in 2003, to investigate the Mahoning County Jail, was too embarrassing to the authorities here, especially since the media has been having a feeding frenzy reporting on the corruption, case-fixing, police brutality, and evidence tampering in the past as well as in the present.

I continued my correspondences with the Justice Department and the media, when my health permitted it. After being released from jail, I immediately contacted my former doctors and some new ones. The staphylococcus infection caused me to get three minor surgeries to remove the infection because the antibiotics were ineffective. I had to have surgery on the outside of both jaws and the back of my neck. Large abscesses had formed in those spots, as well as on the scalp. So much for the jail's doctor's evaluation. I still have it in pristine condition, for any who care to read it. Other than those minor surgeries, I had to get a hernia operation to repair my abdomen. When I originally got patched up from the gunshot wounds to the stomach, I was supposed to return for more surgery, but I ended up in jail for thirteen months. After jail, my intestines were protruding through three separate holes in the wall of my abdomen. I also spent a long time rehabilitating the use of my ankles, legs, and knees.

Thirteen months walking on steel and concrete without my canes, leg braces, or back braces had nearly deformed my skeletal system permanently. In between doctors and hospitals, I caught up on the local news, past and present. I still had an overwhelming number of friends in the area because I had been a good friend to them. There is no doubt that the best friend of all of them was my former girlfriend, Joanna. She was the third girlfriend of my entire life. We went to high school and college together. She is a news junkie and keeps all types of interesting information about the area. In between medical treatments, I submerged myself in her boxes of newspaper articles. I slowly continued to heal, with a little help from my friends.

CHAPTER 19

To Protect and Serve

J oanna had a lovely home, complete with a library, a business office, and a computer room. Sitting in her "command center," I was surrounded by word processors, computers, fax machines, and income tax forms. I usually occupied my time in the command center reading the old newspaper articles. The box of articles that really interested me was labeled "To Protect and Serve." This was the motto of those authorities in the area who were a part of law enforcement. The box didn't just contain articles about the police, it also contained articles about the local politicians, judges, prosecutors, and attorneys in the immediate area.

On September 16, 2007, the *Youngstown Vindicator* ran an article about the thirtieth anniversary of "Black Monday," the day five thousand excellent-paying, steel mill jobs were permanently eliminated, when Sheet and Tube announced that it was closing its local works and moving to Chicago. This was the beginning of the end. A domino effect ensued, as business after business, legal and underground, slowly disintegrated. Most of the gambling, prostitution, and hot goods rackets depended on the steady flow of cash from the mill jobs.

Most of the mill employees had tabs at the local bars that were strategically located around the mills to be of the utmost convenience to the "spenders." "One-stop shopping" was a phrase often heard in the confines of the local pubs. Thousands of more jobs were lost as businesses continued to fail in rapid succession. The community was in a constant struggle for survival, as thousands of jobs and tax payers relocated.

On August 29, 2007, there appears an article in the *Youngstown Vindicator* stating that Youngstown is the poorest midsize city in the U.S.A. While the locals argue that we are not the poorest, they can only argue that we are at worst the seventh poorest. This area has remained among the poorest ever since Black Monday, of 1977. According to the FBI, in an article that appears in the *Youngstown Vindicator*, on November 19, 2007, Youngstown is also the fifteenth most dangerous city. The year before that we were ranked ninth, and at other times we have been ranked as high as fourth. The old days of mob wars in the area caused the area to be called Bombtown, Murder Capital, Dodge City, and the Wild Wild West. Those nicknames of the past have been revisited upon us, presently. It has been a long time since citizens in the area have called our police officers honest or trustworthy. In an article that appears in the *Youngstown Vindicator*, on December 21, 2002, fifty-nine percent of the nation has ranked police officers as the sixth most ethical and honest professionals. Those statistics vary locally, depending on the severity of the police scandals, in the immediate vicinity.

In an article that appears in the *Youngstown Vindicator*, on November 21, 2007, our city prosecutor just got a raise from $66,707 to $73,595. This is approximately what my mailman makes. The same article shows that our police chief just got a raise from $85,354 to $95,627. Just before the very recent Delphi-Packard buyouts, this wage was quite common among the workers at that wire-making facility. The facts that our prosecutors make the same thing as the mailman, and that the police chief makes the same thing as assembly-line workers, have been used to rationalize our authorities taking bribes or indulging in income producing activities in questionable underground circles.

An article appears in the *Youngstown Vindicator*, on August 25, 2005, in which it is mentioned that Youngstown's former chief deputy at the Mahoning County Sheriff's Department, Frank Carbon, has been sentenced to forty-one months in federal prison for selling marijuana and cheating on his taxes. Carbon pleaded guilty to conspiracy to possess with intent to distribute 1.1 to 3.3 tons of marijuana, from early 2000 throughout 2001. The FBI states in the *Youngstown*

Vindicator, on April 15, 2008, that Mahoning County Jail guard, Ivey J. Maybou, figured that he could make enough extra money to pay off some debts by selling cocaine to inmates. Once Maybou was in custody, he admitted everything. According to the article that appears in the *Youngstown Vindicator*, on March 26, 2008, Robert G. Anderson's salary of $30,742, as a corrections officer for the Martin P. Joyce Juvenile Justice Center, just wasn't enough for him. He augmented that salary by trafficking in cocaine all over the city. Not only must he serve three concurrent four-year prison terms, but he also must surrender assets, including three automobiles used in the drug trafficking.

In the August 28, 2001 article, in the *Youngstown Vindicator*, Jennifer Carroll-Kirr, assistant county prosecutor for Warren's Trumbull County, recommended that former Mahoning County deputy, Robert Gore, receive two years in prison, in exchange for his three guilty pleas to trafficking in cocaine. For Gore's guilty pleas, the assistant prosecutor dismissed three felony charges of trafficking in cocaine and a count each of engaging in a pattern of corrupt activity and conspiracy to drug trafficking. If convicted of all charges, Gore could have faced up to fifteen years in prison. One of his co-conspirators, Cheryl Bricker, also a former Mahoning County deputy, received a slap on the wrist, after being indicted on eight counts of trafficking in cocaine and engaging in a pattern of corrupt activity and conspiracy to drug trafficking. Naturally, it is presumed that both of the defendants aided in investigating others in their conspiracy, in exchange for such light sentences.

In the October 3, 2007 edition of the Youngstown Vindicator, a drug dealer and three Columbus, Ohio, police officers conspired to steal two pounds of cocaine from another drug dealer with plans to sell it and share the profit. The conspirators also planned to rob two hundred thousand dollars in drug money from some other unsuspecting soul. The head of the conspiracy, Officer Sean Beck, went so far as to take forty-five prescription painkillers from a victim he stopped for a traffic check, and then had his drug-dealer buddies sell them. Beck also extorted 7,500 dollars from two drug dealers, in exchange for dropping an investigation of them.

All of this pales in comparison to Mahoning County Sheriff Phil Chance's actions.

Chance had a very bad habit of raiding the larger drug dealers in the area. The large amounts of confiscated drugs and money would be replaced with flour and a much smaller amount of money. The drugs would be sold for a very healthy profit by another drug dealer for Sheriff Phil Chance. This went on for years until the FBI stepped in with informants who were wired. Major Budd and his cohorts at the Mahoning County Jail had their reign of terror ended, when one of their own snitched on them to save his own neck. According to the August 15, 2007 article, and another dated November 17, 2005, Major Michael J. Budd was second in command at the Mahoning County Sheriff's Department, when he and eight other officers took it upon themselves to beat the prisoners as if they were slaves. The civil-rights inmate abuse case is only one of many that I wrote the Justice Department and the Akron lawyers about. It took a long time coming, but justice was finally served. Budd and his goons in uniform were convicted of beating three inmates. I know for a fact that there were many more. There were also many female inmates who were forced to surrender sexual favors to the goons in uniform. Major Budd is still doing his eight years, with a projected release date of August 4, 2012.

In the midst of all of this nonsense, the Mahoning County Sheriff's Department somehow influenced a local motorcycle shop, frequented by most of the bikers in this area, to contribute twelve fully dressed Harley-Davidson Hogs to the police department, for its motorcycle patrol program. The *Vindicator* mentions, on July 9, 2005, that "Black Cops Against Police Brutality" says that black officers have to challenge their white counterparts to ensure that justice is dispensed fairly to all. In Champion, Ohio, the spokesman for the organization, De Lacy Davis, stated that all police take an oath to protect and serve. He went on to say that that pledge should be applied with balance and fairness. While race shouldn't matter, it does. Davis stated that black officers often let white officers get away with abuse, even in predominantly black communities, because even there the whites control the police departments.

He went on to say that police culture hasn't changed much in the last one hundred years.

Nearby Pittsburg, Pennsylvania, offered a solution to the growing problem of domestic violence by officers. In the *Pittsburgh Post-Gazette*, dated October 19, 2007, the Pittsburg Police Bureau unveiled new policies on domestic violence by officers, but women say that the penalties are not strong enough. A call is being made that domestic violence by officers will no longer be met with a slap on the wrist but will be met as committed by any other criminal, including punishment to fit the crime and permanent firing from the police force. No one is above the law, especially the policeman. Who polices the police?

Locals call for the resignation of Lisbon's Columbiana County Sheriff, David L. Smith, after he was charged with operating a vehicle while intoxicated. The Ohio State Highway Patrol also cited Smith for speeding and driving outside marked lanes. The patrol reported that Smith had just left a dinner at the Buckeye State Sheriff's Association, a professional law enforcement group, in Columbus, Ohio. That article appears in *The Vindicator*, October 14, 2007. Another article in *The Vindicator*, dated April 19, 2008, states that Smith was sentenced to twenty days in jail, with seventeen of those days suspended. He will remain as the sheriff. Who polices the police? The easier the authorities are on one of their own, the worse it gets. *The Vindicator* asserts in the March 28, 2008 edition that a couple has filed a lawsuit stemming from an August shooting into their home, by an off-duty Mahoning County deputy sheriff, who was aiming for a raccoon. An article appears in the *Buckeye Review*, on January 30, 2008, in which the writer asserts that seven counts of felonious assault, charged against Brandon C. Jackson, were dismissed because the prosecutor claims that she just received exculpatory evidence that might prove the defendant's innocence. The writer of the article presents a convincing argument that the prosecutors of the case had the exculpatory evidence for the two years that the case lethargically crawled forward.

In yet another startling case from Youngstown, involving the police, *The Youngstown Vindicator*, on April 3, 2008, mentioned the possibility of cheerleading coach, Angela J. Jones, filing excessive-force charges against officers who roughed her up and arrested her for pushing a swinging door into one of the officers as she entered Chaney High School, to coach some of the students. Students went to court to testify that the officers body slammed the woman without provocation. Jones actually took the case to court instead of plea bargaining for her probation. A jury found her not guilty of all charges, which leaves the door wide open for her to file civil-rights abuse charges against the officers.

In a case that is too sad to be true, but is, *The Vindicator* ran an article about eightyseven-year-old Mary Rush, who lived alone and suffered from mild dementia. The poor old woman accidentally locked herself out of her home and the neighbors heard her crying in the cold rain, on her porch. Those neighbors continuously telephoned the police, who actually responded on the scene but refused to investigate or do a walk around on the woman's property, because it was raining and the officers didn't want to get wet. The elderly Mrs. Rush was found the next morning, dead from a cut she sustained, when she tried to break a window to get back into her home. She also died from hypothermia; exposure to the elements. It was very cold and wet that night. The article appears in *The Vindicator*, on April 30, 2008. Once again public outrage demands that the local news media do their jobs, by getting to the bottom of this ridiculous fiasco. Who polices the police?

One of my all-time favorite articles, presented in *The Vindicator*, appears in the April 8, 2008 edition. It is in this article that the corruption of the Mahoning Valley law enforcement is typified. A judge dismissed aggravated murder charges against a Mahoning County man over an assertion by Summit County prosecutors, in Akron, Ohio, that Youngstown police "compromised" ballistic evidence in the 2002 slaying of Javan Rogers, twenty-four, of Akron. Summit County had jurisdiction in the case, prosecutors said, because Rogers was abducted from his Akron residence on North Portage Path and found shot to death execution-style, in Youngstown on August 27, 2002. The Mahoning County defendant, Arian S. O'Connor, thirty, was charged in October with the Rogers slaying after Youngstown police tied him to the crime by switching shell casings from that shooting and an unrelated drive-by shooting in September 2002, prosecutors said in open court, in Summit County, in Akron. "When we can no longer believe that the police, law enforcement, are being truthful, it's a very sad day for the justice system," Judge Cosgrove acknowledged. Naturally the Youngstown culprits responsible for planting the false evidence swore that a mistake was simply made and that no one here meant to confuse the issue. Again Judge Cosgrove of Summit County Common Pleas Court attacked, "This is a situation that strikes at the very heart of our democracy and our justice system." An independent investigation was called for to find out who in the Youngstown system instigated such a fraud on the Summit County court, the Akron police, and the people of Summit County. Youngstown policemen were pissing off other Ohio policemen.

Youngstown was so corrupt that even other corrupt Ohio towns distanced themselves from us.

My personal nemesis, Trumbull County prosecutor, J. Walter Dragelevich, now simply a defense attorney, got himself into a little trouble, according to the February 7, 2003 article that appeared in *The Vindicator*, when he altered the odometer on an Oldsmobile Bravada. This information was revealed in U.S. District Court in Cleveland. Dragelevich was facing three years in prison, followed by three years of supervised release, and a fine of up to 250,000 dollars.

This is the gentleman, who was the Trumbull County prosecutor, that I appealed to when crooked cops in his area persecuted me and many others, more than twenty-five years ago. This is the prosecutor who threatened to put me away, regardless of the evidence I had.

I take great pleasure in presenting this charlatan to the American people. Who polices the police? Many times in the past, I've sent mountains of evidence proving that the local officials had perjured themselves, fixed cases, destroyed exculpatory evidence, abused prisoners, and extorted favors and money from the citizens of this area. The response from the media here was usually the same, "We can't make a move until the police and the prosecutor's office give us permission." Most of the news media in Youngstown is a part of the

"Good-Old-Boy Network." It is only when you put the media at risk of exposure as part of that "Good-Old-Boy Network" that they even pretend to do their jobs. As told to me by one of the reporters of one of the local news channels, "We'd starve to death if the police and prosecutors didn't throw us an occasional bone." No one is in a hurry to piss off the authorities in this area, with the truth.

My criticism is not limited to the police, but to any authorities in this area who help to convince the outside world that this is a corrupt place to live. An article in *The Vindicator*, dated March 20, 2008, tells the story of Brian T. Hughes, the former Springfield Township fire chief, who pleaded no contest to a charge stemming from a 2005 barn fire. He was allowed to plead to a lesser charge of disorderly conduct, and pay a hundred-dollar fine. Hughes and the owner of the barn had hatched some plot to burn the barn and profit from it. False reports were filed and 911 services were illegally used. Hughes had complained about being reduced from a full-time pay of $41,130 to a much less part-time pay. He is quoted as saying that he had to make ends meet any way that he could. Nearby, in Harrisburg, Pennsylvania, suspended Superior Court Judge, Michael T. Joyce pleaded innocent to charges of mail fraud and money laundering. He was suspended with pay, when a grand jury indicted him on charges that he bilked two insurance companies out of 440,000 dollars. He continues to receive his salary of $165,342 a year, plus benefits. The criminal case stems from an August 2001 traffic accident, that Joyce claimed left him in such bad health that he was unable to exercise or play golf for more than a year. Prosecutors say that the judge was rear-ended by another vehicle at about 5 mph, and then proceeded to fake his injuries to cash in on the insurance money. The judge was later caught playing eighteen holes of golf, in Jamaica, going scuba diving, participating in in-line skating, and working out in a local gym. He used the insurance money to buy a motorcycle and to make payments on a house and an airplane. The charges carry a maximum prison term of twenty years. That article can be found in *The Vindicator*, August 21, 2007.

The September 7, 2007 and the September 13, 2007 issues of *The Vindicator*, tell the tale of Youngstown's Judge Maureen A.

Cronin. At the time, Cronin was facing jail time after being charged with her second driving-under-the-influence charge, in two years. She pleaded no contest to charges of driving under the influence in 2005, after being stopped returning from the Mountaineer Casino, Racetrack & Resort, in Chester, West Virginia. At that time, her driver's license was revoked for 180 days. She was also sentenced to 180 days in jail, but 177 of those days were suspended. She ended up doing twelve months of non-reporting probation. Cronin retired from the Mahoning County Common Pleas Court bench after serving thirteen years. The latest charge resulted in her getting to wear yellow license plates on her vehicle that signify that she is a convicted multiple drunken-driving offender. She will also have an ignition interlock device on her dashboard that will measure her alcohol concentration when she blows into it. If the reading is acceptable, the car will start. The conviction in 2005 prompted her retirement from the bench. It is truly ironic that this drunk was so hard on offenders who had the same drinking problem that she had. I personally witnessed her sentence a gentleman to eighteen months in the penitentiary for doing the same thing that she did; he too was guilty of two or three DUI charges. Who polices the police? What a joke! To protect and serve. In Youngstown, they only protect and serve themselves. Here is proof that the "Good-Old-Boy Network" actually has a few women in it.

On October 21, 2001, in *The Vindicator*, Bertram de Souza tells the world just what is wrong with Youngstown; it's hopelessly corrupt. He starts off in the article by talking about the Mahoning County Democratic Party chairmen, Don L. Hanni Jr. and Michael R. Morley. de Souza adamantly asserts that both of these attorneys were accused in sworn testimony of participating in case-fixing schemes in Mahoning County. de Souza next mentions two well-known businessmen in the area, Bruce R. Zoldan and Anthony Saadey.

Both of these gentlemen were accused in sworn testimony, in federal court, of paying bribes to fix cases. de Souza then turns to lawyers and prosecutors, who swore in federal court in Cleveland to the alleged case-fixing actions on the parts of Hanni, Morley, Saadey, and Zoldan.

James Philomena, Stuart Banks, Jack Campbell, and Lawrence Seidita are the names of the attorneys who sold out their fellow rats, at the two-week racketeering trial of James A. Vitullo and Russell J. Saadey, in U.S. District Court in Cleveland. This was the stage where these members of the "Good-Old-Boy Network" self-destructed by telling on themselves and their cohorts. Vitullo was found innocent of all charges and Saadey was found guilty of all charges except one. Banks, Seidita, Campbell, and others are cooperating with the federal government in return for lighter sentences for their convictions on charges relating to their participation in a case-fixing enterprise in the county. County Prosecutor Phil Gains has given these snitches immunity from state charges. They essentially have received slaps on their wrists, and Prosecutor Gains has expressed little, if any interest, in going after the local crooks.

Philomena, in his testimony in the racketeering trial of Vitullo, who was an assistant prosecutor under him, and Russell Saadey, who was a prosecutor's investigator in the Philomena administration, claimed that he fixed a murder case with Hanni. Philomena admitted taking bribes to fix many other cases, while there in federal court. *The Vindicator* carries an article about the life and death of ex-prosecutor James A. Philomena, in its September 5, 2007 issue. The article mentions that Philomena's downfall came from bribery, case-fixing, perjury, and a drug problem. There is also a mentioning of the fact that Philomena was allegedly involved in the failed hit on Prosecutor Phil Gains. Philomena was released, in 2005, after serving six years in state and federal prisons. He died in 2007, just two years after his release. He once had aspirations to be Ohio's Attorney General. de Souza's last comment about James Philomena was that these words will forever be etched in the psyche of Mahoning County: "Justice For Sale."

Another of the area's local, golden boys, Marc Dann, surpassed Philomena as a local attorney and actually became Ohio's Attorney General. Attorney General Dann's troubles began when a staffer filed a report with the Columbus Police Department, accusing Anthony S. Gutierrez, her supervisor, of sexually harassing her, including once at a condominium he shared with Attorney General Marc Dann.

Cindy Stankoski and her coworker, Vanessa Stout, also filed sexual harassment complaints against Gutierrez, with the Attorney General's office. The two staffers to Marc Dann also filed charges with the Federal Equal Employment Opportunity Commission. Gutierrez is Dann's Office Director of General Services and a longtime friend. An investigation of the charges led to the paid suspensions of Gutierrez and Leo Jennings, the communications director and another longtime friend of Marc Dann. That story can be found in *The Vindicator*, April 19, 2008.

In *The Vindicator*, April 20, 2008 Bertram de Souza again weighs in on the problems of corruption in this area, after Marc Dann's troubles are made apparent, when two of his female staffers file sexual harassment charges. de Souza starts off in the article by scolding Dann for not learning from the past mistakes of other politicians from this area. de Souza mentions the federal prosecutor, Steven J. Katzman, who later became an assistant U.S. Attorney, who left a warning to those who remained in the Mahoning Valley, after he and other authorities rounded up ex-Sheriff and ex-Congressman Jim Traficant; ex-prosecutor James Philomena; ex-Sheriff Phil Chance; former Judges Patrick Kerrigan, Andrew Polovischak, and Martin Emrich. Katzman and other authorities also rounded up another seventy crooked lawyers, officeholders, and mobsters who were convicted in the federal government's corruption dragnet. Katzman's message was simple: "Public officials should be careful about the company they keep." He characterized the region as a sociologically and politically regressive community mired in corruption. de Souza, picking up where Katzman left off, states that Dann refused to learn the lessons of the past and immediately surrounded himself with his longtime friends and cronies, who just so happened to hail from this area. Those cronies are now responsible for calls for Dann to resign or be impeached. On April 27, 2008, *The Vindicator* dropped another bombshell, when it ran a story about a special agent to Attorney General Marc Dann, who was placed on a seven-month administrative leave, while collecting forty-two thousand dollars, and then was fired, for demanding sexual favors from a fellow member of a narcotics task force. Attorney General Dann's office fired Dwight

L. Aspacher, after a lengthy investigation into his criminal charges of sexual misconduct.

It is indeed ironic that Attorney General Marc Dann came into office on a platform that claimed to clean up the corrupt system that existed in Columbus. It seems that he set a bad example for his employees to follow when he had an affair. This is reported in *The Vindicator*, May 3, 2008. In that article, Dann insists that he won't resign. In *The Vindicator*, May 6, 2008, local party leaders urge Dann to stand firm, while fellow legislators want him to resign or be impeached. I knew Dann personally, when he was with the law firm of Betras and Dann. When I was in the Mahoning County Jail for thirteen months, on the trumped-up gun charge, I wrote to Attorney Dann. At that time, he was in the middle of the campaign for Attorney General of Ohio. He wrote me in jail to say that he was aware of the corruption in local law enforcement, the county jail, the Mahoning Valley, and in the state of Ohio. In his letter to me he stated that he thought that he had a better chance of cleaning up that corruption, even here locally, by getting some real power to make a change; that would be as Attorney General of Ohio. He also wrote that he was well aware of the civil rights abuses and the filthiness at the county jail. Attorney Marc Dann intimated to me that he was very regretful not to be able to take my case and expose the crooked bastards who planted evidence and perjured themselves in my criminal case. He asked me to contact him again, after the election, if I still needed him.

In an article that appears in *The Vindicator*, on May 5, 2008, there seems to be at least seven investigations coming at Marc Dann, because of the sexual harassment complaints that his staffers filed and his admission that he had an affair with another of his workers. Truly it seems that his employees were simply following his lead, when it came to playing with the female coworkers. The article also mentions that Dann got into hot water with the Disciplinary Counsel of the Ohio Supreme Court in 2002, because he failed to adequately represent a client in a divorce case. To protect and serve. How hypocritical!

CHAPTER 20

Business as Usual

I f you ever wondered why the locals on the street love me, and the authorities hate me, consider this. After taking a very serious ass whipping, from the crooked police who stopped me on May 25, 2002, and then being lied on and charged by perjurous officers, I was left to rot in jail for thirteen months, because there was no bond since I was deemed a flight risk. When a bond was finally set, I had suffered a stroke and a heart attack; not to mention that my body was riddled with staphylococcus that I contracted in the Mahoning County Jail. Before my stroke in jail my bond was 250,000 dollars, after the stroke the bond was only 2,500 dollars and I got to go home by paying a bondsman 250 dollars. It was a big secret at the time, but it is common knowledge now that I incessantly wrote to the lawyers in Akron, about the police abuse, the planting of evidence, the destruction of exculpatory evidence, the filthiness of the jail, and the poor medical treatment the prisoners endured. I got nowhere until I got most of the jail's population to cosign my complaints. That was the birth of "The Brotherhood," which grew to phenomenal proportions when we were all finally released from jail and hooked up on the outside.

Whenever I see a fellow former inmate or a policeman, who recognizes me, the conversation turns to my letter writing campaign that ended up with the county jail being shut down and the prisoners being released. I found an article in one of Joanna's boxes in her command center marked, "Mahoning County Jail Class-Action Lawsuit," and dug into it.

I was amazed that she had saved every article beginning with the early complaints in 2003.

In the November 18, 2005 edition of *The Vindicator*, there appears an article that mentions the class-action lawsuit of the prisoners. The entire criminal justice system in Mahoning County was described as "dysfunctional" by Special Master Atty. Vincent M. Nathan of Toledo, who asked all of the players to work together. Nathan, who was appointed by U.S. District Court Judge David D. Dowd to oversee the jail, deserves the thanks of all county residents for not pulling any punches in a twenty-two-page evaluation he submitted to the judge. He contended that the jail's problems "are the result of a dysfunctional criminal justice system" and recommended the formation of a working group to address the myriad of problems affecting law enforcement agencies, the prosecutor's office, the courts, and the jail.

A working group, called the Criminal Justice Review Committee, is in place and has been doing important work in identifying the problems and proposing solutions. Consultants Mark A. Cunniff and Michael R. Jones met with two dozen criminal justice representatives from the sheriff's department, the courts, police, and community corrections programs. Judge Dowd, who is developing a solution to the overcrowding and understaffing at the jail, in the wake of a successful class-action lawsuit filed by the inmates, and Nathan were present at the event. Nathan stated, "For too long, the issue of the jail has resulted in politicians passing the buck."

Cunniff said, "We should not be that fearful of the media that we are unwilling to take a risk." A special notation was made that secrecy and hiding information from the public only breed suspicion and distrust in public officials. The consultants go on to say that there is no substitute for transparency in government. Consider how many defense attorneys I contacted locally and out of town before the Akron lawyers came to my rescue; the others didn't care.

In *The Vindicator*, on December 5, 2006, the University of Toledo professor and Special Master Atty. Vincent M. Nathan, who was hired to make recommendations for the operation of the Mahoning County jail, said that a prisoner population limit of 288 made a lot more sense than a population of 486, which was the prison population on November 16, 2006. Just a few months after the prisoners won their class-action civil rights lawsuit, in March 2005, common pleas judges devised a thirteen-step release program that was supposed to limit the population to 296. A three-judge panel has been overseeing the jail. Another article, concerning the Mahoning County Jail and the inmates' lawsuit is mentioned on September 22, 2007, in *The Vindicator*. In this article the lawyers I contacted in Akron are featured. Mention is made of the fact that Attorneys Robert Armbruster and Thomas Kelley won the class-action lawsuit that involved jail overcrowding and understaffing, on March 2005, on behalf of the disgruntled inmates, whose civil rights were being violated.

As a result of the success of that lawsuit, the main jail, the Mahoning County Justice Center, reduced its inmate population, and the misdemeanor jail closed. There have been conversations, from those in the know, that power has been effectively usurped from the incompetent and corrupt authorities in the area, by outside lawyers, judges, professors, and consultants, for as long as five years. Imagine how the local warden, sheriff, prosecutor, guards, judges, commissioners, and the jail's medical staff must have felt when a large number of them lost their jobs and many others were laid off indefinitely. According to the articles I have just cited from editions of the local newspapers, maybe rooms should be made in the Mahoning County Jail for the corrupt and abusive policemen, judges, prosecutors, and politicians from the immediate area, because they are still doing what they usually do; they are still conducting their sideline businesses as usual. Nothing has stopped or changed. They've simply gotten smarter about their underground activities. The corrupt officials have gone the way of the "invisible" local crime lords. They too are aware of wires and informants aimed at them as they have been aimed at the regular criminals. In Youngstown, mobs only exist because of their connections in law enforcement. Here, everybody has his hand out for a piece of the pie. How absurd to believe that organized crime is dead here and that all of the corrupt officials have been weeded out and jailed! Many of the criminal enterprises that

I will bring to your attention have been doing business as usual for five to twenty years, or more. The police got their cut and that criminal enterprise endured. When a lawbreaker, who is making serious money, gets busted, it's only because he's not paying off or he's paying off and simply gets a slap on the wrist. That usually boils down to probation, early judicial release, community service, or forfeiture of impounded cash and property, followed by a fine. Either way you end up paying to operate in the corrupt official's "territory." And what of the local media? Because they survive on the occasional "bones" that the local authorities throw them, they are reluctant to bite the corrupt hands that feed them.

Just to give you some idea what type of criminal culture exists in the Youngstown City/ Mahoning Valley area, look up the article that appears in *The Youngstown Vindicator*, on May 9, 2008. In that article, local residents celebrate the sixty-seventh birthday of the notorious sheriff-turned-congressman, Jim Traficant. Traficant was imprisoned in 2002, for racketeering, bribery, and tax evasion. A federal jury found Traficant guilty of ten felony charges. He was sentenced to eight years in prison on July 30, 2002, and his projected release date is September 2, 2009. The Royal Oaks Bar & Grille was filled with Traficant's friends and supporters, who say that they may celebrate his birthday every year, from now on. The bar issued Traficant masks to any who would wear them. These people revere Traficant as a local legend. Many of them even recited one of many of Traficant's famous quotes. Crime and corruption go hand in hand, in this area, as business goes on as usual.

Take a look at the illegal money being made in this little town that is geographically positioned midway between New York City and Chicago. The high prices of scrap metal have brought a new type of criminal to Youngstown, the scrap thief. With scrapyards paying nearly three dollars a pound for copper plumbing and wiring, no empty structure is safe from the "copper-stripping thieves," who can easily "collect" four hundred dollars' worth of the precious metal in a few hours. This practice is not limited to abandoned buildings, but includes occupied structures as well. An article in *The Youngstown Vindicator*, on March 27, 2008, mentions that two local men were charged with the theft of 4,500 dollars' worth of copper that they stole from a nearby business.

The two men stole three copper bars, which weigh fifty pounds each, and fifty feet of copper wire, from Truck Electric, of McDonald, Ohio. Boosting, or stealing goods with the intention of selling or trading them for a profit, has gotten very big in this area lately. A good booster can brag of stealing 1,200 dollars' worth of clothing, food, or jewelry in a few hours' time. The booster then "cashes in" to his fence, who probably placed an order with the thief in the first place. The thief usually receives one-third to one-half of the store's selling price for the goods. That would give the booster four hundred to six hundred dollars, for less than an hour's work.

This area prides itself on hunting and marksmanship. It is pretty much a rite of passage, for a father to teach his son or daughter to hunt and kill, at about the age of twelve. An article in *The Vindicator*, dated November 26, 2007, mentions fathers taking their fourteen- to sixteen-year-old sons out for their first hunting and killing experiences. Mention is made of the fact that these fathers teach the children to use shotguns, rifles, and bows to cut down their prey. There is big business in selling guns, locally and out of state. Most of the guns from this area find their way to New York or Chicago, because of the stringent gun laws in those two places.

Older criminals use juveniles to steal firearms, because of the jail time involved; the juveniles usually don't get serious time for their crimes. *The Vindicator* carries a story, in its October 3, 2007 edition, about a sixteen-year-old who burglarized one of the largest gun dealers in the area. His punishment so far was to appear in Juvenile Court, on four felonies, resulting from the break-in and theft, of a store-full of guns, and then be detained in the Juvenile Justice Center. Even though he is charged with felonies, by the Bureau of Alcohol, Tobacco, Firearms, and Explosives, he is not expected to be tried as an adult. Think of the money he could have made off the guns he stole; think of the violence he and his crew could have meted out. As Lying Johnny was so fond of saying, "Ain't nothing like a big pistol and a pocket full of money, to make some fool think that they're Superman."

An article appears in *The Vindicator*, on July 19, 2001, in which reports are made on cockfighting in the area. Members of the Mahoning Valley Drug Task Force found a pit bull that had been used to fight other dogs and eighty roosters used for cockfighting, in the basement of a home raided by that task force. The task force was there to arrest a man indicted by a federal grand jury on cocaine charges. Dave Nelson, an Animal Charity investigator, said the roosters, because of such unsanitary conditions in the basement, would have to be destroyed. Investigators revealed that bettors waged eight thousand dollars, per person, each week, on the cockfights.

Lieutenant Dave Allen, Task Force commander for the Mahoning Valley Drug Task Force, stated in *The Vindicator*, on July 19, 2001, that two inner-urban drug rings had been operating and selling to their "own," for the past ten years, until lately, when suburbanite drug dealers came here for drugs to sell in four of the more expensive and well-to-do suburbs. The drugs taken back to the suburban users were sold at private parties, in private homes, and trendy bars. Twelve to fifteen large-scale drug dealers, from the two inner-urban drug rings, and several of the suburban drug dealers were secretly indicted along with three men from New York. Charges include conspiracy to distribute cocaine, possession with intent to distribute, and using the telephone to facilitate drug trafficking. Another wave of indictments is forthcoming, in which ten more drug dealers will get their date with justice. Nearly half of the defendants moved here from New York, in 1998, to set up their drug rings. Drug sales netted one and a half million dollars per week. Six of those arrested have out-of-the country connections and have been deemed flight risks. For that reason, those six drug dealers have been refused bond and were forced to stay in jail until trial time.

The right kind of cough syrup is very expensive and in high demand in Youngstown.

The yellow-colored Tussionex was selling for fifty to sixty dollars an ounce, or about four hundred dollars plus for an eight-ounce bottle. According to an article in *The Vindicator*, dated April 30, 2003, the cough syrup is now so rare and in such high demand that it brings $125 to $150 an ounce, in some places. That's about $1,000 to $1,200 for an eight-ounce bottle of the liquid. The cough medicine is very potent and contains the same ingredients as Vicodin; its effect is similar to heroin and it's very addictive. According to the article, Tameika Fields and Khaliah Green stole two hundred ounces of the Tussionex cough syrup from a pharmacy in Los Angeles and brought it to Youngstown to sell. The two women flew the liquid to this area and then took a local bus to distribute the syrup to their customers. The bus driver alerted the authorities and the two women were arrested when they got off the bus in downtown Youngstown, at the bus station.

Another article appears in that same edition of the *Vindicator*. In this next article, it is made more than apparent that the drug dealer in question has hired the ex-prosecutor, Gary Van Brocklin. The judge is none other than my judge from the trumped-up gun charge, Judge Jack Durkin. I begged this judge to look into the stolen and planted evidence in my case, to no avail. Newspapers and lawyers in Akron, Cleveland, and Columbus call Judge Durkin and ex prosecutor Van Brocklin part of the "Good-Old-Boy" network; I do know for a fact that Van Brocklin's law firm handled my ex-wife's case when she tried to murder me. They also represented my ex-wife when I sued her for payment of the medical bills I incurred as a result of the shooting. It was Van Brocklin's law firm that suggested that my ex-wife return some real estate that she had in her name, which actually belonged to my family. The apartment building was surrendered to *me* with the stipulation that I drop the lawsuit and pay the medical bills myself. That was the only way that she would surrender the property. She had already looked into selling the property or mortgaging it to the hilt. This is the same Seattle, Washington, apartment building that my brother rented to the D.C. Snipers, John Williams Muhammad and his apprentice, John Malvo. *The Vindicator* article goes on to mention that the drug dealer represented by Van Brocklin, in Judge Jack Durkin's court, received probation, after helping authorities with their investigations of other drug dealers he was "acquainted with."

The drug dealer, Robert Treham, had pleaded guilty, nearly a year before, in Mahoning County Common Pleas Court, to two counts of cocaine trafficking. A charge of engaging in a pattern of corrupt activity was dismissed by prosecutors as part of a plea agreement. Treham had been part of a major cocaine operation in the Mahoning Valley. His sentencing had been delayed because his deal with the prosecutors and the court required him to "assist" authorities in building cases against six other men who faced similar charges. Those cases have now been handled, with Treham's civic-minded assistance. Assistant prosecutor Terry Grenga said in open court that because Treham cooperated with authorities, prosecutors agreed to recommend that he be placed on probation rather than be sent to prison. Judge Jack Durkin followed that recommendation and placed Treham on probation for one year. Keep in mind that this was one of the major drug dealers in the area. His ex-prosecutor lawyer got him a perfect deal with the present prosecutor. Treham also had a very good friend and high school classmate in Officer Jeff Allen, the deputy sheriff assigned to the Mahoning Valley Drug Task Force. Authorities have said that Treham was part of a cocaine ring that supplied cocaine to others, who sold it in bars and private clubs in the city's suburbs. The network sold 330 pounds of cocaine over a ten-year period of time. The reason that I remember this case so well is because I was still in jail for the thirteen months on the trumped-up charges concerning the gun. Judge Durkin was also my judge, and Van Brocklin's firm had represented my ex-wife when she shot me and when I had to sue her to get back the apartment building in Seattle.

This drug dealer bought his way out of jail by dealing with the prosecutor and the judge, through his attorney, the ex-prosecutor, Gary Van Brocklin. This article was written on April 30, 2003. I read this article while I was still in jail and I was not released until after my stroke. My release date from the Mahoning County Jail was June 11, 2003. Business as usual in the "Yo," especially if you can tap into the "Good-Old-Boy Pipeline," by hiring the ex-prosecutor as your lawyer. Here in this town, it's always about who you know.

In *The Vindicator*, October 10, 2007, an article appears that discusses seventy-three-year-old Alberta McGauley and her attempt to supplement her retirement check with some drug money. Police arrested the elderly woman after presenting a search warrant, and then charged her with drug trafficking. Officers found cocaine packaged for selling and 690 dollars in the woman's coat pocket. A loaded nine millimeter handgun was also found under a cushion on a love seat in her living room. In that same edition of *The Vindicator*, Larese Jones was sentenced to thirty-six years to life imprisonment because he drove Richard Helms to David Klamer's residence, with the plan to sell OxyContin to Klamer and then rob Klamer. Klamer got the upper hand and shot Helms in the head. The shot killed Helms. Klamer got a smart lawyer, who argued that Klamer wasn't competent to stand trial because his psychiatric evaluation showed that his drug dependency was a result of a mental disorder or vice versa.

Judge R. Scott Krichbaum sent him to the North Coast Behavioral Health Care Systems in Cleveland for treatment designed to restore him to normalcy. Martin P. Desmond, assistant county prosecutor, declined to discuss the case with the media. Business as usual.

It seems that many of the gainfully employed in Youngstown want to augment their incomes. The small amount paid for salaries in this area is often used as a rationalization by lawbreakers before and after they get caught. On August 18, 2007, *The Vindicator* reports that in nearby Allentown, Pennsylvania, a former middle school principal charged with selling crystal methamphetamine from his school office, his home, and other locations pleaded guilty to multiple drug offenses. A teacher since 1979 and a principal since 2000, John Acerra pleaded guilty to two counts of felony delivery of methamphetamine and one count of felony possession with intent to deliver. Principal Acerra was in his office during the police raid, after school hours. Police and federal agents actually caught the principal with the drugs spread out on his school desk. Acerra resigned his position a few days after his arrest and is awaiting trial.

Andre Johnson also had a very good job, but felt that he needed more income than his firefighter's job paid. His story is reported in *The Vindicator*, April 1, 2008. The fired city firefighter, indicted on felony marijuana possession and trafficking charges, pleaded guilty to a misdemeanor attempted marijuana possession charge and has been placed on six months of non-reporting probation. Fireman Johnson struggled with his would-be robber, Stefin Gantt, in Johnson's basement, as Gantt attempted to rob Johnson of the marijuana he was selling and the 540 dollars Johnson had on him from other drug sales. During the struggle Johnson was shot three times and Gantt's ear was bitten off. The prosecution and the defense agreed to recommend probation to Judge Maureen A. Sweeney, of the Mahoning County Common Pleas Court, on the condition that Johnson would waive his right to appeal his termination from the fire department. He was fired because of the apparent drug activity at his home. Michael J. McBride, assistant county prosecutor, said that his major goal was to keep Johnson off the fire department. An article appears in *The Vindicator*, on October 7, 2007, in which Ohio State Highway patrolmen burn six million dollars' worth of confiscated guns, marijuana, cocaine, and heroin, in a 3,500-degree furnace. Ex-Sheriff Phil Chance also made this claim, when he actually had his own drug dealers sell the confiscated merchandise and split the profits with him and his loyal deputies. The only thing Phil Chance burned was the baking flour he used to replace the drugs he and his deputies stole from the evidence vault.

Prostitution has gotten a little more sophisticated in the area lately. Drug dealers are using their profits to buy old abandoned houses, refurbish them, and then rent them out to the same women that they have prostituting for them. The women are relatively invisible once they are off the streets and the new landlords are guaranteed the rent from a Section 8 contract with the Housing Department that provides low-income housing for some of those who can't afford to live anyplace else. If the woman gets busted for dealing drugs or prostitution, the drug-dealing pimp turned landlord is immune because the property is rented to the hooker. In "The Yo," many in the underground economy are attempting to master the art of invisibility. The pretend gangsters want to be seen and end up in jail many times before they realize the benefits of invisibility. If the truth were told, most of these pretend gangsters never learn the secrets of success in the Yo, and those secrets are really very simple: networking, compromising, and being as invisible as possible. The baggy pants hanging off of your ass, the 2,500-dollar-rims on the 800-dollar-car, the loud car stereo, and the baseball caps turned sideways are dead giveaways to anyone with the common sense of observation. You may as well wear a sign saying, "I'm doing something illegal, and making good money at it; come and get me." According to *The Vindicator*, January 10, 2008, Richard Minich tried his best to be invisible, but he talked too much on the telephone about his drug transactions. When the task force finally raided his place and two other residences, where his cohorts plied the same trade, they found that Minich had almost become a recluse. He didn't go out, but he had quite a bit of company coming to visit him, especially when they came to buy marijuana. Cash confiscated by the task force amounted to 350,000 dollars. Sixty pounds of marijuana were also intercepted. Minich's residence had steel doors with bars over them. The doors were also barricaded from the inside. Three pit bulls patrolled the house and Minich had a video surveillance system in place. An indoor marijuana growing system contained forty-eight plants. Besides some firearms, authorities found a scale and a money-counting machine. Authorities will primarily be following his cell phone records, computer records, and bank accounts during a follow-up investigation.

I have friends from all walks of life. Some of these are new friends and some are old friends. The old ones are the most imposing, yet they are the ones least likely to turn a helping hand. In this town called 'Youngstown, new friends understand networking, compromising, and treating others the way you want them to treat you. In short, they understand the concepts of brotherhood. Most of my old friends have worked long enough to retire and are now coming to the shocking realization that they are not bringing in enough income to make ends meet.

They are old, frustrated, bitter, jealous, and afraid of young people. They have adopted a dog eat-dog mentality. They borrow without repaying and they beg special favors without returning those favors. I have mentioned several times that old friends and relatives have taken advantage of the fact that many wish to embark upon some mutually beneficial enterprises with me, but I have intentionally remained invisible for a number of reasons. Only one of those reasons is my health. You don't disappear from the law for twenty years, then resurface just to reveal the corruption of that system in *The New York Times Magazine*, then shut down the jail, get the guards fired or laid off, then enable outsiders to usurp the power of the county jail managers for five years. In this town, it is advisable that I remain scarce, if not invisible.

Like my ex, private-detective-turned-restaurateur, P, many of my old friends and family used their relationships with me to impress others enough to embark on certain business ventures with some of my other old and new friends while misrepresenting themselves as my agent. Nothing negative has come my way as a result of this charade, but quite a bit of money has come their way and they have sworn that they will give me the traditional ten percent "finder's fee," for that misrepresentation. I might add that these guilty friends and relatives did not reveal to me that they had benefitted financially, by claiming to others that they represented my interests in certain ventures. I had to be told by my ex-private detective and a few other old friends who remained "in the loop." When I confronted certain parties about their dishonesty, they promised to compensate me at some later date, which they never did. I am glad that they didn't because they are all gone to jail for a long time, while I'm traveling the world with Joanna and regaining my health more each day. I couldn't help but laugh to myself when I encountered some of the thieves who profited from using my name.

They expected to see a dried up old man, walking on crutches or two canes. Imagine the surprise on some of their faces when they saw their old classmate looking ten years younger than I did the last time they saw me. Some actually had fear on their faces when they saw that I was able to run up the staircase, two and three steps at a time. I grew up with the members of the biker-club-turned-drug-ring that I am about to reveal to you. Some of these members claimed that they were going to pay me as much as forty thousand dollars for using their relationships with me to gain favor with other "businessmen." As I said, I'm glad that they never paid me.

The Youngstown Vindicator carried an article, on November 20, 2005, about a super huge drug ring that operated coast-to-coast, while using cross-country motorcycling events to masquerade the fact that they were actually transporting drugs. I mentioned earlier that when I went to my many doctors, I often walked to a lifetime friend's home, R.G., one block away from my doctors. I also mentioned that Booker Wellington was one of many who used his friendship with the Holmes family to further his interests with others in the "Youngstown Underground Economy." I mentioned that he sold some bogus goods to another lifetime friend of mine and claimed that the bogus goods came from me. I literally had to force him to return the man's money and explain that I had nothing to do with the transaction. This same Booker Wellington, who promised me forty thousand dollars, when I found out that he had been benefitting financially, by falsely presenting himself as my agent, was literally taking 250 dollars from a blood relative of mine, J, every time he saw him. I don't know the nature of their business and I don't know how J ended up owing Booker. I just know that R.G. told me that he witnessed J paying Booker three times, and that I should put an end to it. Booker had accumulated quite a bit of money and muscle. He was "power tripping," a term we apply to those with too much money and muscle, who become abusive in their attempts to prove how "gangsterous" they are.

I had to threaten to send some of "The Brotherhood" to visit Booker before he relented in his constant extortion of the 250 dollars from J. Booker, like everyone else, had heard the story about B-Boy and K-Dog whipping Ron's ass, when he pulled the knife on me. Booker knew that I was constantly surrounded by the best killers money could buy. Those killers hoped to get me indebted to them so that they could argue that I owed them a silencer. That was my claim to fame; that is why I constantly found myself being courted by hit men; that is why so many businessmen wanted to do me favors. It was always about "the tools of the trade," the silencers. All I had to do was to mention that I was trading a silencer to one of the up-and-coming young killers, who I wanted to do a little "work" for me, and all of a sudden my enemies loved me again. Silencers bring "crazy loot," in a town of professional killers.

Booker's gang is discussed extensively in *The Youngstown Vindicator*, on November 20, 2005, just eight months after the

Akron lawyers won the civil-rights lawsuit for the prisoners at Mahoning County Jail, in March 2005. That lawsuit essentially shut the county jail down.

Imagine how pissed off the local authorities were that the Feds were running things here. *The Vindicator* mentions that seven local residents were among the ten men charged in a federal indictment for distributing cocaine in the Youngstown and Sharon, Pennsylvania, areas. A New York man, Juan "Lenny" Francisco Melo, is listed as the main supplier to Youngstown's Booker Wellington, who in turn supplied his partners: Marvin L. McWilson, Cleveland G. Hightower, Ralph R. Stoddard, Gerald R. Baker, Dorian W. Christian, and Joseph N. Flaviano. Just to show you the networking and franchising benefits of the Brotherhood, consider this: Eliminating racism creates a less hostile environment for making money; Melo is Hispanic, the rest are black. In Youngstown, networking, compromising, and invisibility equal money. Unfortunately, Booker and Marvin had too many vehicles, too many homes, and they talked too much on the telephone. They had a sham of a construction business as a front, but they never filed taxes on the "legal" business. Recall how Booker put on the parade for me, with the four cars, the two trucks, and the two motorcycles, when I made him refund the money he made off a friend of mine by selling him bogus goods that Booker claimed that he got from me. These old-ass men are my age. We grew up together; we raced cars and motorcycles together; we boxed and practiced martial arts together; but their weakness was the same as that of younger "showboats"— they were too anxious to be seen and heard. They, like most of the younger gang bangers in this area, "showboated" in such a way as to essentially say, "Look at me making all of this money. Come and get me." Other *Vindicator* articles state that Booker's gang supplied drugs from New York to California. The indictment states that the gang sold drugs from 1993 to 2005. Booker's entire gang was sentenced to Fed time: five to ten years. All of their vehicles, houses, and cash were forfeited. If they decide to "roll over" on somebody bigger than they are, the Feds will cut them a deal involving much less jail time.

As quiet as it's kept, drugs do not bring the largest and the safest money in the Youngstown area. Hot cars do. Simply go to a junkyard that sells new wrecks, buy the vehicle, trade the identification numbers from the wreck to the stolen car, and then trade the GPS unit from the wreck to the stolen car. New wrecked vehicles are going for 800 to 2,500 dollars in this area, from junkyards and insurance companies. A little work changing the necessary identification items will easily yield a profit of twenty thousand to thirty thousand dollars, or more, for high-end luxury, sport or SUV vehicles. Keep in mind that I'm talking about the profit from just one vehicle.

Most of the hot vehicle racketeers operate for years, until someone tells on them. *The Vindicator*, on March 22, 2008, carried a story of just such a theft ring. From what I've heard from the friends and attorneys of the alleged thieves, somebody informed on them. That's how it works in this town. If you get busted, just give up someone else who is a little bigger.

In the before-mentioned *Vindicator* article that was issued on March 22, 2008, Ohio Attorney General Marc Dann poses for a picture with Mahoning County Prosecutor, Paul Gains to answer questions about the arrests of fifteen people charged with being part of a burglary ring. The burglary ring was so sophisticated that prospective clients only needed to place an order and the thieves would fill that order. Eventually someone snitched on the burglary ring of fifteen, and they were charged with a total of sixty-eight counts, including racketeering. More than four hundred thousand dollars' worth of stolen goods were recovered by the task force that included James Ciotti, of the Ohio Bureau of Criminal Identification and Investigation, formerly of the DEA, who went to Ohio Attorney General, Marc Dann, to ask if the organized crime commission would get involved in investigating with a task force that needed more help and manpower. A multi-jurisdictional task force was necessary because of the many jurisdictions burglarized by the thieves. Again, various races came together to make money. Authorities believe 125 burglaries have been solved with the arrest of the theft ring. This burglary ring was the third of four. Two rings had already been taken down; now the third has been brought down; a fourth burglary ring of super sophisticated thieves is about to be arrested.

Two of the key players in the burglary ring were Albert Alli and his wife Laura Alli. He is the son of Al Alli, the late former president of the United Auto Worker's Local 1112, at the Lordstown auto building complex. Stolen cars had the identification numbers altered, as did several motorcycles that the theft ring stole. Horse trailers, commercial riding lawn mowers, air compressors, scooters, all-terrain vehicles, backhoes, brush hogs, computers, power tools, large-screen televisions, furniture, safes, and a Jacuzzi were among some of the items recovered from the burglary ring. Some of the task force members voiced a particular concern over the fact that the thieves had stolen police jackets from Red Diamond Uniforms in Austintown, Ohio. It was revealed that the thieves planned to rob several of the larger drug dealers, by wearing the stolen police jackets and pretending to be policemen. In addition to the obvious charges, most of the thieves in the burglary ring have been charged with violation of the "RICO" act. This is a special charge for those involved in gangs and organized crime.

The October 3, 2007 copy of *The Vindicator* carries an interesting article about a Canadian truck driver who was pulled over by the Pennsylvania State Troopers for not having the proper stickers on his truck's plates. The troopers found more than 250,000 dollars in heat-shrunken plastic packages that were hidden in the truck's cab. The money later tested positive for cocaine and heroin residue. Ebrahim Mansouri, fifty-three, of Toronto, Canada, pleaded guilty, in U.S. District Court, to transporting currency to avoid a reporting requirement. Federal law requires people to declare more than ten thousand dollars, in cash, when they cross the U.S. border. Mansouri told the troopers that the money was from his gambling winnings and his savings from his trucker's pay. The money was forfeited under federal law, because of the declaration laws. Mansouri went to jail without bail until trial because he was a flight risk. The government advises big spenders that it is illegal to cross the U.S. border, coming or going, with more than ten thousand dollars, unless you declare it.

In that same *Vindicator* issue, October 3, 2007, there appears an article about an exaccountant, for the Cleveland, Ohio Catholic Diocese, who funneled 784,000 dollars in kickbacks to a diocese official and later was convicted of conspiracy and fourteen other counts. Anton Zgoznik arranged the payments to his former boss, Joseph Smith, from 1997 through 2004, in what prosecutors portrayed as unauthorized kickbacks, in return for having diocesan accounting work contracted to Zgoznik's private business. Zgoznik was convicted of conspiracy to commit mail fraud, eight counts of mail fraud, one count of conspiracy to defraud the IRS, one count of corruptly trying to obstruct, one count of aiding preparation of a false document, and three counts of aiding preparation of a false tax return. The prosecutor was reluctant to say very much to the media, because Zgoznik's former boss, Joseph Smith, who was chief legal and financial officer for the diocese when the payments were made, still had his case pending. He was charged with twenty-three counts, including making false personal income tax returns, money laundering, mail fraud, and conspiracy. Zgoznik was facing twenty years in jail, but is expected to serve much less time because of his "cooperation" with investigators.

Zgoznik's defense attorney, claimed during the trial, that the payments amounted to extra executive compensation, authorized by the church officials, in a pattern of secret financial dealings. Zgoznik then said that he was a middleman, who handled payments between diocesan leaders and a valued lay employee, who could have commanded a higher salary elsewhere. He went on to say that the diocese boosted Smith's compensation through him but that he did not know it was wrong to do so. He said that he was loyal to the diocese when the payments were made. The diocese, which includes eight counties and about 780,000 Catholics, has claimed that it was victimized by the scheme. The diocese issued a statement to the media saying it has implemented policies and procedures in recent years to strengthen its financial controls. The statement said that it was unfortunate that Mr. Zgoznik chose to defraud the diocese. Retired Bishop, Anthony M. Pilla, said that he felt betrayed when he learned about the fraud. Zgoznik maintains that the church authorities were a part of the scam.

Just about anything goes in the Youngstown area, if it will bring a healthy profit. I went to one of the local hospitals for some minor surgery and encountered one of the nurses whom I had met on an earlier occasion. She was quite candid when she told me that her uncle, whom I knew, had given up his racketeering sideline and was now a legitimate businessman, specializing in construction and hospital supplies. She pointed out that the very pillows I was lying on bore his name brand on the label.

An article in *The Vindicator*, on April 19, 2008, once again shows that when racism and hostility are eliminated, networking can provide opportunities that were not available before. Four of seven men charged in an arson-for-profit case were in federal custody, pending pretrial detention hearings. The defendants in custody were Majeed Bazazpour, Mohammad Fard, Iraj Nasseri, and Frank Tenney. Remaining defendants are believed to be on the run in Iran.

They are Cyrus Ghassab, Farideh Jamali, and Jamshid Ghassab. All seven of the men are named in a twenty-one-count indictment that charges them with arson, mail fraud, and money laundering. At least 695,112 dollars of unlawfully obtained proceeds from insurance schemes was laundered. The first four men mentioned made their initial appearances in Youngstown's federal court. Magistrate Judge, George J. Limbert, ordered that they remain jailed because they were flight risks. The case was being personally prosecuted by the assistant U.S. Attorney, Phillip J. Tripi. Once again, ex-prosecutor Gary Van Brocklin's law firm was representing the interests of some big-money defendants.

Between 1994 and 2005, nine fires were set at commercial buildings in Mahoning and Trumbull counties by one or more of the coconspirators. The arsonists concealed what they were doing by making misrepresentations to their insurance companies. To throw suspicion away from themselves, the defendants consistently named a business competitor as the likely arsonist. Money made from the insurance claims was used to buy homes in the United States and Iran. The arson ring also used the insurance money to travel, to relocate businesses to Iran, to reinvest in other businesses, and to divert assets to other countries. To make money here in Youngstown, Islamic and white boys came together to make some real money.

Business does indeed make strange bedfellows. But this is business as usual in Youngstown. To survive in this area, one must put aside petty bickering for the common good: money.

An article appears in *The Vindicator*, on April 5, 2008, in which the police threaten to monitor high-crime areas with surveillance cameras. The authorities mentioned that even though lawbreakers will be aware of the cameras at first, later they will disregard the cameras and do what they do naturally: break the law. Five hot spots are the targets for the high-tech, spy-in-the-sky. Cameras will be mounted on the tops of buildings and telephone poles.

Need big money fast. Why not get it the old-fashioned way—steal it. According to *The Youngstown Vindicator* article, of November 27, 2007, that's exactly what Roger Lee Dillon, a security guard and armored car driver, did with the assistance of his girlfriend, Niki Boyd. The pair have been nicknamed "The Modern-day Bonnie and Clyde." The business is an armored car company called A-T Systems. Its employees pick up cash and checks from businesses and take them to various banks; sometimes storing the money for a short time at the transfer station, in Liberty, Ohio, just outside of Youngstown. Last night, two drivers came back from a run to Cleveland to find someone had cleaned out the place. Liberty Police Chief, Tony Slifka, believes it's an internal affair and that the culprit had help. The money was deposited in two safes and was removed from the safe and premises. Whoever did it knew the alarm codes to get into the building and the safes. The thief then re-armed the alarms as he left. He also took the surveillance videotape. It leads police to believe their suspect is twenty-two-year-old Roger Lee Dillon, who worked there. The FBI was called in when it was suspected that the robbery duo had fled the area. The crime is very reminiscent of a similar crime of eleven years ago, in which Leeza Mazon, an employee at the Wells Fargo depot in Youngstown, helped Jeff Chicase steal 2.3 million dollars. That pales in comparison to the $7.4 million heist that Dillon pulled, which is being touted as the largest in Ohio's history.

Dillon's employer put a one-hundred-thousand-dollar reward up for information on his whereabouts. In just a few days, the FBI found Dillon, his girlfriend, and Dillon's mother, Sharon Lee

Gregory, only 250 miles away, in Pipestem, West Virginia. They were all arrested without incident. All of the money was there, except for 3,500 dollars that Dillon used to buy a 1989 van, to haul the money in.

The FBI said that it took Dillon three months to plan the heist. The capture date for Dillon, his girlfriend, and his mother was December 1, 2007. They are all expected to spend the larger part of the rest of their lives in prison, for conspiracy, interstate transportation of stolen property, and stealing federally insured bank money from an armored car company. Sentencing is scheduled for May 22, 2008, with the probability of the trio doing fifteen to twenty-five years in prison.

Youngstown is really famous for its gambling rackets. Our state is surrounded by states that practice legal gambling of all kinds. We almost stand alone as one of the non-gambling states of modern times. However, there is a very lucrative underground gambling network, in this town and several smaller surrounding Ohio towns, that will rival the gambling income of the legitimate gambling houses in other states. This is why gangsters fought so hard for a piece of the turf in this area, that was first established when the steel mills were at full production and everyone here was making a fist full of money. For a number of reasons, the legal gambling issue has been defeated, time after time, in this immediate area. Now we are about to vote on that issue again, in November of 2008. Dwayne Hickman, of the old *The Many Loves of Dobie Gillis*, is very active in advertising on television and billboards, to vote for the legal gambling in Ohio. He points out that thirty-eight states have already passed the law for legal gambling. With arguments pro and con, on the gambling issue taking up television network time, one cannot say which way Ohio will vote. Whatever happens, there will still be the underground gambling rackets here, because the underground gambling "wins" pay bigger percentages.

Our embattled attorney general, Marc Dann, was being threatened with impeachment for the sexual scandals and the appearances of corruption in his administration. It is indeed ironic that he was voted into office on a platform claiming to rid Ohio of corruption in politics. The following *Vindicator* articles point out what was really going on when he cracked down on illegal gambling in this area.

The Vindicator, August 23, 2007, states that Gov. Ted Strickland established new administrative rules that more clearly define legal amusement games and make it illegal to operate so-called skill-based machines that pay cash prizes. Attorney General Marc Dann sent cease-and-desist orders to hundreds of known or suspected operators of such machines and is giving them three days to get the units off of their premises. "If they need to use my pickup truck to get those illegal gambling machines out of the public domain, they're welcome to do that," Dann was quoted as saying at a press conference in the governor's Cabinet Room at the Statehouse. He added, "I think three days is more than enough time to do that." The governor and the attorney general claimed that they were tired of the illegal use of the gambling machines in bars and storefronts. Such machines have gone from twenty thousand to fifty thousand units, in public and private bars, in the last six months. Seven hundred cease-and-desist orders were sent out to the offending parties, who were discovered by undercover law enforcement.

The article lists Leo Jennings as a spokesman for Attorney General Marc Dann, when Jennings stated that, "We didn't get them all, but we will." Ohio Governor Ted Strickland, Ohio Attorney General Marc Dann, and Dann's spokesman, Leo Jennings, are all on record as being against the illegal gambling machines, and for the criminal charges and the twenty-five-thousand-dollar fine. Gov. Ted Strickland went on to say, "The people of Ohio have made it very clear, time after time, that they do not wish to expand gambling interests in their state."

Again, Dann's spokesman, Leo Jennings, made a statement in *The Vindicator*, on October 28, 2007, stating that the new law not only forbids the use of the illegal gambling machines, but it also outlaws the ownership of the machines. The machines have been ruled as being the same thing as slot machines. On March 22, 2008, *The Vindicator* ran an article about a couple from nearby Warren, Ohio, who were raided for illegal gambling, on January 12, 2008, in violation of the new Ohio gambling law that Gov. Strickland and

Attorney General Dann warned them about. A Chicago, Illinois, man was also arrested. One of my former attorneys, Thomas Zena, who is in with the law and politics network in Youngstown, represented the accused, Phillip M. Cassidy and his wife Janet. Zena argued that the Cassidys are retired, have no criminal records, and were "working" at the place, Wild Cherry Gaming, to supplement their retirement incomes. Meanwhile, an arrest warrant was issued for Michael C. Pesola, of Chicago, Illinois, the actual manager and operator of the illegal gaming house. Pesola had the gambling house electronically monitored in such a way, as to be able to watch who was playing the machines at Wild Cherry Gaming from his home in Chicago. In another raid of the same type in February 2008, police seized thirty-two of the gaming machines and money at Treasure Island Gaming. Those who played the machines earned points that they exchanged in another room, for cash, minus a 10 percent service fee.

I mentioned earlier about the push to get legal gambling passed in the state of Ohio.

According to the article featured in *The Vindicator*, on May 3, 2008, there is an organization that hopes to have a casino built in Ohio and they now have a new partnership with a casino company. The two entities stopped in this area to drum up support for getting legal gambling.

The issue will be decided at the polls in November 2008. A 600 million-dollar facility is planned for nearby Clinton County, in southern Ohio. It will be completely furnished with five thousand slot machines, one hundred table games, a 1,500-room hotel, stores, entertainment bars, and restaurants. To get this on the ballot, petitioners must register 402,000 signatures in favor of the endeavor, but 700,000 signatures will be collected, just to be sure. So far, Ohio voters have rejected casino-styled gambling three times in the past twenty years. Promoters of the venture promise thirty percent of the casino's profits will go to the state's counties.

Mahoning County is projected to collect $4.8 million annually from the project, Trumbull County is to collect $4.2 million annually, and Columbiana County is to get $2.1 million. Timothy Cope, chief financial officer of Lakes Entertainment, said that one percent of the casino profits will be dedicated to creating a fund for individuals in the state with gambling addictions.

Cope went on to say, "This is something that will bring upwards of five thousand jobs to Ohio, and spread the wealth to all the counties equally. We think we finally have a good proposal for the state of Ohio." It will take three years for the facility to be built. Perhaps voters will finally pass the law for legal gambling, since Delphi-Packard just went from six thousand workers to only six hundred overnight, because of layoffs, buyouts, and early retirements. Ohio is job poor.

Cope then went on to state, "It's all about jobs and making a major investment in the state, plus keeping people from leaving the state to gamble elsewhere. We have a tag line: 'What plays in Ohio, stays in Ohio.'" As I said many times before, whether the issue of legal gambling in this area is passed or not, there will always be a thriving underground gambling network here, simply because the "wins" pay higher percentages; that is the big draw. ·

Youngstown-lawyer-turned-attorney general, Marc Dann, was facing articles of impeachment, because his confessed extramarital affair set the on-the-job atmosphere for the other male workers to sexually harass the female workers. The articles of impeachment also mentioned that he knowingly allowed one of his employees to use the state computer to operate a private construction company. Just a short while earlier, Dann and Governor Strickland waged a campaign against using gambling machines in public places. That campaign got even hotter when they got more serious by declaring it against the law to own the machines. Undercover law enforcement was used to locate the machines, identify the owners, and then arrest the culprits. Our attorney general rode into the state capital on an anti-corruption platform; he then took it upon himself to wage a personal war against gambling.

How ironic it is that what really got him to resign on May 14, 2008, was not the articles of impeachment mentioned in *The Vindicator*, on that date, but revelation of the fact that he was linked to certain gambling interests. *The Vindicator*, on May 13, 2008, carried an article that spoke of the FBI being asked to investigate Marc

Dann by a task force that is part of Dann's own office. Sources who spoke only on the condition of anonymity told "The Dispatch" that the investigation's focus is Dann's dealings with gambling interests, not the ongoing sexual-harassment scandal in his office that has cost four people their jobs and triggered calls by Gov. Ted Strickland and other Democratic leaders for Dann's resignation or impeachment. Dann has admitted to his spokesman, Ted Hart, that he was aware of the fact that the Ohio Organized Crime Investigations Commission had initiated a gambling investigation, and that he was a possible target of that investigation.

Dann, who is actually the chairman of that commission, recused himself from that investigation from the very beginning. The commission's six members are appointed by the governor. The group works closely with law-enforcement organizations to investigate specific criminal issues, including violent crime, burglary, and foreclosure scams. State Auditor, Mary Taylor, said that she is expanding her annual audit of the attorney general's office to take a deeper look into financial operations, including expense reports. The audit is expected to be released in the fall. The gambling issue surfaced last year amid a heated public debate about whether so-called skill games should be allowed in Ohio. As a candidate for attorney general in 2006, Dann had accompanied two leaders in the state's then-legal gambling industry on fund-raising visits to gambling parlors. At the time, Republican Attorney General Jim Petro was cracking down on "Tic Tac Fruit" and similar games, which were allowed under a loophole in the state's gambling law. Game operators said Dann assured them that he would ease off from Petra's more-aggressive stance if elected.

Dann raised more than two hundred thousand from gambling interests, said Jay Young, the former president of Ohio Skill Games and the man who drove Dann on his fund-raising tour. They were accompanied by skill-game distributor Jeff Mayle. Dann raised a total of $1.3 million to fuel his come-from-behind victory over Republican Betty D. Montgomery, who had signaled a tougher stance against gambling. Dann is quoted as saying, "I'm not going to be prejudiced against you. I don't have a problem with this," meaning that Dann had no problem with the gambling machines, but that was before he got elected with the money the gambling interests put together just for him. Skill-game distributor, Jeff Mayle, added that, "Marc Dann called game operators and asked them for money because he was for skill games and wouldn't do anything to stop them." After first attempting to regulate the games as legal last spring, Dann abruptly changed course in June and attempted to drive them out of business. The effort culminated in October with a state law banning the machines. Dann's office coordinated raids on businesses and homes owned by Young and Mayle, among others, to amass evidence of a criminal conspiracy. At the same time, Dann took 33,500 dollars of the gambling interests' money to buy alarm systems, cameras, and other security enhancements for his home just outside of Youngstown, in Liberty, Ohio. Dann claimed that he had been receiving threats from the gambling interests, whose money he had taken and then backstabbed them. This is one of the reasons why so many people get killed or disappear, in this area. Dann will no longer have his bodyguards since resigning from office. He is too easy a target. Didn't he think about the consequences of his actions? Hasn't he learned from all of his experiences, as a lawyer in Youngstown, how backstabbers are dealt with? Does he understand that if he can't be "reached," that certain people will go after his family? Dann is deluding himself by believing that it's business as usual, when in fact it's not. Believe me, exAttorney General Marc Dann knows better.

CHAPTER 21

Tools of the Trade

Dann's backstabbing of the gambling interests is exactly the type of situation that leads professional killers to me, in search of the tools of the trade: silencers. Selling them my blueprints and prefabricated parts is legal and as far as I'm willing to go, for any amount of money. I have been begged and offered a king's ransom to assemble the silencers myself, but that's against the law. In a very few areas in the U.S.A., silencers can be bought legally with a special federal firearms license and insurance. The thought has crossed my mind to get the proper licensing, then get federal permission to legally assemble one of my silencers myself, to compare to the government's military-grade silencers. I can't say how I know, but let it suffice to say that my silencer design renders a product that endures longer than our military's, costs less to manufacture, and is much quieter. Eventually, I will get around to having a legal comparison of my invention to Uncle Sam's version, and I already know which is the better product. Perhaps I will sell my design to the government. After all, it's a safer idea than selling the blueprints and parts on the Internet, where any old crazy can legally get his or her hands on such an effective weapon.

Like I said before, completed silencers are sold legally, in many parts of our country, and can be acquired simply by qualifying for and paying for the desired license and insurance. I have been acquainted with professional hit men in the past and lately, have been courted by them, all over again. All of them have the same general complaint; either they have never been able to find a silencer, or if they did find one, it was no damn good. An article from *The Vindicator*, way back on May 25, 1999, makes it crystal clear that the biggest, richest mob figures in the history of organized crime in this area, for some reason or another, could no longer get their hands on quiet, reliable silencers. Black, Hispanic, and Italian remnants of former mobs and gangs that had been decimated by law enforcement, gang wars, and the RICO statute, came together in the Youngstown area and formed a network of franchises that was known as "The Enterprise." This venture had the best of everything: Italian mobsters' connections in law enforcement and in politics; black drug dealers' money; and Hispanic connections on potent, but cheap, cocaine and heroin. To protect this money-making enterprise, "real killers" were retained in bulk, for a show of force or to be dispatched to an actual job. Anybody who had to be "hit" was hit; no exceptions, but as you will see, these killers lacked the proper tools of the trade.

In *The Youngstown Vindicator*, May 25, 1999, when hit man Mark A. Batcho answers questions about shooting to kill or to wound, he sounds like an at-attention Marine talking to his commanding officer. "It was a group mission, sir," Batcho, an ex-Marine, told a prosecutor of the mob's plan to incapacitate a lawyer. "I was given strict orders to only shoot attorney Gary Van Brocklin." (This is the same Van Brocklin, whose law firm represented my ex-wife when she shot me and when I sued her for the medical bills and ended up with the house in Seattle that the D.C. Snipers used as their headquarters.) Batcho testified in Mahoning County Common Pleas Court that he was told by Jeff Riddle to shoot Van Brocklin, on April 1, 1996, in his downtown office. With the lawyer injured, a court case pending for his client, Lavance Turnage, would be delayed "I felt it was an extreme measure," Batcho said, turning to face the six-man, six-woman jury. He said he did it, though, because he liked Turnage and wanted to help "the kid." (Batcho is white, Riddle and Turnage are black. This was part of the plan to mix races, connections, and money into a new Youngstown order.)

Special Prosecutor A. Steven Dever wondered why Batcho was chosen by Riddle, thirty-nine, of Youngstown, for the job. "They needed a white guy, sir," the thirty-two-year-old Batcho, of Campbell,

Ohio, answered. "They" refers to Riddle, Turnage, and George E. Wilkins III, all of whom are black. Batcho said that Wilkins accompanied him inside Van Brocklin's office on Boardman Street and carried a .357 handgun, to hold on the secretary, while Riddle stayed in the getaway car. Using Dever, the prosecutor, Batcho demonstrated for the jury how he used a .22-caliber handgun, with a silencer, to shoot Van Brocklin in the left knee. Batcho testified that he wasn't pleased with the performance of the silencer, because it didn't really muffle the gunshot.

"You had a piece of junk?" the prosecutor asked.

"Absolutely," Batcho replied.

Batcho testified for fifty minutes that day and was due back on the stand the next day to testify in the racketeering trial of Bernard "Bernie the Jew" Altshuler, sixty-eight, of Liberty, Ohio, just outside of Youngstown. Batcho was also to testify in the racketeering trials of Riddle and Turnage, both of Youngstown. The men are accused of being associates of mob boss Lenny Strollo and of carrying out his desire to have organized crime figure Ernie Biondillo Jr. and county Prosecutor Paul J. Gains killed, and Van Brocklin wounded. In exchange for their testimonies, the trigger men were not charged with pulling the triggers. They pled guilty to lesser charges and cooperated with the government, as did Batcho, who has admitted shooting Gains and Van Brocklin. Batcho said that when he confessed all of his past crimes to the prosecutors, he also admitted to being part of a burglary ring and to killing Lawrence Sisman, sixty-six, of Boardman, Ohio, who was found March 23, 1996, in his car, at his apartment complex, with a bullet in his head. Sisman had been a partner in the Palace in the Pines Bar. Batcho testified that he killed Sisman because the manager of the bar, Bob Pacillo, disliked Sisman because he was ruining the business by being too possessive of the nude dancing girls. Batcho also mentioned that Frank Lentine, an associate of the late mob boss, Joey Naples, also voiced displeasure in Sisman's behavior.

Batcho described Biondillo as his best friend in the whole world, "He was like a father to me." Batcho rolled up the sleeves to his orange prison jumpsuit to show the jury the picture of Ernest Biondillo that was tattooed on his left bicep. Batcho has admitted being friends to Biondillo and Strollo, even though the two men were rivals. Strollo, Altshuler, Riddle, Turnage, and Batcho were some of the bigger players in that one faction, called "The Enterprise." Assassinated mob boss Joey Naples and the late Ernie Biondillo were of another faction.

Melissa Rich, Biondillo's daughter, was outraged when she got all of the facts, that Bernie Altshuler and Lennie Strollo had her father killed, then attended his funeral and hugged her. Batcho admitted that "the mob" that he worked for was plagued with subpar weapons. The only reason that Paul Gains lived when Batcho went after him, in Gains' Boardman, Ohio home, on December 24, 1996, when he was prosecutor-elect, was the fact that the gun that Jeff Riddle gave him to do the job with jammed after firing just one shot, only wounding Gains. Batcho was paid three thousand dollars by Riddle to kill Gains; this was his initiation into "The Enterprise."

Prior testimony has shown that Strollo felt he was able to fix cases when Prosecutor James A. Philomena was in office, and he didn't want Gains in that position. Cleveland Blair, who was one of the trigger men who killed Biondillo, spoke of running from the passenger side of the front of Biondillo's Cadillac, on June 3, 1996, and then opening fire on Biondillo, with what he described as an old raggedy shotgun. George Wilkins, the other Biondillo assassin, stated that he fired once into the driver's side of Biondillo's Cadillac, but didn't know how to operate the pump action shotgun to get another shot. Blair was paid 3,500 dollars for shooting Biondillo in the head with the shotgun. Biondillo, aligned with Joey Naples until Naples was "knocked off," was apparently "knocked off" by the same faction, who craved the turf that Naples and Biondillo owned. The break in the Biondillo case came when one of the hit men was seen wearing Biondillo's ring, as a souvenir of the hit.

With everyone taking deals to save their asses, Strollo had no way out and nowhere to run. He surprised his minions, who were telling on him, by telling on them and many more. Lenny Strollo is almost single-handedly responsible for the decimation of the Italian mob in this area, by a policy of assassination followed by turning "federal informant." Strollo turned government witness as the state trial ended and the federal trial began in Cleveland, Ohio. He testified against his codefendants, who were all found guilty and sentenced to life in prison without parole. Strollo and most of the confessed shooters are only looking at twelve years, except for Batcho, who is facing eighteen years. I'll say it one more time; Strollo is the reason that the Italian mob in this area was so weakened that it had to form alliances with the Hispanics and the blacks. To survive in this town, various factions and various races came together.

These days it doesn't pay to trust anyone. I know lawbreakers who have committed murder, yet a deal was offered to them if they could "net" someone of a higher value to law enforcement. Then some genius in law enforcement will use that case hanging over some poor sap's head to send him or her undercover, with no regard for the sap's life or for the lives of the members of his or her family. I mentioned that the younger people who are seeking me out are working under orders from the old crowd that I used to run with. The old heads still fear, after eight years of my being back on the streets of Youngstown, that I might be working for law enforcement or that I plan on taking over their hustles. The problem is that I have more to fear from them than they have to fear from me. In this area, it pays to be paranoid.

It has taken eight years for my old partners to start revealing themselves to me, personally, and that is only because they need silencers or someone is sending them to set me up. Most of the few who have revealed themselves have had ulterior motives that proved to be counterproductive to me. R.G. grew up with the five Holmes brothers. We affectionately called him "cousin," even though he was not related to us at all. My mother even spoke of him as "another one of her kids." R.G. took his early retirement from his job and collected a pocketful of money. Unfortunately, there were also "early withdrawal penalties" for dipping into his retirement funds a little too early. R.G. incurred a tax penalty of five thousand dollars a year, for three years in a row. Who did he come to, after all of the big-named tax preparation companies refused to touch his tax dilemma? Yours truly, his good buddy the tax man, Ben Holmes Jr. It took me a month to find a loophole that allowed him to declare a portion of his contributions to the retirement fund as "untaxable." I was able to negate the five thousand dollars tax penalty and get a nine-thousand-dollar refund for R.G. The only thing I asked for was fifty dollars for my services. Even though he was sitting on the seventy thousand from his early retirement, he claimed to be broke and we agreed that he would pay me when the refund check came. It was his idea to give me one-third of the check, three thousand dollars for waiting for the refund to come.

After waiting way too long for him to pay me, while he was still sitting on the seventy thousand, claiming to be broke, and lying about receiving the nine thousand refund check, I contacted one of my cousins and his wife. She was one of the managers at the local IRS office. She told me when R.G. got the check, where he cashed it, and how much he sent to his two daughters, out of town. It really bothered me, in my time of need, that one of my lifelong friends was playing me over money that he obviously didn't need. I discussed the matter with another lifelong friend. This one was a lot smarter and a lot more trustworthy. Mike, "The Mouthpiece," so called because of his genius in the field of law, literally had to talk me out of having someone shoot this thief in the ass with some buckshot, over my three thousand dollars that he promised me and had spent. The Mouthpiece actually had to remind me why we all had nicknames, back in the day.

Names and nicknames defined us. Psychologically, what's in a name? A name, whether positive or negative, can make you or break you mentally. My old running buddies—Big Pimping, Lying Johnny, Crazy Gene, the Wizard, and the Mouthpiece—were just what their names designated. Mike, the Mouthpiece, reminded me that I was nicknamed "The Thinker" for a reason. Mike broke it down to me just like this: "Come on now, brother, you're supposed to be the Thinker. Get to thinking and out think this asshole. After all, if you shoot this fool or have someone else shoot him, you still won't have your money."

The Mouthpiece reminded me that I had out-thought the crooked police who were after me for twenty years, I out-thought more corrupt policemen when I filed the class-action lawsuit against the jail, while incarcerated there on trumped-up charges. That lawsuit led to the jail being closed, the prisoners freed, and power taken from the hands of the jail's corrupt managers and given to an overseeing committee, out of town. The Mouthpiece even reminded me how I out thought death, by not panicking, but by having the consciousness of mind to lower my blood pressure and plug the bullet wounds with my fingers, after my ex-wife tried to murder me in my sleep. While Mike was on a roll convincing me, I thought of a few other times when I had to outthink an opponent. I thought about the time that I had to send three thousand dollars' worth of photographs and audio tapes to members of my ex-wife's family, her coworkers, her church members, the police, and the prosecutor to prove to them that she was lying when she said that she hadn't seen me for twenty years, when actually I had been living with her and my daughter, the whole while that she was engaged to and married to another man, whom she did not allow to come to our home, that we made with our daughter. Mike was right. I went home to my mother's house, stretched out in the bed, and in five minutes I had the solution.

When R.G. came to me the next year, which he actually had the nerve to do, to do his taxes, just as I had done that past year, when he lied about the refund, I agreed to do them, with the stipulation that he give me temporary power of attorney, only when it came to representing him to the IRS. He had no problem doing that, especially with another nine-thousand-dollar payday coming up from my hard work on his taxes. The backstabber never saw it coming.

Having the power of attorney over R.G.'s taxes gave me the right to change the address to which the refund check was sent. I had it sent to my mother's house, where I was living. When the check arrived, I overwhelmed R.G. with a show of force; I had several of the well-known "killers in training" escort R.G. and me to the bank to cash the check. There were no problems, and again I realized how differently things went; even though I was sick as hell and walking on a cane, I had a whole lot of backup from people who were dying to make a reputation off a backstabbing "welcher," like R.G. Once again, the Brotherhood came through for me. When all of this was over, I had a minute to reflect by playing the whole thing over again in my head like a videotape or a DVD. The immortal words of Willis Southerland came to mind: Brother Southerland was my mentor for the ten years that I worked with him at the Ohio Edison electric company. When asked by some nut, under some circumstances that I don't even remember, to trust him, Willis responded, "What the hell do I look like trusting you? I don't even trust myself half the time. As a matter of fact, I usually record myself when I'm sleeping, just to make sure that I don't tell anything in my sleep." I actually tried recording myself during sleep, and I am proud to say that I don't talk in my sleep.

I am convinced that when my lifelong associates, Booker Wellington and Ernie "The Hit Man," were caught by me carrying voice-activated recorders and talking about things that they shouldn't be talking about, that this was an attempt to save their own necks by hanging me. Both of them had very serious cases over their heads and both were facing serious time. Ernie overdosed on bad dope and Booker is doing a long stretch, all because they couldn't set me up or anyone else, for the law enforcement authorities who make deals like that.

Once again I am reminded of Lying Johnny's parting words, "Just because you're paranoid doesn't mean that there isn't someone out to get you." That strange and twisted "Johnny speak" was making more sense every day. You can imagine, with all that I've been through, that I have trust issues. When I relate to you how scandalous and untrustworthy some of my friends and relatives have become since I've been resurrected, you will probably want to put a hit on them yourself. I've had family members ask me about alternative IDs, then they don't come for the paperwork themselves; they send a known snitch to pick up the documents. This same relative had his wife call me on the telephone and discuss going out on a date. When I asked about her husband, she revealed to me that he was the one who suggested that she call me with the offer. She further related that he was on the telephone listening to our every word. I challenged him to make himself known on the other end of the telephone and he did. What was that all about? Fortunately I was not interested in his wife, and did not compromise myself in the conversation.

I have cosigned for cars and furniture for most of my relatives, and have ended up paying for those items myself. One of my relatives had a bad habit of getting me to cosign for him to buy cars, then blow the motors, and refuse to pay for the item. I'd end up putting a motor in the car and keeping it or selling it. That same relative had a wife who left him every few months. He'd stop payments on the household items that I had cosigned for, and I'd have to pay for the items or sell them. Depending on who's counting, his wife left him three to five times.

Each time I was stuck with paying for something that he refused to pay for. My mother spent $2,500 and I spent $4,000 hiring lawyers to recover property for this relative. When this relative got on his feet, he offered to go in with other family members to buy my mother some storm windows for her home. Three hundred and fifty dollars were left over from the cost of the windows and this asshole has been crying like a baby over that chump change for way too long. He never paid me or my mother for getting the property back for him that was worth $250,000, but he cried like a bitch over the extra $350 dollars that my mother spent on food. This same relative came into $355,000 cash money. Instead of sending my mother some of it, if he really wanted her to have some of it, he asked another relative, J, what should he get for my mother; what did she need. J, looking for a loan from this relative himself, told him that my mother didn't need anything because J was holding more than twenty thousand dollars for her.

Not too long after that, my mother received a summons to court, because J was challenging her competence to handle the Social Security funds that she was receiving for herself and for my father, who is confined to a nursing home. In my absence over the years, my mother has come to trust and depend on J. She even put his name on her bank account. Not only did he take possession of her twenty thousand dollars and deposit it into his credit union, he also took the direct deposited Social Security checks, just as fast as they were deposited, without buying her groceries, paying her bills, or paying for her medications on a timely basis.

By the time he got around to spending some of my mother's money on the things she needed, I had already paid for them. Utility disconnection notices came in the mail every day. The final insult to my mother and to me came in the mail in the form of the court summons concerning his getting custody of her Social Security checks to insure that I did not steal them. The weather was bad and my mother didn't feel well. Even though she was eighty years old at the time and badly crippled by arthritis to the point that she too was walking on a cane, I think that she was too depressed to contend in court with one of her blood relatives, over her own money. She asked me to go to court in her place. I went to court and I took Joanna with me. After all, when I didn't have the money to buy my mother food, medicine, or to pay bills, Joanna stepped up to the plate and refused to be reimbursed.

When we got to court, J had retained an attorney to accompany him. I have no doubts that he used my mother's money to hire the attorney, since the bank withdrawals correspond with the date in question. But then again, J was always stealing large amounts of money from my mother's account anyway. The judge hearing the case was a classmate to J and to me. When he realized that this was a family matter, he recused himself and another judge heard the case. J thought that he had the upper hand because he had an attorney with which to make statements and to ask questions. Not having an attorney put me at a disadvantage. I could only answer the questions I was asked and I couldn't ask the court, J, or his lawyer anything. Then I did the same thing to J in court that I did to my ex-wife Addie, when we went to court over her shooting me. I simply pulled out a handful of documents, while I was on the stand, started shuffling through them, and waited for the judge to ask me what they were. They were bank statements and withdrawal slips, showing when and where J withdrew money from my mother's account. The judge determined that my name was not on the account, therefore I was not the culprit absconding with the funds; J was. J was recalled to the stand by the judge and J's lawyer looked at the floor and shook her head. Then Joanna started shaking her head.

The judge joined the two and started shaking his head. The judge did my work for me after seeing the bank statements and the withdrawal slips. He had a few questions to ask J. "Where is Mrs. Holmes' money?"

J replied that the money was in his credit union. He went on to say that he put the money in the credit union to keep me from getting it.

The judge was quick to point out that my name was not on my mother's account, but J's was. "You and only you are responsible for the amounts withdrawn from this bank account. How much of the money is still in your credit union?"

J responded that better than twenty thousand dollars was still in his personal account in his credit union.

The judge asked, "Is anyone else's name on your credit union account?"

J replied that his wife's name was also on the credit union account. The judge asked J what was he doing with the money. J answered that he paid off his house and some other bills; probably including the three new cars that were sitting in his driveway. J claimed that he intended to replace my mother's money when he got his retirement money, which he had already gotten and refused to repay her. When asked why he didn't repay Mrs. Holmes after he got his retirement money, J just shrugged his shoulders like a six-year-old and said, "I don't know why I didn't repay her twenty thousand dollar."

Then the judge asked him the question that made him answer what will probably go down in history as the dumbest thing to say to a judge in court: The judge asked him, "If you died today or tomorrow, Mrs. Holmes wouldn't get her money, your wife would get it. Don't you think that that is unfair?"

J again shrugged his shoulders like a six-year-old and replied, "No, I don't think that's unfair at all." That was it. The fool had hung himself. Consequently, the judge ruled that J had taken money without replacing it.

Furthermore, he wasn't using the money for what it was intended: taking care of my mother.

The judge ruled that J was not fit to be a guardian over my father's and my mother's estate. The judge ruled that there was an "issue of trust" or distrust involved here, since J admitted that he took my mother's money and used it, but couldn't explain why he hadn't returned the cash after he received a very generous retirement package from his employer, Delphi-Packard. The judge ordered that Family Services would be investigating the matter and that they would act as my parents' guardian.

Days later, I couldn't believe my eyes when Joanna and I came out of the local Walgreen's store and happened to look across the street at J coming out of the National City Bank with my mother; and she was wearing the red jogging outfit that Joanna and I bought her for Christmas.

I later found out that J had talked her into putting his name on her bank account again. He also took her to his credit union to see the balance in the account that only bore his and his wife's names. He did not put my mother's name on the credit union account, as the judge, the Social Security case worker, and the Family Services agent suggested. Based on what my mother's life insurance agent is saying, J has taken over the life insurance account that my mother has been paying on for thirty years. I don't know if my mother voluntarily signed the life insurance account over to J, or if this is some scheme contrived by J and the insurance agent. This is also being investigated. So far, J has not turned my mother's money over to her or any of her family. Most of my classmates and many of my relatives worked at Delphi-Packard, until they all recently retired, before they got laid off indefinitely.

Whenever I see them in the stores, they are quick to point out that J worked, had lunch, and socialized in the same areas as my ex-wife and her new husband. No less than fifty have sworn that J witnessed my ex-wife Addie and her new husband kissing at the entrance door, to the plant, as they separated to go to their individual departments. Relatives who worked with J and Addie swear that J knew about Addie dating James and many other men. They also swear that J knew about Addie's and James' engagement; he was even heard commenting on the engagement ring. And yes, he definitely knew that they had gotten married, while I was still living in the house with Addie.

No wonder James and Addie were so mad at J, when he accompanied me to court when Addie shot me. They thought that he had ratted them out. He certainly knew every move that they made, but he never told me a thing. When I bugged the telephone in our house and caught my ex-wife Addie talking to her new husband about a ring, I played the audio tape for J and asked him who the man was. He swore that he had no idea. But he did. For many years before Addie started seeing James, I lived in our home with her. When she went to work, my father came by the house in the mornings to check on me and J came by every night after work to do the same. My daughter Benita was gone away to college by this time, but she knew about the affair as well. Her saving grace was that she refused to give Addie away, in the wedding, in Virginia; the same place where Addie and I got married. She asked her mother, "How are you going to marry this man when you already have a husband living in our home in Youngstown?" I don't know whether Benita or J had any idea that Addie's solution was to shoot me, but I do know that it has crossed their minds that if they had warned me, I would never have been shot. James, the new husband, may have been the only one who didn't know that there was no longer a case against me and that I planned on turning myself in to the proper law enforcement authorities. Addie and I had already agreed that I would leave the area to surrender to the police, since there was no longer a case against me and I had no wish to get my ex-wife, my daughter, my mother, my father, or J arrested for harboring a fugitive from justice for twenty years.

I was satisfied that I had thrown a monkey wrench into J's plans to steal more from my mother, until I witnessed him taking her to the bank. I guess that he wasn't pleased with my showing the judge the withdrawal slips he used to take money from my mother's account, because he called me at Joanna's house, where I had been finishing one of my books for the last six months, to curse me out and to threaten my life on the answering machine. You might recall the last time that someone threatened me, when K-Dog and B-Boy had a "conversation" with Ron, after he threatened me with a knife. I have saved J's threats from the answering machine for posterity. You never know when you might want to look back at the way things used to be and wonder over how things have changed. In case you haven't been paying attention, J was the family member who had gotten in the hole to Booker.

Booker was the head of a drug ring and R.G., for whom I did the income taxes, informed me that Booker had taken $250 off of J on three occasions. I put a stop to the bullying and my reward is for J to steal from my mother and to threaten me. Also on the answering machine's audio tape is a threat from J to Joanna. On that tape he tells her not to bring my mother anymore medicine, food, Christmas presents, birthday presents, or Mother's Day presents. J was also adamant about Joanna not riding my mother in her car or talking to her on the telephone. He went on to warn Joanna that she will suffer the same fate as I will.

I'm accustomed to threats and "pretend gangsters," who cry like little girls when the lead starts flying. Then they want to cry "foul," or they will claim that they were just kidding; but by that time it's just a little too late. I've had too many close bouts with death and I'm not in the best of health. A threat to me is very serious, because I already have one foot in the grave and the other one is slipping fast. That's where my "friends" come in. I call the Brotherhood my friends because that's what they are. They have done more for me and charged me less than many of my own "Holmes Family" members. The occasional threat quickly becomes an apology, when my "friends" come to my rescue. I don't get into their rackets and I don't want any of their money. They have muscle if I need it and it's good to have options. In return, I do what I've always done: I provide them silencer blueprints and the prefabricated, unassembled parts. From there, they make their own tools of the trade. Isn't it indeed ironic that I once had to use the Brotherhood to stop Booker from bullying J?

CHAPTER 22

Survival Skills

W hen I get the longing to hang around with some of my "old, old, school crew," as the younger people call us, I drop in on Gutknecht Towers. Gutknecht Towers is a high-rise apartment building that caters to those fifty-five years old and up. The tenants are usually the retired and the disabled. A funny thing happened to them on their way to retirement; they got old, their jobs moved away, and they found out that their retirement checks just weren't enough to make ends meet, in this super-high, inflationary economy. "Old heads" who have no desire to starve, while trying to live on their retirement checks, are quietly, secretly slipping back into the old hustles they used to have. These are usually lightweight endeavors that are part-time, relatively safe, and carry very little jail time. It is common to hear them say, "I'm just trying to supplement that little-ass check. I got to make ends meet somehow."

Gutknecht has become a meeting place for most of my old friends because it is in the center of everything, close to downtown, only a few steps from our entertainment center, and in the back yard of Youngstown State University. When these old players are not watching the young girls at the university, they watch the hookers strolling the same area. Occasionally someone will actually have something to say that's worthwhile. Mike, the Mouthpiece, lives there and I stopped in to ask him if he had heard that Lying Johnny had gotten sick and died. The Mouthpiece set my mind at ease; Johnny had been sick, but he recovered. He was still in the land of the living. Our conversation covered a number of things and as usual the subject turned to current events. Gutknecht had become an active information network. By that I mean that you could always find someone who knew what or whom you needed to know. If someone living there or visiting there didn't know something, they certainly could point you to someone who did. Naturally, to supplement their "little-ass" retirement checks, these "walking encyclopedias" charged for information and for "introductions" to the right people. At Gutknecht, knowledge is money.

I told the Mouthpiece about my day in court, representing my mother when J decided to take the rest of her money through the court. Mike was already aware of what I thought was going to be news to him. He knew that J wasn't satisfied going after my parents' Social Security checks; he also wanted the house, my mother's perfectly preserved 1979 Cadillac, and my deceased brother's 1970 GTO. Both cars were probably worth a king's ransom. The Mouthpiece turned the conversation to the many racing cars we both used to own back in the old days, as if that conversation would take my mind off of J's treachery. When the Mouthpiece saw that he couldn't divert my attention from delving on the subject of people taking advantage of my mother, he came right out with what he was thinking, "Well, we're both men of the world and we've both been around the block a time or two. You know like I know that some of these clowns need a good ass whipping every now and then. As a matter of fact, some of them are going to make someone kill them, and rightfully so." I responded that Mike was beginning to sound a lot like Vinnie, when he went to jail for nearly beating his mother to death, with a metal, fold-up chair. You may recall that Vinnie was the cartoonist who uncontrollably wrote about my leading the Brotherhood to world domination. Vinnie also had half of Youngstown believing that he was one of my lieutenants or generals or something. After nearly killing his mother with the metal, fold-up chair, Vinnie was declared "criminally insane" and sent to a mental institution for two years. That was on May 2, 2008. The article appears in *The Vindicator* of that same date.

Mike was very impressed that Vinnie could escape an attempted murder rap by pleading temporary insanity and making it work for him. Mike called him the smartest crazy man that he had ever met. I remember the effect Vinnie's cartoon had on a number of people when he wrote that I had psychic abilities, that I was clairvoyant, that I could project thoughts, and that I could read minds. He really freaked people out when he told them that I could talk to animals, but that wasn't as bad as the time that he wrote about my hypnotizing women with my voice and eyes.

Vinnie lived two blocks away from me when I moved into my mother's house after my ex-wife shot me. When Tish or Tasha took me to my many doctors' appointments, Vinnie often caught a ride with us to his doctors as well. As a result, we were usually stuck with him most of the time. He was cool, as long as he took his medicine and didn't have any "spells." It was only when he was off of the epilepsy medications that he got into trouble. I remember the time P, my private detective-turned-restaurateur, let me drive his red Lincoln for a few days and I went to the car wash to have it done. Earl and Charmaine were detailing cars that day, when Earl challenged me with some rude behavior and a "near threat." This was the time that Charmaine sucker punched him in the chest with both hands, knocking the breath out of him and sending him to the ground. Vinnie wasn't present to witness that event, but that didn't stop him from creating a cartoon about the incident. In his cartoon, Vinnie wrote that I projected my thoughts to Charmaine and caused her arms to move, striking Earl as I would have struck him.

I used to work at the electric company and I've had plenty of experience with electric transformers being struck by lightning. Vinnie and I were present at Lomax's house when a fierce thunderstorm came out of nowhere. I could see by the lightning pattern that the lightning was being conducted to the electric transformer. I called it, and the lightning struck the telephone pole and the transformer. There was a hole in the transformer the size of a softball. Vinnie and Lomax were both convinced that I had called the lightning down from the heavens. My guess is that they were both super high off something.

I used to walk to my doctor's office when my car wasn't running or when I couldn't catch Tish or Tasha. One day Vinnie and I were walking to our doctors' offices, while sharing a box of Kentucky Fried Chicken. A vicious dog approached me and started growling. This was the same dog that had eaten several of the smaller cats and dogs in my neighborhood. Vinnie had run off and I was on my own. I was walking on a metal cane and I knew that if I had to strike the dog, the metal cane would do the trick. I asked the dog if he preferred some of my chicken or a rap upside his head with my cane. I then told the dog that I didn't hear his response and that he should shake his head, yes or no, if he wanted the chicken. The dog shook his head up and down, meaning yes he wanted the chicken. I gave it to him and I never had a problem with him again. As a matter of fact, I often found him on the back porch of my mother's house, waiting to escort me on my walk to and from the doctor's office. At night he would walk in front of me and point whenever another person popped up on us. Vinnie witnessed all of this and made a cartoon about it. Soon people thought that I had mesmerized their dogs, led them away, and probably had them stashed somewhere. It got so bad that people started asking me where their dog was and what had I done with it. One girl saw her dog in front of my mother's house and yelled to the dog, "Once you dogs go to the Holmes's house, you never want to come back home. The only thing that my mother and I were doing to the dogs was feeding them the scraps from our many steak dinners. Max, the vicious dog that escorted me at night, for a piece of Kentucky Fried Chicken, was shot to death by his owner, because the dog obeyed me more than he did his owner.

On another occasion, Tish had taken Vinnie and me to and from one of my doctor's appointments, when she decided that she wanted to try out my binoculars by bird watching in our local Wick Park. She and Vinnie smoked their cigarettes and took turns watching the birds with my binoculars. They didn't see the irate drunk, who came out of nowhere and mumbled something about us being in his spot. His slow deliberate walk toward us became a speedy walk, and that suddenly became an all-out blitz. This crazy was running up on us and Vinnie and Tish didn't even notice. A falcon let out a shrill warning cry and swooped down on the drunk, striking him in the back of the head. The falcon knocked the man to his knees and drew blood from the gash in the bald spot of the drunk's head. When the drunk was able, he retreated very quickly. Vinnie and Tish spread the tale that I made the falcon attack the drunk, because the drunk appeared to be initiating an attack against me. Vinnie went ballistic when he spotted a falcon in my backyard later that same day. He and Tish swore that it was the same falcon from Wick Park. Naturally, Vinnie had to make a cartoon about it all.

Vinnie has two years to do in the nut hospital, then he'll be loose on the streets again. God help us all. Athletes, lawyers, gamblers, thieves, drug dealers, whores, hit men, and cops are all very superstitious beings, who have no problem speaking of good or bad luck. Each of these professions is filled with people who actively seek good luck and try to find a way to ward off bad luck. Every one of them is looking for an edge. Can you imagine the effect Vinnie's cartoons had on the people I came into contact with after they read his highly circulated cartoons about my being able to read their minds, hypnotize their women, and turn their dogs against them? A handful of people feared that I might actually be psychic and distanced themselves from me, but most of my associates chose to endear themselves to me because they preferred to have me on their side and not against them. The pseudopsychic thing was actually working for me.

No one cared to remember that my deductive reasoning skills had been finely honed by my criminology professors in college, by my friend P the private detective, and by surviving on the run for twenty years. It was easier for them to believe that I was psychic.

After all, it made good gossip conversation when there was nothing on cable.

Brother Mike, the Mouthpiece, snapped me back from my trip down memory lane. He was tired of hearing about crazy Vinnie. He was more concerned with making some quick money to pay a few bills. Then he said it, "You don't have to worry about money, especially since your brother got that half-million-dollar reward from turning in his buddies, the D.C. Snipers." I responded by stating that my brother's money was his and not mine.

That didn't stop the Mouthpiece, who came back with, "Man, you know how to make money in this town. I know you got a wad stashed. You got skills." I asked Mike what kind of skills was he referring to, and he replied, "You got survival skills. When everybody else is dying, you're living; when everybody else is starving, you're eating; and when everybody else is in a brain fog, you're thinking. As long as you know how to make those silencers, you'll never starve in this town. Ain't nothing here but killers, and they'll pay you whatever you want for the silencers. Yeah, brother, you got survival skills."

I liked the term "survival skills," and I don't think that I had ever heard it before. The very phrase started me to thinking about my skills at survival. When I had to disappear, twenty years ago, my main source of income was selling blueprints to the silencers in the backs of gun magazines. Not only was I running from crooked cops, but from varying factions of gangs and mobs also. Now the offspring of those gangs are courting "Uncle Ben," to gain his favor, because these killers want silencers. The richest and most powerful network of gangs this area has ever seen can't get their hands on reliable silencers. I am a very valuable asset to them. I can get anything I want from them—the finest women, the finest cars, the finest homes, the finest vacations, bodyguards, and a pocketful of money. Instead of selling my product in the back of gun magazines like I used to do, I can make two hundred thousand dollars a year by setting up a website on the Internet to sell my product. Just think of it. Five sheets of paper will bring me two hundred thousand dollars a year. Nobody who ever bought my silencer blueprints and the prefabricated, unassembled parts ever complained about the endurance, the accuracy, or the quietness of the silencer. If anything, written and oral responses lauded the ease of assembling the product and many customers were amazed at the effectiveness and low cost.

I often hear young and old bitching about how hard life is. Everyone is crying about what it takes to make ends meet, especially in this job-poor area They all whine about how hard it is to survive. These pitiful specimens couldn't last one day on the run. They would never think to put their fingers in the bullet holes to hold on to life for just a few minutes more. Would they remember Hezekiah's prayer in the grip of certain death? Could they sit in the county jail for thirteen months, while suffering from bullet wounds, a stroke, heart disease, and bone disease, and still have the will power to attack their jailers by filing civil rights, classaction lawsuits through out-of-town lawyers? Now I've perfected a two-hundred-thousand-dollar mail order business that I can take with me anywhere in the world, with no inventory, and no costs. No, these brothers and sisters couldn't last a day in my shoes. The sad thing is that anything I have ever had, I was willing to share, even with lazy, stingy people who would not do the same for me. Now I have found myself surrounded by a bunch of crybabies who are looking for something for nothing, and that includes members of my family. At least the people in the Brotherhood have something to offer me for what they want from me. At least they are interested in a fair exchange. At least they are there when I need them. Yes, Mike was right. I had survival skills, and as long as killing was still in style in Youngstown, I'd survive. But sometimes just surviving isn't enough. Sometimes you have to feed that aching hunger for just a little more.

CHAPTER 23

Mob Deep

I was leaving Mike's apartment, at Gutknecht Towers, when I heard someone call me.

It was Capelli, aka, Capone. He was parked in his 1979, black Cadillac Fleetwood; right behind my mother's 1979, yellow Cadillac that I had been test driving after a minor tune-up. I went over to the black Cadillac and got in the back with Capone. His two bodyguards were on the front seat. He quickly explained that he recognized my mother's yellow car and surmised that I must have been driving it, since she no longer drove, because of health reasons. He introduced me as "Fam" to his henchmen, which was short for "Family." That is what we used to call each other in the old days, when we used to hang out at Joey Naples's bar, Dee's Lounge. Joey Naples had been one of the local mob bosses, until he got knocked off. Capone and a few other young Italians were the heirs apparent, who floated to the top of organized crime, after the old heads eliminated each other or informed on each other. These new young mob bosses called themselves "Warlords."

Capone had carved out a piece of territory for himself by synthesizing crystal methamphetamine and cocaine. The combination was called Zoom, and he had taken a large portion of the crack cocaine trade with the new product. Now he needed guns and silencers to protect his new enterprise from renegades. He proposed a very lucrative arrangement for the two of us and mentioned that he had heard about the trouble and threats I was getting from my brother Jerry, aka, J, and some of his crew. Capone knew all about my brother taking my mother's money and trying to put her in the nursing home. Capone was crazy about my mother and he didn't like what he was hearing about the whole mess. When Capone called me family, he meant it.

We went a long way back together. I first met Capone when we were about twelve years old, and I was working at my father's gas station, just one block from the Capelli family home. My father, the Capellis, and a few others ran the numbers racket out of my father's gas station and their homes. Often, young Capelli, aka Capone, would transport numbers and cash, back and forth, between his family's home and my father's gas station. My father also owned two houses that were located side by side. One of the houses was our home, but the other was "The Joint." Anything you could imagine to make money from went on at the Joint. My father bought a new Buick every year, paid for several homes, and a one-hundred-acre farm from the income that came out of the Joint; and at the age of twelve, I was the bouncer. I remember being tall for my age and carrying a long-barreled, .22 caliber pistol in my belt. In retrospect, it is a wonder that I didn't blow my penis off, since I carried the gun cocked, in my belt, and pointing to my groin. The Capellis and many other Italians were constantly present at the Joint and at our gas station. Our families remained friends forever.

Young Capelli and I raced cars and motorcycles out of my shop when we got old enough. Young Capelli became "Capone" when he and thirty of his crew came to my rescue after I was surrounded by a gang that was protected by some policemen, who wanted me to make drugs and silencers for them, exclusively. I won't go into the details for fear of opening a can of worms that needs to be left permanently sealed, but let it suffice to say that even though crooked policemen and rival gangs were involved, Capone earned his nickname that day.

Capone was not satisfied that he was convincing me to sign on with his crew, so he again dropped the family card on me. He went way back to 1966, when his family got my parents out of jail for running the Joint. The finest designer clothing, the most expensive guns, the best food, and untold amounts of jewelry came through the Joint. Any type of gambling you could think of was practiced there, and the finest prostitutes and strippers Youngstown had to offer plied their trade there. When the Feds raided the joint, my parents and many other regulars were looking at a lifetime of charges. Someone in the Capone family showed up at the jail with lawyers and a big bag of money. Not only was everyone released, but the charges were all dropped, and no one even got probation. The guns that were taken from my parents' home were returned to them, and I have them today. Capone dropped all of that on me in his efforts to exclusively recruit me. The kind of money he was promising me rivaled the president's salary, and that was just for my working in an advisory capacity.

Something startled the two bodyguards, who were glued to the front seat of the big, black Caddy, watching anything that moved outside of the car. Someone was approaching the car and the hired killers were about to go into attack mode, as they made mad dashes to their armpits to grip their weapons. I quickly allayed their fears by telling them that I recognized the figure approaching the vehicle; it was Mike, the Mouthpiece. The bodyguard driving the car lowered the rear passenger window on my side to let Mike talk to me. He said, "I know that you're all right, and I recognize Capelli's pimp mobile. How you doing, Capone? Holmes, can I holler at you for just one minute?" I excused myself and got out of the car to talk to Mike, who said, "Man, don't get yourself into any shit by letting them deal with your fucked-up brother. You know that once you let them do anything for you, that you're 'in' for life. I told you too many times before that you're 'The Thinker;' you're supposed to be able to outthink your brother."

I thanked Mike for his concern and sent him on his way, as I got back into the black Caddy to resume my deal with "the devil." One thing Mike had said resonated in my mind, "If you let them do anything for you, you're in for life."

I could forgive my brother for stealing from my mother, but he also threatened my mother, Joanna, and me, several times. To make matters worse, he had taken steps to get her committed to a nursing home after he intentionally brought about her poor health by starving her and by withholding her medications, which I entrusted to him as

I made preparations to go out of town on business. His first attempt at legally taking the rest of the little my mother had left fell flat when I thwarted his efforts in court, with evidence that he had mishandled funds that my mother entrusted to him. The second attempt involved having her hospitalized for dehydration and malnutrition. His argument was that she was too fragile mentally and physically to feed herself or to take her medications. He further argued to my mother's doctors and to the hospital staff that I had abandoned my mother to pursue a business venture, and that he didn't have the time to do my job, which was taking care of my mother. She had lost forty pounds in just two months. Every test that is imaginable to mankind was given to her, and the only problems that she had were potassium deficiency, dehydration, malnutrition, and a bad set of knees. Not bad for an old woman of eighty-one. After she spent five days in the hospital, her doctor determined that she would be better off in a nursing home if no one would be available in her home to make sure that she got her meals and medicine properly. Jerry thought that he had won, until I met with the doctor to confirm that I would delay my out-of-town trip until I got my mother back on her feet; I would be staying with her, in her home.

Three weeks later, my mother had regained thirty pounds, and she had met all of the mental and physical requirements of her six therapists, five nurses, and three doctors. All of them released her. Lillie B. Holmes would not be residing in any nursing home anytime soon. My brother Jerry was pissed off to the nth degree and suggested more physical and psychological tests to the doctors who had just released her. Then he tried to trick her into going to other doctors who might see things his way. She refused to go.

To stop Jerry from having access to her Social Security checks, which were being directly deposited into an account bearing his and her name, I had lawyers from Family Services take the checks, pay some utilities, and personally deliver the balance into my mother's hand.

On one occasion, Jerry popped up at Family Services Headquarters just as my mother and I were about to receive the check from them. Jerry presented a power of attorney document dated March of 2008. This was supposed to deliver her check and all of her assets into his hand. The Family Services agent was about to give the check to Jerry when I pulled out my trump card—my own power of attorney document, dated and signed, August of 2008. This happened on September 15, 2008. Mom received her check and we left the agency, with Jerry following closely behind us, cursing and threatening, as usual. I had anticipated his every move, and when he followed our car in his, I already had a third car following him. When the third car blew its horn to make its presence known, Jerry broke off the chase. That act made my mind up for me. I didn't want Capone to have him killed or crippled, but it was good to have options.

Sitting in the car with Capone and his killers, I decided upon the lesser evil of letting myself be seen in the company of killers, to dissuade any who deluded themselves into believing that they were gangsters, or that I didn't have backup. I was running with the real thing. Capone and his crew were doing very well with their new enterprise. Their clothing reminded me of what the old gangsters used to say when I was a kid: "Real gangsters wear Armani." Once again Capone played the family card on me, when he reminded me of the trust his family had in my father, when they helped him get his farm. In return, my father reserved a hidden corn-patch for the Italians to grow "whatever" they chose. My father had a legal contract to sell his produce and meat to a number of Italian, Greek, Irish, and Jewish restaurants.

Capone reminded me that all of this was done for him by his friends. Capone and I came to an agreement, of which I will not disclose at this time. But let it suffice to say that Joanna, my mother, and I would be well taken care of from then on. I rationalized that it was better coming in as a boss than as a slave. I sealed my deal with Capone with a handshake, and then I left the black Caddy. It was late and I had a lot to think about.

Flat on my back, in bed, knocked out, at three o'clock in the morning, I had a brainstorm. I suddenly remembered what Jerry had admitted in court, when the judge questioned him about his misappropriation of my mother's assets, at the guardianship hearing. My brother, Jerry, aka J, was recorded in court, admitting that my mother had entrusted him with a sum of money, in 1998, when my father went into the nursing home for Alzheimer's. He stated that it was his idea to hold the money in his credit union, in his and his wife's names. He admitted that my mother did not know that he was actually hiding assets from the Social Security Administration, a felony. He further admitted that he had used her money to pay off his home and some other bills. He claimed that it was his intention to repay the money when he got his Delphi-Packard retirement money. He further admitted that he had already received his retirement money and refused to repay my mother. That constituted fraud, theft, and misappropriation of funds. Subsequently, I acquired the transcripts of the court hearing and ran to an attorney to file a lawsuit against Jerry for my mother's assets; the threat of criminal charges was used for leverage, but I would actually follow through with those threats at a later date. It gave me a real pleasure to overhear him on the telephone begging my mother to drop the lawsuit. He tried to convince her that she wouldn't get all of her money if she pressed the lawsuit now, because the stock market was down drastically, and he had her money in stocks and bonds. She told him that the matter was out of her hands and into the lawyer's hands. I took it upon myself to brag about the "insurance" I had bought, since he had a very bad habit of doing his dirt under the influence of drugs and alcohol, then swearing that his high blood sugar was the blame for his insane actions. I reminded him that Capone's crew had the magical ability to make crazy people very sane. He relented.

Since that day that I agreed to the deal with Capone, by shaking his hand, I have often thought about what my father used to say about the mob: "Once you get in, you never get out. If you don't watch out, you can end up being a slave." Most of my life I had been trying not to get too close to the vacuum, for fear of being sucked all the way in. Now these killers were actually acting as my saviors. I was no longer just affiliated with the mob; no longer was I simply connected. All of a sudden, I was knee-deep in the mob. I was "Mob Deep."

Everything worked out fine for my mother, Joanna, and me. So far I haven't had to release my hounds on anyone, but there's always tomorrow. Capone and the Brotherhood have fulfilled all of their promises to me. Now it is my tum to hold up my end. I have already provided blueprints, parts, and training for the silencer project. Now they are asking me about the rumors that I am well trained in "remote control" devices, and I'm convinced that they are not concerned with programming their DVD players or their televisions.

Benjamin Robert Holmes Jr. was born on December 11, 1951. He is sixty-six years old and resides in Youngstown, Ohio. Because of his height, six feet five inches, he looked older and his father, a race car builder and driver, let him race cars at the local tracks at the age of twelve.

A product of the public school system, he graduated from the Rayen High School in 1969. Later he worked as a heavy equipment operator at the local electric company and as an investigator at a local law firm. He studied engineering for two years at Youngstown State University, then he transferred to Eastlands College, in the United Kingdom, to study engineering mechanics and management. Benjamin presently holds a bachelor's degree in those studies and is two hours short of a master's degree.

He is most known as the innocent man in the Discovery Channel series, *I Faked My Own Death*. In that series he was approached by mobsters and crooked policemen who wanted him to build gun silencers. After refusing them, his home was firebombed and he was falsely charged and threatened with death. He was on the run for twenty years, until his wife shot him several times over another man she had secretly married.

Tape recordings he had made over twenty years cleared him of the false charges, revealed public officials' connection to the mob, and revealed his wife's plot to eliminate him. Even more amazing than his being on the run for twenty years, using many false identifies, is the fact that he survived his wife's gunshots by plugging the bullet holes with his fingers, until he got to the hospital.

9 781645 310310